DNA and Social Networking

DNA and Social Networking

A GUIDE TO GENEALOGY IN THE TWENTY-FIRST CENTURY

DEBBIE KENNETT

All trademarks used herein are the property of their respective owners. The use of any trademark in this text does not vest in the author or publisher any trademark ownership rights in such trademarks, nor does the use of such trademarks imply any affiliation with or endorsement of this book by such owners.

Facebook is a Trademark of Facebook Inc.

First published 2011

The History Press
The Mill, Brimscombe Port
Stroud, Gloucestershire, GL5 2QG
www.thehistorypress.co.uk

British Library Cataloguing in Publication Data.
A catalogue record for this book is available from the British Library.

ISBN 978 0 7524 5862 5

Typesetting and origination by The History Press
Printed in Great Britain
Manufacturing managed by Jellyfish Print Solutions Ltd

Contents

Foreword

by Chris Pomery

This book is timely as it catches family history at a point where it is changing from being predominantly a solitary pursuit and becoming more and more a group endeavour. The networking methods that Debbie reveals in this book – and the collaborative skills that she teaches – can be used by every genealogist to help widen our searches and accelerate our research.

We're all aware that the last decade has seen an explosion in the amount of family history data arriving online. The days when most genealogical research started out with day-long trips to record offices armed with a notepad and pencil have now passed. Today the first place people look when they begin their research is on the web. This has to be a good thing. More people have access to the data, they have equal access to it and they can access it from anywhere around the world at any time they choose. These changes have also led to an increase in the number of people researching each source, and to many more people placing the results of their research online, either as a tree, a website or even simply as a note on an online bulletin board.

While some research is always going to be of a less than high quality, the increased sharing stimulated by the web helps each of us to move our own research forward quicker. That's a clear improvement on the pre-email past, but the main benefits of the internet age are truly found when we learn to work together; building up a team of researchers and collaborators who by working together achieve more than any one individual ever could, and more quickly. This book explains how everyone can start to reap the benefits of that networking process, regardless of whether you're running a DNA project or not.

A major section of the book you're holding describes the latest developments in the fast-changing field of genetic testing for genealogists. Next to the arrival of the internet, the application of genetic tests for use by family historians is the second great genealogical revolution of the past decade. Long used by population scientists to unravel how mankind spread across the planet from our origins in Africa, we now have ten years' experience of using DNA testing to advance our family history research.

Today many thousands of DNA projects are currently underway around the world; run by ordinary people like you and me, the vast majority of them analysing whether men who share the same surname are genetically related to each other and, therefore, belong in the same family tree. The pool of around half a million Y-chromosome DNA results that has now been built up is helping each of us develop a clearer picture of how our surnames came into being, how and why they grew as they have done and how related we are to each other.

Genetic testing increasingly looks set to become an integral part of everyday genealogical research in the years ahead. A decade ago, a DNA test was seen as something exotic and tangential to the main work of the genealogist, which was visiting archives and transcribing the data in them. Today it's possible to run a parallel DNA project and to use the DNA results to confirm we have identified the correct people within each line and tree. While the first generation of tests looked only along two of our many lines – the direct paternal and maternal lines – the good news is that the new, second generation of DNA tests is going to be even more useful, as they help identify anyone who descends from any one of our great-great-grandparents.

This is a book that has been waiting to be written, and Debbie is the right person to write it. Well known within the Guild of One-Name Studies as an expert on social networking, she has been promoting her own surname DNA project, which is investigating the origins of the West Country surname Cruwys, for many years. This book summarises her experience in a highly readable format, which serves both as a primer for family history researchers, and as a resource that anyone can dip in to in order to learn more about social and online networking, and about DNA testing.

www.DNAandFamilyHistory.com

Preface

The first decade of the new millennium has been an exciting time for the family historian. I took my first tentative steps on the internet in December 2000 and one of the first searches I performed on Google was for the surname Cruwys (pronounced Cruise), my own maiden name. There were probably no more than a few hundred results and I was able to work my way right through to the end of the search list. A similar search today returns around 30,000 hits. When I first started to research my family history I purchased censuses on CD and microfiche, and scrolled through reels of microfilm at the library. Now all the UK censuses from 1841 through to 1911 are transcribed and indexed and, for the price of a subscription to a commercial provider such as Ancestry.com or Findmypast, digital images of the original census pages can be viewed online or downloaded on to a home computer. New datasets, such as wills and parish register collections, are being added on a regular basis and the challenge now is that there is so much available on the internet that it is difficult to find the time to search through all the new records. The increasing availability of online records has in turn fuelled a growing interest in family history research in the UK, helped in part by the popularity of television programmes such as *Who Do You Think You Are?* which first hit our screens back in 2004.

The world of genetic genealogy

DNA testing has developed in parallel to these new developments in the family history world. The first commercial DNA tests for genealogists became available in the year 2000, the same year in which scientists published the first draft of the human genome. By the end of 2001 there were about 100 or so DNA projects in existence. Four years later the number of projects had grown to over 2,500. By the end of the decade there were well over 6,000 projects. I first became aware of the possibilities of DNA testing when I joined the Guild of One-Name Studies in 2006. Two Guild members, Susan Meates and Chris Pomery, were among the early pioneers of DNA testing. Susan published a series of articles in the Guild's journal on the Meates DNA project, and Chris had already published his first book on the subject with a second to follow in 2007. I set up my first project for my Cruwys/Cruse one-name study in September 2007. There are distinct advantages in being one of the second-phase adopters of a new technology. I was able to draw on the collective knowledge of my fellow Guild members and other project administrators, both here and in the US, and learn from their mistakes and experiences. If ever I had a difficult question or an unusual result there was always someone who could provide the answer. Boosted by the success of my surname project, in March 2009 I set up a new DNA project for the county of Devon, and later that same year I became a co-administrator of the mitochondrial DNA haplogroup U4 project. I now have responsibility for over 550 project members, which has given me a very broad insight into the range of results that might be expected across the full spectrum of tests. I learn more as each new result comes in and, through the process of explaining DNA test results to a large number of project members, I have come to understand the questions that can arise and the problems that people have understanding their results. In the few years since I have been involved in DNA testing the science has not stood still. New initiatives have been launched, new features have been added to existing products and a major new DNA test has been added to the toolbox for the family historian. I have been able to monitor these developments as they have happened and have tested either myself or members of my family as appropriate.

The first part of this book is devoted to this exciting new world of genetic gene-alogy. The book starts by explaining the basic principles involved and then goes on to look in depth at the three different DNA tests that have a direct application for the family historian. It is not necessary to have a degree in genetics to understand the results of a DNA test, but there are just a few key pieces of terminology that need to be mastered. As with any new tool, it is all very well understanding the theory, but it is only when you start to put that theory into practice and take a DNA test for yourself that it begins to make sense. I hope that I have explained the ben-efits sufficiently well to encourage you to take that important first step if you have not already done so.

Making connections

The rapid growth of the internet has not only transformed family history research but has also revolutionised the process of making contact with other researchers from all over the world. There is only so much that one person can achieve on his or her own, and the research process becomes much easier and more productive if you can share the burden and collaborate with other researchers. Not all the answers can be found on the internet and you will also want to track down living people to fill in some of the gaps in your own genealogical jigsaw puzzle. Another family member might have a copy of the long-lost family bible, an archive of family photos or a collection of handwritten letters that will add context to your research. If you become involved in a DNA project you will have a particular interest in tracking down living relatives or other people who share your surname as you will hope to persuade them to participate in the project. The second part of this book therefore looks at different ways to network and collaborate with other researchers. If you are contemplating setting up your own DNA project you will be able to use some of these methods to promote your project. Some of the websites covered are designed specifically for the genealogist, but the mainstream social media websites also have an important role to play. If you are trying to get to grips with these developments for the first time it can be very difficult navigating the internet to find the most relevant sites. I have, therefore, provided a comprehensive collection of links at the end of each chapter for background reading and further information.

The ephemeral nature of the internet means that there is no guarantee that all the websites I have featured or listed will still be in existence by the time you read this book. Similarly, there will no doubt be other innovative new websites on the horizon which I have not anticipated. In writing this book I have made full use of all the new social media to keep me informed of the latest developments, but it has been quite a challenge keeping up with all changes. New social networking websites were being launched, existing websites underwent major redesigns and once-popular websites fell out of favour and were closed down. New companies appeared on the scene while others were taken over or went into liquidation. New DNA tests were introduced to the market and new features were added to existing tests. Inevitably in a book of this nature there will be omissions, for which I take full responsibility. If you feel that I have missed out something important I would love to hear from you, and I would hope to rectify any errors in an updated edition of the book in the future. Regardless of any errors, omissions or subsequent developments, the basic principles and techniques described in this book will still apply.

I have assumed that anyone who is motivated to read a book on DNA and social networking will already have some knowledge of the basic principles of family history research. The wider topic of surnames is also beyond the scope of this book, but there are a number of excellent books on the subject and I have included a comprehensive list in the bibliography, together with a list of surname websites in Appendix D.

I hope that you will share my enthusiasm for DNA testing and social networking, and that by the time you have finished this book you will be inspired to get your own DNA tested and to make the most of all the social networks to help with your own family history research.

Acknowledgements

I am fortunate that I joined the world of DNA testing at a time when genetic gene-alogy had already come of age. We owe a huge debt to the scientists who made it all happen, and to the pioneering project administrators who embraced this new tool from the beginning and shared their experiences in books, magazine articles and on mailing lists and websites. This book would not have been possible without them and I have merely distilled the combined knowledge of my predecessors to bring the subject up to date.

I am very grateful to Chris Pomery for writing the foreword to this book, and for all his encouragement over the last few years. Tim Janzen kindly read the draft of the DNA section and provided many helpful comments. John Sloan gave me some useful insight and commentary for the Y-DNA chapters. I enjoyed many friendly discussions with James Irvine and Ralph Taylor on the subject of surname distribu-tions and the management of large surname DNA projects. Susan Meates was one of the early pioneers of DNA testing within the Guild of One-Name Studies, and I have benefited from her advice and experience. Ron Scott, my co-administrator on the U4 project, has been an invaluable source of knowledge on the topic of mito-chondrial DNA testing. Princess Maria Semeonovna Sviatopolk-Mirski generously shared with me the results of her unique mitochondrial DNA test. Jill Whitehead provided an interesting perspective on Jewish DNA. Wendy Archer set me straight on the subject of mailing lists and message boards. Tom Hutchison collaborated with me on the ISOGG (International Society of Genetic Genealogy) Wiki, and helped me to understand the technical aspects of wiki creation. Polly Rubery joined the blogging community at the same time as me, and was a friendly sounding board for my early blog postings.

Who Do You Think You Are? Live (WDYTYA), the family history show organised by the Society of Genealogists at Olympia in London, has become a meeting place for genetic genealogists from both sides of the Atlantic in recent years – largely thanks to the work of Katherine Borges, the director of the International Society of Genetic

Genealogy, and Brian Swann, the England and Wales co-ordinator of ISOGG. I would like to thank both of them for the many enjoyable discussions we have had both over the phone and in person. I am also indebted to my genetic geneal- ogy friends and colleagues in America who came over to England for WDYTYA and shared their knowledge and insights with us during the show and afterwards over drinks and dinner. My thanks go out to Emily Aulicino, Terry Barton, Doron Behar, John and Ann Blair, Max Blankfeld, Candy Jones Campise, L.A. Chancey, Bennett Greenspan, Michael Hammer, Kenny Hedgpeth, Linda Magellan, Derrell Teat, Megan Smolenyak, Johnna St Clair and Cynthia Wells.

The ISOGG project administrators' mailing list is always a source of advice and knowledge, and I would specifically like to thank Roberta Estes, Colleen Fitzpatrick, Bill Hurst, Julie Frame Falk, Kathy Johns, CeCe Le Moore, Nancy Kiser, David Pike, John Robb, Ann Turner and Larry Vick for their helpful contributions.

I am grateful to the many family historians from around the world who have generously shared their research with me for the benefit of my Cruwys/Cruse one-name study. I am indebted to the 550 or so people from twenty-five different countries who have participated in my various DNA projects, and given me access to a wide range of DNA test results. There is nothing like trying to explain DNA results to other people to help you to understand the process yourself! I have had many enjoyable email exchanges with my project members and even had the pleasure of meeting some of them in person.

I would like to thank Penny Law from *Family History Monthly* for recommending me to the publishers, and Katharine Reeve for putting her trust in me and patiently waiting for the delivery of the manuscript long after the due date. Abbie Wood and Lindsey Smith from The History Press have worked hard behind the scenes to bring this book to fruition, and Lindsey has patiently dealt with all the many amendments that had to be made to keep the book as up-to-date as possible prior to printing.

Finally I would like to thank my family who are totally bemused by my interests in DNA and genealogy, and who will no doubt be relieved that normal life will now be resumed after the completion of this book.

I

THE GENETIC GENEALOGY REVOLUTION

1

The basic principles

… the idea that within each of our body cells we carry a tangible fragment from an ancestor from thousands of years ago is both astonishing and profound. That these pieces of DNA have travelled over thousands of miles and thousands of years to get to us, virtually unchanged, from our remote ancestors still fills me with awe, and I am not alone.

Bryan Sykes, *Blood of the Isles*

It is now over ten years since the first DNA tests for the family historian came on the market. DNA testing is no longer a tool deployed by a few brave pioneering surname project administrators, but is rapidly becoming an essential part of the research process for many genealogists. In the early years there were just a few basic low-resolution tests available at comparatively high prices from a handful of companies. In the intervening years the range of tests available has grown and prices have dropped to a more affordable level. The number of companies offering DNA tests has also expanded. Today around a million people from around the world have had their DNA analysed, either for genealogy purposes or to learn more about their deep ancestry. We have not yet reached the stage where a DNA test is ordered by everyone as a matter of routine when they begin their family history research, but most people are at least aware of the possibilities of DNA testing, even if they do not fully understand the process and have not taken a test themselves.

All humans share over 99.5 per cent of their DNA. It is the few differences in the remaining 0.5 per cent of our DNA which distinguish us from each other. A DNA test will look at those few genetic markers in our DNA that do vary from one person to another. In general terms the more DNA we have in common with another person the more closely related we are, and the more markers that can be measured the more accurately the relationship can be predicted. This brings us to the first important point which relates to all DNA tests. A DNA test on its own reveals very little. The value of the test lies in the comparison process, and the more people you can compare your results with the better.

Types of test

When the first genetic genealogy tests became available in the year 2000 there were two different types of test that could be purchased: a Y-chromosome (Y-DNA) test and a mitochondrial DNA (mtDNA) test.

A Y-DNA test explores the direct paternal line, that is, your father, your father's father, your father's father's father, and so on back in time. In most cultures the Y-chromosome usually follows the same path as the surname. For this reason, the Y-DNA test is the most popular and most useful test, and is usually the first exposure that family historians will have to DNA testing. A Y-DNA test can only be taken a by a man, as only men inherit a Y-chromosome. Women who wish to explore their surname through DNA testing, therefore, need to recruit a male relative, such as their father, brother, uncle or cousin, to take a test on their behalf. The first Y-DNA tests only looked at 10 or 12 genetic markers. Today a standard Y-DNA test will analyse a minimum of 37 markers and it is possible to be tested on 100 or more markers.

A mitochondrial DNA test is a mirror image of the Y-DNA test and follows the direct maternal line – your mother, your mother's mother, your mother's mother's mother. Both males and females inherit mitochondrial DNA from their mothers, but only the female can pass it on to the next generation. An mtDNA test can, therefore, be taken by both men and women. The early mtDNA tests looked at a small number of locations in the most variable region of the mitochondrial genome. Today the gold-standard mtDNA test is a full sequence of the entire mitochondrial genome.

The Y-chromosome and mitochondrial DNA are passed on virtually unchanged from father to son and mother to child. They effectively contain a historical record of the DNA, not just from our recent ancestors but from our ancient ancestors on the paternal and maternal lines going back for thousands and thousands of years. Y-DNA and mtDNA tests are, therefore, used not just by family historians but also by anthropologists and population geneticists who are endeavouring to reconstruct the migratory paths of our distant ancestors as they left Africa and spread out to populate the world. Consequently, these tests come with an added bonus as they will not just help with your family history research, but will also provide some insight into your deep ancestry on your direct paternal or maternal line.

The third type of test used by family historians only came onto the market at the end of 2009 and is currently available from just two companies: 23andMe and Family Tree DNA. This test analyses hundreds of thousands of autosomal DNA markers and can help us to explore all the lines on our family tree. We inherit a mixture of autosomal DNA from both our parents, but it is shuffled up and diluted with each new generation, crisscrossing all the branches in our family tree. Although an autosomal DNA test can be used to help with our research on all our family lines, it is most effective for finding relatives within the last five generations or so. In some cases it can help locate relatives within the past five to fifteen generations. These tests can be taken by both men and women.

Uses and limitations

The uses and limitations of each different type of test will be explored in detail in the following chapters of this book, but we will first of all take a look at a few of the basic principles that apply to all of the tests. Firstly, it needs to be made clear that a DNA test is not a magic solution and will not provide you with an instantaneous family history. A DNA test is just one tool which can be used as an aid to research, and it works best when it is used in conjunction with traditional documentary research. If you are lucky you might get a match with someone who is researching the same line as you and who can supplement the information that you already have. A DNA test can also, in some cases, save time and money by providing a narrower focus for your research. If, for example, you have reached a brick wall with your research in London but your surname is found in many different counties, a Y-DNA match with a well-documented line from a specific town or parish will enable you to target your research on one particular county rather than having to scour records across the whole country.

As DNA testing is essentially a match-making game, the success of a DNA test depends on whether or not you get any relevant matches. The chances of getting a match very much depend on who else is in the database. If you test with a long-standing surname project, which has representatives from most of the trees for the surname, you will have a good chance of finding a match. If there is no project for your surname, or the project only has a few members, you might be in for a long wait before you learn anything from your DNA test result. Some of the American-led projects only have participants from the US, and even if you do have a match it will not be particularly meaningful as your match is unlikely to know where in the UK his line originated. The autosomal tests from 23andMe and Family Tree DNA are still both very new and it will take time for the databases to build up in size. DNA testing is, therefore, very much a question of numbers, and the more people who participate the more we will learn. Many people do simply order a DNA test just to add their results to the company's database and see if they get any matches, but if you wish to have an immediate return on your investment it is better to test within a structured surname project or have a hypothesis in mind and select the appropriate candidates in advance for testing.

One important limitation of DNA testing is that it is very good at confirming that two people are related, but it will never tell us the name of the ancestor we share in common or when he or she lived. You are instead given a range of probabilities as to the timeframe when the common ancestor might have lived. The accuracy of the prediction also depends on the resolution of the test. If two men have identical Y-DNA results with a low-resolution test comparing a small number of markers, the results might indicate that they have a 90 per cent probability of sharing a common ancestor within the last twenty-four generations. A high-resolution test with more markers might perhaps give a 90 per cent probability of sharing a common ancestor within four generations. A 90 per cent probability also means that there is still a 10 per cent chance that the match will fall beyond the expected range.

Who to test?

The choice of who to test is partly decided by the type of test which is being taken. Both men and women can take an autosomal DNA test and a mitochondrial DNA test, but only a man can take a Y-DNA test. If a choice of candidates is available it is always preferable to test the oldest generation, but this is especially important for the autosomal DNA tests, which work within a more limited timeframe. What happens, however, if the person you would like to take a DNA test is no longer alive? People often ask if it is possible to extract DNA from a stamp licked by a deceased relative, a locket of hair, fingernail clippings or other similar items. Sadly, in nearly all cases, the answer is no. In the first place there is the risk of contamination, and there is consequently no absolute guarantee that the DNA is from the required person. Secondly, such testing is expensive as it has to be carried out in a specialist laboratory, and the success rate is low. To extract DNA from hair, the hair shaft is required. Even if any DNA can be extracted, it is highly likely that the pieces of DNA you need will not have survived. There is a greater chance of success in recovering mitochondrial DNA because there is much more mtDNA in each cell, whereas there is only one Y-chromosome, but for genealogy purposes it is usually the Y-DNA which is needed. The other related question which sometimes arises is whether or not it is possible to exhume a body in an attempt to extract DNA. Here the chances of success are even lower as DNA degrades rapidly over time, especially if it has been exposed to the elements. There is also a further hurdle to be overcome as permission is required from the church authorities before any exhumation is allowed, and it is rare for such permission to be granted. In view of all these difficulties, if you are considering getting a DNA test done on a relative it is very important to get the testing done while they are still around to provide the sample.

Choosing a testing company

Once you have decided which test you wish to take, the next stage will be to decide on a testing company. If you are considering taking a Y-DNA test, or getting a relative

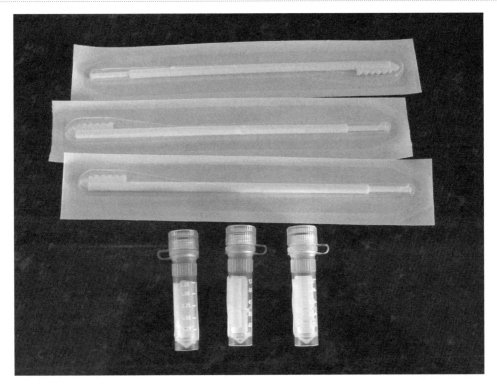

Figure 1   A typical DNA test kit consisting of vials of preservative together with some brushes for scraping the cells from inside the cheek. Three samples are usually required.

to test on your behalf, in most cases the choice will be dictated by the testing company hosting the relevant surname project. If there is no pre-existing surname project and you are interested in starting your own project I have looked at some of the issues to consider in Chapter 6. There is more flexibility with a mitochondrial DNA test, but there are many advantages to be gained from testing with a company with a large database which hosts geographical and haplogroup projects in order to maximise the chances of finding a meaningful match. These issues are explored in detail in Chapter 4. The new generation of autosomal DNA tests are reviewed in Chapter 5. The choice of company will very much depend on whether you are more interested in taking the test for health or ancestry purposes. A list of testing companies is provided in Appendix B along with brief descriptions.

It is important to remember that the DNA testing market is constantly evolving. Some companies have been at the forefront of the latest developments and continue to introduce new tests and extend their product offerings. In contrast, some of the smaller companies that appeared to be a good choice a few years ago have been taken over or have gone into liquidation. The range of tests offered will be an important consideration. It is not always easy to predict in advance the additional tests that might be required, but if you test with a company which only offers a limited range of tests, if you need to upgrade and the test you need is not offered, it would then be necessary to pay to be retested elsewhere. It is always best to get recommendations from other people who have taken DNA tests and to learn from their experiences. The best way to do this is to make use of the resources, such as mailing lists and forums, listed in Appendix A.

Taking a DNA test

Having decided on a testing company, the actual process of taking a DNA test is very straightforward and simple. There is no need to visit a doctor or have a blood sample taken. The DNA kit is sent out in the post and everything can be done in the comfort of your own home. The kit consists of some small brushes that look rather like mini toothbrushes and a few vials of preservative. The brushes are used to scrape some cells from inside your cheek. It is a completely painless process – the most difficult part is refraining from eating and drinking for at least an hour beforehand! Once the swab has been taken, a plunger is pressed on the brush to release it into the vial. The pots are then sealed up and go back in the post to the testing laboratory. You will usually be asked to provide samples to fill three vials. One testing company, 23andMe, collects DNA in a different way, and requires you to spit into a container. Whichever method is used, once your kit has been received in the lab, it will take anything from four to eight weeks to receive your results. All the major companies will allow you to access your results online and will provide various educational resources to help you to understand your results.

Having discussed the basic principles, we will now move on to explore the different types of test in depth, beginning with the Y-chromosome DNA test and its particular application within surname projects.

2

Surnames and the paternal line

The most popular and widely used DNA test for family history purposes is the Y-chromosome DNA test, colloquially known as a Y-DNA test. The Y-chromosome is passed on from father to son and carries the gene which determines the male sex. Conveniently for the family historian, the path of Y-chromosome transmission usually corresponds with the inheritance of surnames, making the Y-DNA test a very valuable tool as an aid to traditional documentary research. For family history purposes Y-DNA tests are usually co-ordinated within surname projects. Commercial Y-DNA tests first became available in the year 2000. By the end of the decade several hundred thousand men had had their Y-DNA tested, and there were in excess of 6,000 surname projects. Women cannot, of course, take a Y-DNA test as they do not inherit the Y-chromosome. Most women will, however, have a father, brother, uncle or cousin who can take the test in their place.

The Y-chromosome is passed on from father to son virtually unchanged. Indeed when scientists first began to explore the Y-chromosome they found so few differences that it was thought that it would not be very useful for genealogical or evolutionary studies! Gradually, however, as the sequencing technology improved and new techniques were developed, scientists began to spot patterns in the millions of letters that make up the Y-chromosome and discovered that there were particular locations or 'markers' which did sometimes change. These markers are known as short tandem repeats (STRs). A number of studies have been published comparing these markers between father and son to establish the rate of change – the mutation rate. It has also been discovered that some markers mutate at a faster rate than others. Once the mutation rates have been established for the various markers it is then possible to infer the relationship between two men purely on the basis of their DNA results and the number of differences between them. Fortunately, we do not have to worry about doing any complicated calculations ourselves. The testing companies do all the maths for us and will provide you with a list of your matches in their database, together with an estimate as to the time when you most probably shared a common ancestor.

Y-STR (short tandem repeat) markers are repeating sequences of DNA found in the Y-chromosome. STR markers are given names usually beginning with the letters DYS (which is an abbreviation of DNA Y-chromosome Segment). STR markers are then given a unique identification number such as DYS 19 or DYS 390.

DNA consists of a sequence of just four letters – A, T, C and G – combined in pairs in a spiralling ladder structure. Sometimes the DNA appears to stutter and a sequence of letters will be repeated. On marker DYS 393, for example, many men have a series of thirteen repeats of the letters AGAT:

CTGTCTG AGAT AGAT AGAT AGAT AGAT AGAT AGAT AGAT AGAT AGAT AGAT AGAT AGAT TCTGCC

The number of repeats is counted on each marker to give you a value or **allele** for all the markers tested. The example above would be written as DYS = 13. Normally a son would have the same Y-STR markers as his father. Very occasionally an error in the copying process occurs and a son will have a different value to his father. The son will then pass on this new mutated value to his own sons who in turn will pass it on to future generations. The mutations are generally harmless and usually have no medical implications.

Typically, a commercial Y-DNA test will provide results for 37 or 43 Y-STR markers, with higher-resolution tests being made available at 67 or 111 markers. A Y-DNA test result will be shown as a set of numbers representing the alleles for each marker tested. The combination of numbers for all the markers tested is known as a **haplotype**.

Table 1   Y-STR markers, alleles and haplotypes.

A standard Y-DNA test will include a panel of Y-STR markers. When Y-DNA tests first became commercially available in the year 2000, only 10 or 12-marker tests could be purchased. These tests are now considered to be low-resolution tests because a large number of men with many different surnames will have identical results when tested at 10 or 12 markers. As more markers are added to the mix the irrelevant matches start to disappear, leaving only the matches which are of genealogical significance. The standard Y-DNA test today uses at least 37 or 43 markers. Some companies offer the option to test additional panels of markers which can bring the total number of markers tested up to over 100. A Y-DNA test result is received in the form of a string of numbers representing the values for each of the markers tested. On its own this string of numbers is essentially meaningless. The value of the test comes when you start to compare your numbers with other people and, in particular, with men who share the same surname. Close relations, such as father and son, uncle and nephew and first and second cousins, will in most cases match each other on 37 out of 37 markers. This is known as a 37/37 match. In other words, they will have an identical set of numbers on all 37 markers. The further back in time you go the greater the chance of finding a mutation. Two third cousins might, therefore, match on 36/37 markers. Two sixth cousins might match on 35/37 markers. The more matching markers the two men share the more closely related they will be. If they mismatch on too many markers they will not share a common patrilineal ancestor within a genealogical timeframe, or in other words in the 900 or so years since surnames began to be introduced.

A DNA test is, therefore, a very effective tool to determine whether or not two people with the same surname are related, but it will not give you the name of the common ancestor or tell you when that ancestor might have lived. The names and dates can only be determined by traditional documentary research.

Surname projects

A Y-DNA test is best taken within a structured surname project and the value of the test will grow over time as more people join the project and a picture of the surname's distribution and origins begins to emerge. The Y-DNA test can be used within a surname project in a number of ways. Firstly, it can be used to verify the existing documentary research. With the increasing availability of online records such as civil registration indexes and census records, it is generally a reasonably straight-forward matter to trace a British line back to the beginning of the nineteenth century. However, as you go further back in time through the parish registers the links between each generation become less conclusive, especially if no other sup-porting evidence can be found such as a will or an obituary. You might, therefore, find a baptism record in one parish which matches the age given in a burial record

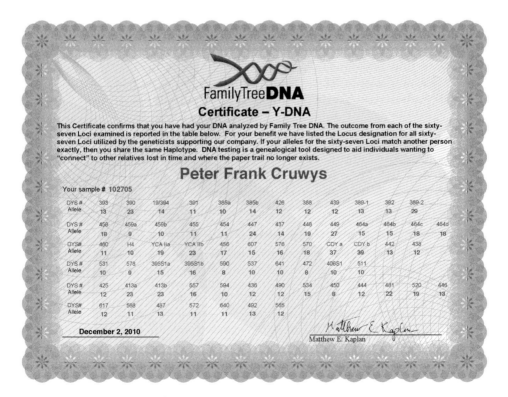

Figure 2   A certificate showing the results of a 67-marker Y-DNA test from the author's father.

in a neighbouring parish. With a rare surname it is usually safe to conclude that you have found the right baptism but it is often easy to make false assumptions, especially if the parish registers for the neighbouring parishes are not readily available online. A Y-DNA test, therefore, provides the opportunity to check the validity of your research, providing that the appropriate candidates for testing can be found.

A Y-DNA test can also be used within a surname project to test a particular hypothesis, such as whether or not two lines are related. It is often the case that two people will be researching the same surname but are unable to find any link in the paper trail – one line might trace back to the 1600s in Devon and another line might be stuck in the 1700s just across the county border in Somerset. If a male descendant from each line takes a Y-DNA test it will be possible to establish once and for all whether or not the two lines are related on the paternal line. A match will provide conclusive proof of the hypothesis, but the lack of a match does not rule out the possibility that the two men are related on a female line. If the lines do not match, it is advisable to test a second candidate from each line so that the lines can be verified back to the earliest possible date, thus ruling out the possibility of a break in the link between the Y-chromosome and the surname in more recent times.

Most surname projects will want to test people from as many different trees as possible to see which lines are related. As projects grow in size the chances of finding a match within the surname project will greatly increase. My own Cruwys/Cruse DNA Project now has almost sixty project members. Although I still have quite a few singletons awaiting matches, many of the other results are beginning to cluster together into

Cruwys/Cruse/Crewes DNA project - Y-DNA Classic Chart

* Haplogroups in green have been confirmed by SNP testing. Haplogroups in red have been predicted by Family Tree DNA based on <u>unambiguous</u> results in the individual's personal
* is in the HAPLO field then we feel that the comparative results are not clear and unambiguous and if the kit holder wants to know their SNP with 100% confidence they may consider o

To read more about how to understand this chart please visit the FAQ here

Markers: [Y-DNA12 ▾]   Page Size: [500]   ☑ Show All Columns

Kit Number	Paternal Ancestor Name	Country	Haplogroup	DYS393	DYS390	DYS19	DYS391	DYS385	DYS426	DYS388	DYS439	DYS389I	DYS392	DYS389II	DYS458	DYS459	DYS455	DYS454	DYS447	DYS437	DYS448
a. Cruwys group 1																					
122936	George Cruwys b. c.1782 Mariansleigh?, Devon	England	R1b1a2	13	23	14	11	10-14	12	12	12	13	11	29	18	9-10	11	11	24	14	19
102705	Hannibal Cruse, m. 1597, Winkleigh, Devon, England	England	R1b1a2a1a1a4	13	23	14	11	10-14	12	12	12	13	13	29	18	9-10	11	11	24	14	19
111477	James Cruwys b.1848 PEI, Canada son of William	England	R1b1a2	13	23	14	11	10-14	12	12	12	13	13	29	18	9-10	11	11	24	14	19
118547	George Cruwys b.1850 PEI, Canada, son of William	England	R1b1a2	13	23	14	11	10-14	12	12	12	13	13	29	18	9-10	11	11	24	14	19
107091	John Crewes m. 1554 Liskeard, Cornwall	England	R1b1a2a1a1	13	23	14	12	12-14	12	12	12	13	13	29	18	9-10	11	11	24	14	19
130860	James Cruise of James & Dora Doyle b. 1859 Dublin	Ireland	R1b1a2a1a1a4	13	23	14	12	12-14	12	12	12	13	13	29	19	9-10	11	11	23	14	19
a. Cruwys group 2																					
115384	John Cruwys m. Elizabeth Prichard 1817 Westminster	England	G	14	22	15	10	14-14	11	13	10	13	11	30	17	9-9	11	11	23	16	21
107548	John Cruwys m. 1708 Oakford, Devon	England	G	14	22	15	10	14-14	11	13	11	13	11	30	17	9-9	11	11	23	15	21
121449	John Cruwys m. Elizabeth Prichard 1817 Westminster	England	G2a3b1	14	22	15	10	14-14	11	13	11	13	11	30	17	9-9	11	11	23	16	21
127489	Simon Cruse m.1759 Kilkhampton, Cornwall	South Africa	G	14	22	15	10	14-14	11	13	11	13	11	30	17	9-9	11	11	23	16	21
a. Cruwys group 3																					
121968	William Cruwys m Sarah Taylor 1820 Witheridge, Dev	England	R1b1a2	13	25	14	12	11-14	12	12	11	13	13	29	18	9-9	11	11	25	15	19
b. Cruse group 1																					
127487	William Cruse d.1717 Ogbourne St George, Wiltshire	England	R1b1a2	14	24	15	10	11-11	12	12	12	13	14	29	19	9-9	11	11	25	15	19
135505	William Cruse d.1717 Ogbourne St George, Wiltshire	England	R1b1a2a1a1b3	14	24	15	10	11-11	12	12	12	13	14	29	19	9-9	11	11	25	15	19
113779	William Cruse m.1706 Compton Beauchamp, Berkshire	England	R1b1a2	14	24	15	11	11-11	12	12	12	13	14	29	19	9-9	11	11	25	15	19
106068	Henry Cruse m. 1848 Worcester, South Africa	England	R1b1a2	14	24	15	11	11-11	12	12	12	13	14	29	19	9-9	11	11	25	15	19
b. Cruse group 2																					
127491	William Cruse b.1769 Woolfardisworthy, Devon	England	I2b	15	23	15	10	14-15	11	13	11	14	12	32	15	8-8	11	11	24	14	20
134832	Edward Cruse d. 1795 Ashburton, Devon	England	I2b1	15	23	15	10	15-15	11	13	11	14	12	32	15	8-8	11	11	24	14	20

Figure 3   A display of Y-DNA results from the Cruwys project. The men with matching or closely matching results are grouped together.

distinct genetic families. I have often been surprised at the lines which do match. Other lines which I was convinced were related turned out to be not connected at all!

In the early days of a surname project the focus will probably be on locating a single representative of each documented line to participate in the project. In the long run it is advisable to test at least two people from each line to verify the tree back to the point where the men share a common ancestor. If you have successfully documented a tree back to the 1600s or earlier, it is advisable to test descendants from as many of the different branches as possible. If enough people are tested from each branch it is sometimes possible to identify, by a process of elimination, specific mutations which are unique to a particular branch. Mutations do, however, occur at random and there is unfortunately no guarantee that a crucial branch-defining mutation will occur where it will be of most use! Family trees also come in all shapes and sizes, and some are more reproductively successful than others. Often one branch will flourish and have multiple living descendants, whereas other branches have become extinct or might only have a handful of living descendants. It then becomes a matter of priority to trace those descendants and persuade them to share their DNA.

All projects will have a number of lines which are stuck in more recent times. London research is particularly problematic, especially if your ancestor unhelpfully died before the 1851 census and, therefore, left no indication as to his place of birth. The 1841 census does at least provide the birth county, but it can still be quite a difficult task narrowing the search down to a particular parish within that county. The ancestor who gives his place of birth in 1841 as Scotland or Ireland presents even more of a challenge, especially if he has a particularly common surname! It can also be difficult researching emigrant lines, especially to Canada and the US where civil registration started very late, and in many cases not until the early 1900s. Although census records are available they do not provide sufficient information on the place of origin to be useful to the family historian, and it is only usually the birth country which is recorded. DNA testing can be a very useful tool in such scenarios. The chances of success depend very much on the size of the surname project and the range of lines tested, but if there is a match with a well-documented line originating in a particular town or village, your research will have much more focus and there will be a much greater chance of finding the link in the paper trail.

I have a good example of how this process works in my own project. One of my project members is descended from a shoemaker and saddler by the name of Henry Cruse. Henry appears to have begun his career as a mariner. According to family legend he was the sole survivor of a shipwreck off the coast of South Africa in the early 1840s. He then stayed in South Africa, married and had a family. The only record which provides any information about his origin is his South African death notice, which gave his age at death, the name of his mother, Mary Cruse, and indicated that he was born in Great Britain. Despite a dedicated search in British records it proved impossible to make any progress on his ancestry. However, a DNA test on one of Henry's descendants provided the vital breakthrough. He matched with another line which was already well researched and could be traced back to the small village of Ogbourne St George in Wiltshire. We now know where the South African line originated and we have also been able to identify a possible link in the paper trail, which we hope eventually to prove by further DNA testing.

Illegitimacy

Illegitimacy is another problem that can sometimes be solved through DNA testing. These tests are usually best conducted within a surname project. A surname project is interested in collecting DNA samples from all bearers of the surname, and it is important to research the illegitimate lines to build up a picture of the illegitimacy rate for the surname over the centuries.

Illegitimacy rates have varied considerably in the last 500 years. Peter Laslett and Karla Oosterveen published a detailed survey of illegitimacy figures extracted from parish registers and the reports of the registrar general in 1973.[1] According to their statistics the illegitimacy rate was around 4.5 per cent in the late 1500s. In the next fifty years the rate dropped sharply to a low of 0.5 per cent between 1551 and 1560. The number of illegitimate births then grew steadily, with a particularly sharp increase in the late 1700s, to reach 6 per cent by 1800. Between 1845 and 1921, 5.3 per cent of births recorded in England and Wales were illegitimate. With an increasingly secular society and a decline in the popularity of marriage the number of babies born out of wedlock has increased dramatically in recent decades. Figures from the Office for National Statistics show that 46 per cent of births in England and Wales in 2009 occurred outside of marriage. However, 84 per cent of births were registered to parents living at the same address whether married or co-habiting, a figure which has barely changed in the last decade.[2]

In practice, therefore, many people taking a DNA test will bear a surname that descends from an illegitimate line. Often the illegitimacy will already have been established from the documentary research. For births in England and Wales from 1837 onwards the father's name will be absent from the birth certificate, and the baby will be registered with the mother's surname. Prior to the beginning of civil registration in 1837 the baptism will be recorded in the parish registers, but the father's name is rarely given. Sometimes the child will be given the father's surname as a middle name. If you are lucky a bastardy bond will be found, naming the father and the amount of money he paid to the parish overseers to support his child. Parish records might also reveal the existence of a bastardy order, whereby the mother was called to testify before the parish officials and was examined under oath to reveal the identity of the father. The father might then be ordered to pay the mother, or the parish, maintenance payments to support his reputed child. If research has revealed a possible surname for the father, DNA testing is a very useful tool to test the hypothesis, provided that a suitable candidate for testing can be found for the surname in question.

Most people who discover an illegitimate birth in their tree will probably struggle to find any clue in the paper records as to the identity of the father. In such cases a DNA test might, in time, provide the breakthrough by providing a high-resolution match with a different surname. Ideally the match will also have ancestry from the same town, village or county as your own ancestor. The process is still something of a lottery, but the chances of success will improve over time as the DNA databases grow in size and more surnames are represented in DNA projects. When searching for a match with a different surname it is advisable to order the maximum number of markers possible to rule out coincidental matches. If you are lucky enough to find a match with another surname you can join the DNA projects for both surnames.

The Swinfield DNA project has an excellent example of an illegitimacy which was resolved through DNA testing. William Swinfield was born in 1841 in Earl Shilton, Leicestershire. According to his birth certificate he was the legitimate child of Thomas and Sarah Swinfield, who had married in 1829. However, at the time of the 1841 census Thomas was no longer living with Sarah and had set up home with another woman in Nottinghamshire, while Sarah stayed behind with the children in Leicestershire. William's younger brother Joseph was born in 1843 in the same parish, but the pretence of a marriage had by now been abandoned and the space for the father's name was left blank on his birth certificate. Male descendants of both William and Joseph took a Y-DNA test. They both matched each other, proving that they had the same father. A descendant of Thomas Swinfield's brother was also tested but he did not match the other two Swinfields, so it was clear that Thomas Swinfield was not the boys' genetic father. Interestingly, however, the illegitimate Swinfields had DNA matches with a number of men with the surname Brown. It just so happened that in the 1841 census an unmarried man by the name of Thomas Brown was lodging with Sarah Swinfield and her children! He continued to live with Sarah and her family until his death in 1892. The most likely explanation, therefore, is that the lodger was the boys' father. It now remains to find a descendant of Thomas Brown to take a DNA test to confirm the hypothesis.

Non-paternity events

Sooner or later, within any surname project, a situation will be encountered when a surprising DNA result is received and a person does not match the expected people within the project. There are a number of reasons which can account for a break in the link between the Y-chromosome and the surname. The rather clumsy phrase 'non-paternity event' (NPE) has become a catch-all to describe these situations. Other phrases have been suggested, such as misattributed paternity, non-paternal surname, false-paternity event and non-patrilineal transmission, but none have caught on within the genetic genealogy community. Regardless of the terminology used, there are a number of reasons which can account for the lack of the expected match:

Faulty research The first course of action when results do not match as expected is to check the research of both parties to ensure that no false assumptions have been made. I have seen a lot of researchers go astray when they find what they think is a matching baptism online in the IGI (International Genealogical Index). They will then merrily pursue their line back for several more generations in blissful ignorance of the fact that their supposed ancestor was buried just a few months after birth! The correct baptism might well be found instead in a neighbouring parish whose records have not been made available online.

Illegitimacy As we have already seen, illegitimacy is the primary reason for a break in the link between a surname and the Y-chromosome. If the illegitimacy has occurred in the last few hundred years there will usually be documentary evidence. A lack of a match could, however, be caused by a more deep-rooted illegitimacy which has not yet been uncovered in the course of the research. If the illegitimacy occurred prior to the introduction of parish registers in 1538, or if the early parish registers have not survived, there is little chance of finding any documentary proof of the event.

Aliases Aliases rarely appear in written sources today but can often be seen in early parish registers, wills and other documents. George Redmonds provides a detailed discussion of aliases in his book *Surnames and Genealogy: A New Approach.*[3] He cites numerous examples from Yorkshire sources such as 'John Jempson alias Morritt' from the West Haddlesey parish registers in 1598, and 'William Cockell alias Stringer' in Kirkburton in 1646. The earliest reference he found dated back to 1446. M.D. Hooper performed a detailed study of aliases in a variety of sources in Devon. He reported that aliases were most commonly used between 1600 and 1650 and had all but disappeared by the early 1800s.[4] He further found that 'The more common a surname is the more likely is it to have aliases associated with it. Thus there are significantly more aliases for names like Adams, Andrews, Baker, Bennett, Clarke, Cooke, Hill, Hooper, Smith, Stephens, Wood or White.' Mike Brown has been interested in aliases for many years and maintains an index of all the incidences he has discovered in Devon sources. He found that the origins of the vast majority of aliases in his index were unresolved, but were often very localised, being confined just to one parish or a small group of neighbouring parishes.[5] He suggests that 'this factor points strongly towards the use of many aliases in order to protect the inheritance, or interests, of children in a single generation'. The use of the term 'alias' in the written record usually disappears within one or two generations, with all future descendants bearing a single surname which will in most cases not tally with their Y-chromosome lineage. Whatever the reasons for the adoption of aliases, it is clear that they will account for some instances of unexpected DNA mismatches. With assiduous research it might well be possible to resolve some of these cases, but many more will remain a mystery.

Change of surname In England and Wales it is perfectly legal to change your surname at any time, providing there is no intent to deceive or defraud another person. There is no legal procedure to follow in order to change a name. You simply start using the new name. No records are available of the number of people who have chosen to change their surname, though many people opt to change their name by deed poll to facilitate the transition to the new surname. The UK Deed Poll Service reports that it has changed over 200,000 people's names in the last five years alone.[6] Historical records of surname changes can sometimes be found in aristocratic or gentry families where surnames were often changed in honour of a famous ancestor, or to preserve a more prestigious surname. I have one such example in my Cruwys one-name study. George Sharland (1758–1831), the son of George Sharland and Harriet Cruwys of Cruwys Morchard, changed his name to Cruwys by Royal Licence in 1831. He was thenceforward known as George Sharland Cruwys. All his male descendants to this day bear the Cruwys surname.

Adoption From 1927 onwards all adoptions granted by the courts in England and Wales, and some overseas adoptions, are recorded in the Adopted Children Register. The register is not open to public search or inspection, but adoptees and their parents can apply to receive adoption certificates. Prior to 1927 an adoption was a private arrangement and few records are likely to exist, though records for some charities such as Dr Barnardo's have survived. Most people today will know that they were adopted but an adoption in an earlier generation will not necessarily be apparent from the available records. To cover the shame of illegitimacy a child was often informally adopted by his or her grandparents or other family members, who then passed off the child as their own. Suspicions will be aroused if a young child appears in a census with an unusually mature mother, though the birth certificate will generally reveal the real mother's name. Informal adoptions often occurred in the case of a second marriage with the children being brought up by a stepfather and adopting his surname. These adoptions will generally be uncovered during the course of your research by checking the appropriate sources. If no birth certificate can be found or, in earlier records, if no baptismal record can be located, an adoption might not necessarily be apparent. The use of DNA testing to find out the surname of the biological father is discussed later in this chapter.

False paternity False paternity, or misattributed paternity, occurs when the alleged father of a child is not the biological father. Such a situation can arise when a mother conceives a child by a man who is not her husband or live-in partner, but passes the child off as her partner's. The term 'paternity fraud' has been coined in more recent times to describe a situation where a woman wilfully misattributes paternity for financial gain. Estimates of the rate of false paternity vary wildly from 1–30 per cent, but reliable data are understandably hard to come by. Many of the studies that provide statistics on non-paternity rates are provided by paternity-testing laboratories. These studies are strongly biased towards men who have reason to have suspicions. In one of the most thorough cross-cultural studies reported to date, it was found that even when paternity confidence was low, the suspicions were mostly unfounded and only 29.8 per cent of men could be excluded as the biological fathers of the children in question.[7]

Fortunately, non-paternity events, whatever the cause might be, are relatively rare. The rate of NPEs is estimated to be somewhere between 1 and 5 per cent.[8] Within a surname project NPEs will, however, have a cumulative effect, and even projects focusing on low-frequency surnames can expect to have a number of distinct genetic clusters. No surname project will have a uniform set of 100 per cent matching results.

Finding a surname project

If you are thinking of taking a Y-DNA test or, if you are female and are hoping to persuade a male relative to take a test on your behalf, it is usually best to order through a surname project. Kits can be purchased at the discounted project price and you will have the chance to compare your results with other people who share your surname. There are currently just two companies which host surname projects: Family Tree DNA (FTDNA) and Ancestry.com DNA. A third company, the British-based DNA Heritage, was acquired by Family Tree DNA in April 2011, and customers were given the option of transferring their results to the Family Tree DNA database. Family Tree DNA was one of the first two companies to offer Y-DNA tests when they became available in the year 2000. It is now the market leader, offering the widest range of tests and hosting the largest number of surname projects. By the end of 2010 there were over 6,000 surname projects at FTDNA, with over 100,000 unique surnames represented in their database. Ancestry.com joined the genetic genealogy market in 2007 when they partnered with the now-defunct company Relative Genetics. Ancestry does not provide information about the number of surname projects they host, and no public lists are provided, but its database can be searched by surname to see if a relevant project exists.

   Family Tree DNA previously maintained a proprietary database and did not accept Y-DNA results from other testing companies. Following on from their acquisition of DNA Heritage, the database was upgraded in August 2011 to allow customers from some other companies to upload their results for a small fee. Nearly all the DNA projects hosted at FTDNA maintain public websites where the DNA results can be freely viewed. Ancestry projects are known as DNA groups. The groups also serve as collaborative websites for teams of researchers working on a surname. Customers of other testing companies can also upload their results to Ancestry.com and join the DNA groups. The membership numbers for the Ancestry.com groups do not, therefore, reflect the number of people who have tested with the company. Most of the groups are closed and you can only see the DNA results if you join the group. The larger surname projects at Ancestry.com are mostly those which were previously hosted at Relative Genetics. For some surnames, particularly the more common surnames, there are sizeable projects at both FTDNA and Ancestry.com. If your surname is found in two different projects it is worth contacting the project administrators of both projects to find out which project would be most suitable for your circumstances. The testing companies use different panels of markers, which makes it more difficult to compare results between companies. It is therefore in your interest to test with the project that has the most relevant results for your surname.

Surname projects come in all shapes and sizes. Some of the pioneer projects, which were set up when Y-DNA tests first became available, now have a large number of project members. Other projects might have only just started out and will only have tested one or two people. As might be expected, there are large projects for all the most common British surnames. The two largest surname projects, Williams and Johnson, had over 800 members by the end of 2010. Some projects will focus on a surname in a particular geographical area whereas others will have a worldwide focus. The Smiths, for example, are subdivided into three separate projects: one for Smiths worldwide, a second project for Smiths in the northern states of America and a third for Smiths from the southern states. As the main purpose of the test is to compare your results with other people, the initial success of your test will, therefore, depend on the number of people and the number of lines represented in the surname project. If you are joining a well-established project you might get a match straightaway. If you join a newer project you will probably have to wait longer for a match. You can help to speed up the process by encouraging other people with your surname to join the project as well.

By testing with a surname project you will also, in most cases, benefit from the advice of an experienced surname project administrator. Surname projects are run by volunteers who all have their own methodologies, and so some projects are better organised than others. Project administrators do not receive any remuneration for their work and the amount of time they can devote to their project will vary considerably. Real life can sometimes get in the way! Larger projects will often have a co-administrator or a team of co-administrators who will take on specific functions within the project. The administrators of projects for high-frequency surnames will probably have a good overview of the structure of a surname and the number of different lines represented in the project, but will understandably not have the time to get involved in the genealogical research of individual project members unless there is a match with their own particular line. They will take responsibility for placing matching DNA results into groups or clusters of 'genetic families' for display on the project website, but will leave their project members to contact their matches and compare genealogical notes. The better organised projects will encourage project members to submit a pedigree for their direct paternal line. This information will either be stored by the project administrator or displayed on the public website where applicable. The administrators of DNA projects for less common surnames will often take a more proactive role in the genealogical research, though their research will often be restricted to one country or a specific geographical region within that country.

The most advanced DNA projects are run in the most part by members of the Guild of One-Name Studies. Guild members are committed to researching 'facts about a surname and all the people who have held it, as opposed to a particular pedigree (the ancestors of one person) or descendancy (the descendants of one person or couple)'. The majority of Guild-registered one-name studies currently focus on less common surnames, though some high-frequency surnames, such as Phillips and Fisher, are also being studied. For low-frequency surnames of British origin, Guild members will typically collect all the birth, marriage and death references for their surname from the General Register Office indexes from the beginning of civil registration in 1837 to the present. Over time the member will attempt to reconstruct all the trees for the surname using censuses, wills, parish registers and other documents. The member will also try to identify the countries where name-bearers have emigrated and collect records from these countries too. The process is often hastened by the receipt of pedigrees and background information from other interested researchers. A growing number of Guild members are now adding a DNA project to their one-name study. The combination of whole-surname reconstruction with a comprehensive corpus of DNA results can provide a unique insight into the origins and distribution of the surname. This dual documentary/DNA approach is described in detail by Chris Pomery in an article published in the *Journal of Genetic Genealogy* in 2009.[9] The methodology was discussed in a follow-up paper published in the same journal in 2010.[10]

There are currently around 300 DNA projects run by members of the Guild of One-Name Studies, though many of these projects are still in their infancy. Some Guild members were, however, amongst the early pioneers of DNA testing. Guild member Alan Savin embarked on the first ever Y-chromosome surname project back in 1997, three years before the tests became available on a commercial basis. The study was carried out in collaboration with Dr Mark Thomas, Professor of Evolutionary Genetics, at University College London. Other pioneering Guild projects include those for the surnames Carden, Meates, Plant and

Pomeroy. Preliminary results from some of these projects have been published and the appropriate links can be found on the project websites, which are listed in Appendix C. The majority of Guild DNA projects are run by project administrators in the UK, but a growing number of American-based DNA project administrators are now registering studies with the Guild.

The vast majority of DNA projects are, however, currently based in the US. Often the initial focus of these projects was to test descendants from an early colonial line or to focus on a surname in a particular US state. As the project progresses and the benefits of DNA testing become apparent, the administrator will seek to broaden the project and attempt to study the surname on a more global basis – but with a particular emphasis on the country of origin, which is often, though not always, in the British Isles. Such projects will often have a large body of DNA results from the US and few, if any, results from the UK and Ireland. If a project does have a large percentage of American testees you might well have to wait longer for a match. The early emigrants to the US only consti-tuted a tiny fraction of the British population, and so representatives of most of the British lines for each surname will not be found in America. The situation is likely to be more pronounced with English surnames, as proportionately more people emigrated from Scotland and Ireland. Conversely, some British lines will have become extinct in their home country but might still thrive in the US. If you wish to speed up the matching process you could take a more proactive role and encourage more people from the UK to join the project for your surname. If a project does have an all-American focus another alternative is to set up a new project for the surname in the British Isles. However, unless a surname is particu-larly common, it is normally best to co-ordinate all the results in one project, as surnames are not respectful of country or county boundaries!

A few lucky people will find that they are eligible for a free Y-DNA test. Some surname projects are co-ordinated through family associations and the money raised from membership subscriptions is used to fund the cost of a test. Other projects will receive donations from its members to pay for tests for candidates from a particular line of interest, and usually one which is not yet represented in the project. Some of the large American projects have been able to galvanise their project members into sponsoring tests for UK residents. The Phillips DNA project has been particularly successful at fundraising and is able to offer a free Y-DNA test to anyone with the surname Phillips who lives in the UK, Ireland or mainland Europe and is able to supply a Phillips family tree that traces back at least five gen-erations. There are a number of other surname projects, such as Pitts and Graves, which have similar offers.

Geographical projects

For some people a surname project will not be an appropriate platform for DNA testing, and a geographical project might be a more suitable option – while still providing the facility to obtain the discounted project pricing and to benefit from the guidance of a project administrator.

Most English-speaking countries started to adopt surnames from the twelfth century onwards, though surnames began to appear in Ireland in the middle of the tenth century. However, in many countries and cultures surnames are a relatively recent innovation. In Wales, patronymic names such as 'John ap Robert' (John son of Robert) were used until at least the sixteenth century and sometimes much later. Scandinavian countries also adopted a patronymic naming system with the suffix *son* or *sen* added to the forename, to produce names such as Karlssen and Eriksson, which reflect the forename of the child's father and not the paternal lineage. Patronymic names only became fixed as surnames in Scandinavia in the nineteenth and twentieth centuries. In Eastern European countries surnames often did not come into usage until the late eighteenth and early nineteenth centuries. Iceland continues to use patronymic and sometimes matronymic names to this day. Surname projects are obviously not appropriate for patronymic and matronymic surnames. Instead a range of geographical projects has been established to collate DNA results from particular countries or regions. All the large geographical projects can be found at Family Tree DNA. Most of these projects will also collect mitochondrial DNA results, and some will also co-ordinate the results from the new generation of autosomal DNA tests (see Chapter 5). There are now projects for most of the major European countries, such as France, Germany, Denmark, Norway, Finland, Spain and Portugal, as well as a growing range of projects for countries in other continents. As with surname projects, many geographical projects initially started in America, but many now have project administrators or co-administrators living in the home country. The Finland project is a particularly successful example. It was established at the end of 2006 by a Finnish project administrator and he and his very active team of co-administrators have succeeded in recruiting over 2,000 participants. A list of the major European geographical projects is provided in Appendix C.

Another scenario where a geographical project might be the best option is when there is no pre-existing project for your surname. The subject of setting up a surname project is covered in Chapter 6. It is not a difficult process, but does require a certain amount of commitment and not everyone will be ready to take on the challenge. If you test through a geographical project you will be able to compare your results with other people from the same region or country and get a feel for how the testing process works. Over time, other people with your surname will join the project and when you or someone else is ready to establish a surname project there will be a

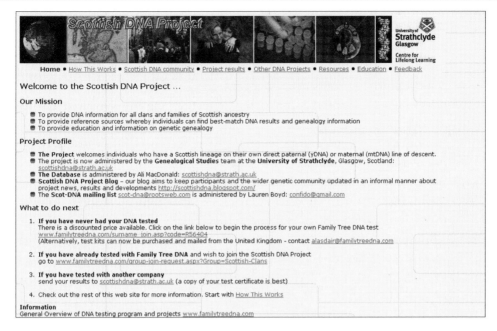

Figure 4   The Scottish DNA Project (formerly the Scottish Clans Project), established in October 2001 by John Hansen, was one of the earliest geographical projects. The project is now administered by the Genealogical Studies team at the University of Strathclyde, Glasgow, and collects both Y-DNA and mtDNA results.

ready–made set of results to get the project off to a good start. A geographical project is also a useful solution if you are hoping to get an elderly relative to take a test on your behalf. You will want to ensure that his DNA is stored before it is too late, and there will not necessarily be time to wait until a suitable surname project has been established. The project system is very flexible and it is possible to belong to a surname project and several geographical projects at the same time.

There are a number of different projects for the British Isles and a full list is given in Appendix C. There are large projects for Wales, Ireland and Scotland. There are also numerous projects for the various Scottish and Irish clans. The Clan Donald and Clan Fraser projects now each have over 1,000 project members. Curiously there is no overall project for England, though there is instead a very large general project for the British Isles which had attracted over 4,500 project members by the end of 2010.

Island populations make an ideal subject for a geographical study because of their relative isolation, which consequently produces a limited pool of surnames. There are well–established DNA projects for the Shetland Islands and the Hebrides, and a new Manx DNA project was set up in 2010. A more recent innovation is the introduction of projects for specific English counties. There are currently projects for Devon, Hampshire and Northumberland as well as a project for East Anglia. No doubt other similar projects will be set up in due course. I set up the Devon project in March 2009 when I realised that there was an unfulfilled need for such a project. Many of my project members have names which are not yet represented in a surname project. One project member was able to get her father's DNA tested through the project after he was diagnosed with a serious illness. I have some people in the project who are descended from illegitimate lines and are hoping to find a match with a different surname to enable them to pursue their documentary research. A number of my project members are conducting mini surname projects under my guidance within the framework of the Devon project, and the Challacombes and Brownings have got off to a particularly good start.

Geographical projects, like surname projects, are run by volunteer project administrators who set down their own criteria for project membership. Some projects have very strict requirements and applicants will be required to supply a pedigree or to have a specific surname associated with the region. Other projects will have much broader entry criteria and will accept anyone with a presumed heritage from the country or region in question.

Adoptions

Y-DNA testing can be a very useful tool to help a male adoptee in the quest for the surname of his biological father. If you have no idea of your father's surname or the county, region or country where your father originated then a surname project or geographical project will not be appropriate. To fill the void, Family Tree DNA set up a special project for adoptees. The Adopted DNA project reached the 1,000-member milestone in the autumn of 2010. The company now claims that between 30 and 40 per cent of adoptees who test through this project find a match with a potential ancestral surname. The majority of project members are in America and the success rate will probably be slightly less for British adoptees as there are comparatively fewer British people in the database, and only a small proportion of genetic lines from Britain are represented in the American population.

Ordering a test

There is now such a broad range of projects available that most people should be able to find a suitable project, and the choice of testing company will, therefore, be decided for you. If you are thinking of setting up your own surname project you will need to decide which company to choose to host your project. The subject of choosing a testing company is covered in Chapter 5. Once you have found a relevant project the next stage will be to decide which tests to order. If you are also interested in taking a mitochondrial DNA test or an autosomal DNA test then it is usually more economical to order these together in a bundle.

When Y-DNA tests were first introduced on a commercial basis only low-resolution tests at 10 or 12 markers were available. Family Tree DNA introduced a 25-marker test in the summer of 2002 and a 37-marker test at the end of 2003. Their gold-standard 67-marker test was launched in the summer of 2006 and a 111-marker test became available in February 2011. DNA Ancestry.com, meanwhile, announced the launch of their DNA testing service in October 2007 and currently offer tests for 33 and 46 markers. Ancestry.com, rather confusingly, counts their markers in a somewhat creative way by including in their testing panel 3 markers which normally have null values. The other companies routinely test for these markers and report values if found, but do not include them in their marker count. Family Tree DNA uses the laboratories at the University of Arizona and also does some tests in their own Genomics Research Centre in Houston, Texas. Ancestry's DNA tests are carried out in the Sorenson Genomics laboratories in Salt Lake City, Utah. There is considerable overlap in the range of markers offered by FTDNA and Sorenson, but there are a few markers which are unique to each laboratory, making it more difficult to compare results.

The low-resolution 12-marker test from Family Tree DNA is now rarely used for genealogical purposes. As the company's database grew in size it became apparent that the test was not capable of distinguishing between different genetic families. At 12 markers people will often have matches with lots of different surnames, and someone with the most common 12-marker haplotype will have several thousand matches. A mismatch at 12 markers can sometimes prove that two men are *not* related on the paternal line, but a match is not conclusive proof that they are related within a genealogical timeframe. Conversely, an apparent lack of a match at 12 markers can mislead one into thinking that two related men are not related. This happened in my own project when a mismatch on 10/12 markers turned into a 35/37 match. The addition of extra markers will gradually reduce the number of false positives and false negatives. For surname projects a high-resolution 37- or 43-marker test used will usually suffice. There are, however, some situations where a 67-marker test is useful. If you are taking a Y-DNA test to resolve an illegitimacy, or you are an adoptee searching for your biological surname, you should take the highest-resolution test available to rule out coincidental matches that might not be relevant. A 67-marker test is also beneficial if you have a common haplotype and have matches with a number of different surnames at 37 or 43 markers. At the time of writing, the 111-marker test had only recently been launched by Family Tree DNA and only a limited number of results were available, making it difficult to assess the impact of this test. It seems likely, however, that it will be particularly useful for refining matches with other surnames and might also prove useful in splitting up large matching groups into subgroups if no branch-defining markers have been discovered with the previous tests.

Understanding your Y-DNA results

All the testing companies will report your Y-DNA results online when they become available. You will be given your own personal page on the company website where you can see your matches and view further information. A certificate is also sent out in the post. If you have tested within a project, the administrator should be able to help you to understand your results and how they relate to the other project members. All project administrators are volunteers and some have more time than others to devote to their project. The knowledge of the project administrators also varies considerably.

The results of your DNA test are presented as a string of numbers representing the values for all the markers that were tested. The combination of numbers is known as a haplotype. These numbers on their own mean very little and the real value of a DNA test comes when you start to compare your results with other people. It is rather like playing a number-matching game – you are hoping to find other people who have the same numbers as you on all or most of their markers. If you have tested with a surname project you will, of course, be hoping that you will have matches with other people who share your surname.

Fortunately, the testing companies take care of the matching process for you. Family Tree DNA will automatically compare your results, either within your project or in the wider FTDNA database, depending on how you have set your preferences, and will notify you by email of any close matches as and when they are received. The names and email addresses of all your matches are also displayed on your matches' page and you can then contact them to see if you can establish how you are related. An option is provided to exclude the low-resolution results from your match list. Project administrators also have the facility to compare results within a project, which allows them to spot any borderline matches that do not meet the automatic matching criteria. Ancestry.com allows results to be compared within a surname project and matches can also be viewed within the wider Ancestry.com database, although low and high-resolution matches are all listed together.

The testing companies have their own criteria for determining what constitutes a match, which broadly correspond with the 'rule of thumb' guidelines provided in Table 2. In addition to the number of matching markers, the genetic distance between the two men needs to be taken into account. When markers mutate the numbers normally change in a single step and the value can go up or down. One man might have a 12 on a particular marker and his son might have a 13 on the same marker, whereas all their other markers have identical values. This is known as a single-step mutation. The genetic distance between these two men is one – as their results differ on just 1 marker by one number. Father-son studies have shown that most Y-STR (short tandem repeats) mutations occur in a single step. In some instances, however, a bigger change will occur. A value of 12 in a father might mutate to a 14 in the son.

Two men are considered to have a 'match' and will therefore share a common ancestor within a genealogical timeframe if they share the same haplogroup and match on the following markers:

Family Tree DNA – 37-marker comparison
34/37, 35/37, 36/37, 37/37 matches

Family Tree DNA – 67-marker comparison
60/67, 61/67, 62/67, 63/67, 64/67, 65/67, 66/67, 67/67 matches

DNA Heritage* and Ancestry – 43-marker comparison**
39/43, 40/43, 41/43, 43/43, 43/43 matches

DNA Heritage – 58-marker comparison
53/58, 54/58, 55/58, 56/58, 57/58, 58/58 matches

The above are guidelines only based on the match protocols provided by the testing companies. Mutations are random and do not always follow rules of thumb! Results falling just outside the above ranges will need careful reviewing in conjunction with the documentary evidence. In these instances it is advisable to test other men from the same line in an attempt to find 'inbetweeners' with fewer mutations to bridge the gap. If you have a borderline result at 37 or 43 markers it can help to upgrade both samples to the appropriate higher-resolution test. A 33/37 mismatch might then become a 63/67 match.

* DNA Heritage was aquired by Family Tree DNA in April 2011. DNA Heritage results can be transferred to the Family Tree DNA database free of charge. The DNA Heritage 58-marker test was only available for a very brief period before the company was sold.

** Ancestry includes three markers which normally have a null value in the vast majority of the male population. Matches on these markers are therefore of no significance and are excluded from the calculations.

Table 2   Are we related? Some rule-of-thumb guidelines.

This is known as a two-step mutation. In this instance if the two men match on the same number of markers but have a two-step mutation they will have a genetic distance of two. The number of matching markers and the genetic distance between the two men are then used in combination to determine the probable Time to the Most Recent Common Ancestor (TMRCA).

Fortunately, you will not need to go back to school and brush up on your maths as the scientists and mathematicians have provided a number of tools that do the job for us. Family Tree DNA have a proprietary tool known as the 'Time Predictor' (FTDNATiP™), or 'TiP' tool, which compares two DNA results and provides a range of probabilities as to the time when the two men shared a common ancestor. The tool can be accessed by clicking on the blue and orange fork icon next to the email address of your match. The tool will compare your results against your match and give you a range of probabilities as to when the common ancestor might have lived. The TiP tool takes account of the genetic distance and the different mutation rates of the various markers. A sample TiP report is shown here with fictional names. This report is based on the real-life DNA results of two men who match on 36/37 markers with a genetic distance of one.

In comparing 37 markers, the probability that Joe Bloggs and John Bloggs shared a common ancestor within the given number of generations is:

Generations	Percentage
4	58.85
8	88.95
12	97.44
16	99.45
20	99.89
24	99.98
28	100

Table 3   A sample Family Tree DNA TiP report comparing the DNA results of two men who match on 36/37 markers with a genetic distance of one.

In this particular case we have already concluded from our genealogical research that the common ancestor lived nine generations ago, and we believe both men descend from two brothers who were born in the late 1600s in Berkshire. The TiP tool shows us that there is a 97.44 per cent probability that the two men share a common ancestor within twelve generations. This result has, therefore, effectively verified the documentary research.

Mutations occur at random and sometimes the results are not as close as one might intuitively expect. The following is a TiP calculation for another real-life scenario involving two second cousins once removed who match on just 35/37 markers and have a genetic distance of two.

In comparing 37 markers, the probability that Michael Doe and Mark Doe shared a common ancestor within the given number of generations is:

Generations	Percentage
4	28.94
8	68.67
12	89.14
16	96.71
20	99.08
24	99.76
28	99.94

Table 4   A sample Family Tree DNA TiP report for two second cousins once removed who match on just 35/37 markers and have a genetic distance of two.

We already know the exact relationship between these two men, but the TiP tool predicts that there is only a 28.94 per cent probability of the two men sharing a common ancestor within four generations. This does not mean that the TiP tool is wrong or there is a mistake in the paper trail. It is simply a demonstration of the random nature of mutations, which means that the more improbable scenarios can sometimes happen. If you put the prediction another way it tells us that if 100 men were tested and had these same marker values, twenty-nine of the men will have a common ancestor who lived within the last four generations, and seventy-one men will have a common ancestor who lived five generations or more ago. The results are, therefore, not the most probable outcome but are well within the expected probability range.

The other testing companies do not have an equivalent of the FTDNATiP. Ancestry.com provides an estimate of the number of generations to the most recent common ancestor but does not give any indication of the range of results or the probabilities. For the more experienced genetic genealogist there is a useful DIY tool created by Dean McGee, which enables comparisons to be made between Y-DNA results to calculate genetic distance and TMRCA. The tool can be found at **www.mymcgee.com/tools/yutility.html**.

In the two examples shown opposite, the genealogical relationship between the men was already known and the DNA results were used to verify the existing research. The situation is slightly more complicated if two men have a match and the relationship is not known. As we have seen, a Y-DNA test is a very useful tool for confirming whether or not two men are related within a genealogical timeframe but it is not as good at telling us exactly when their common ancestor might have lived. Instead we are given a very wide range of probabilities – the common ancestor could have lived 100 years ago, 900 years ago or at any time in between. For this reason DNA results are best interpreted within a structured surname project and in conjunction with all the available paper evidence. If a surname project has successfully built up a collection of DNA results for each tree, new DNA results can easily be slotted into the existing framework. If you are lucky, you might have a particular marker that is only found in one specific branch. Even if the testee's own paper trail is sketchy, he will at least have a renewed focus for his genealogical research and might, with time and patience, be able to establish the connection.

Matches with other surnames

The number of matches that people get in the companies' databases varies considerably. At Family Tree DNA, which has the largest Y-DNA database, some men can have 1,000 or even 2,000 12-marker matches with a huge variety of surnames. At 25 markers the number of matches is reduced but there might still be over 100 matches.

At 37 markers there will probably still be a few matches remaining with other surnames. At the other extreme some men take a Y-DNA test and find that they do not
have a single match, even at 12 markers. Most men will probably fall somewhere in
between these two extremes. The number of matches is partially a reflection of the
bias in the database. There are, for example, disproportionate numbers of samples
from North America and particularly from North Americans of British and Irish
origin. In contrast, there are relatively few samples from men of Indian or Chinese
ancestry. The other factor to bear in mind is that family trees do not come in uniform shapes and sizes. Some branches are thick and bushy, whereas others are long
and straggly. You will probably notice this effect in your family history research and
you will discover that some of your ancestors have far more descendants than others.
You might get lots of enquiries from people researching some of the surnames in
your tree, whereas other surnames attract little or no attention. The surnames that
attract the most interest will often be from lines which include an emigrant to North
America, Australia or New Zealand, simply because these lines thrived in the new
country and were more reproductively successful. In addition, some men will father
lots of sons who in turn produce many sons, whereas other lines eventually become
extinct if the only surviving children are daughters. Genetic genealogists describe
these lines as 'daughtering out'.

If you take a DNA test and have a number of high-resolution matches with other
surnames do not immediately assume that you have uncovered a dark family secret
that has remained hidden for many years. Sometimes it will simply be the case that
no one else with your surname has yet tested. In such a situation it is always best to
get a second person from your line to take a DNA test to compare results, and preferably someone who is more distantly related to you such as a fourth or fifth cousin.
If the two results match you will have verified the line back to the point where you
both share a common paternal ancestor, and you will have ruled out the possibility
of a non-paternal event in both lines from that time, right through to the present day.

The reason for the matches with other surnames is that the Y-chromosome changes
very little from one generation to the next and we are all descended from the same
relatively small gene pool. As an example, the population of England at the time of
the Domesday survey in 1086 has been tentatively estimated at between 1.25 and
2 million, and we can probably safely assume that around half the population was
male.[11] Today there are around 25 million males living in England, and millions of
men of English origin living in America, Canada, Australia and many other countries
around the world. All these men will carry the Y-chromosome of one of those million
or so men who were living in England in 1086. Surnames were introduced gradually
in the ensuing centuries. Some matches with other surnames will, therefore, reflect
a match with a shared ancestor tracing back to a time before the introduction of
surnames. Other matches will occur because of a deep-rooted illegitimacy or other
event which has broken the link with the Y-chromosome, and for which no historical

record will be found. A match with another surname will only be of any conse-
quence if it can be shown that the ancestors from both lines lived in the same town,
village or perhaps county in more recent times when written records are readily
available. In some testing scenarios, such as illegitimacy and adoption, a match with
another surname is, of course, the desired result. In these situations it is always recommended to test the maximum number of markers to refine the matches to a more
manageable timeframe. According to the predictions provided by Family Tree DNA,
if you have a 67/67 marker match, 50 per cent of the time the common ancestor will
have lived within the last three generations, and there is a 90 per cent probability
that he will have lived within the last five generations. With Family Tree DNA's new
111-marker test, an exact match gives a 95 per cent probability that the common
ancestor lived within five generations.

Introducing haplogroups

A Y-chromosome test also provides another piece of information, which is not of
direct relevance to your family history research, but which instead gives you an insight
into your deep ancestry on your direct paternal line. In addition to the haplotype –
the string of numbers that is used for matching purposes – you will also be given
a prediction of your haplogroup. A haplogroup is a broad population grouping of
people who belong on the same branch of the tree of mankind. A complicated alphanumeric system has been adopted to name the haplogroups. Letters of the alphabet
from A through to T are used to denote the base haplogroups. As new branches of
each haplogroup are discovered, alternating letters and numbers are used to name the
various sub-branches. A majority of men of British origin will, for example, learn
that they belong to haplogroup R1b1a2 (formerly known as R1b1b2). Others will
belong to haplogroups I1, I2, R1a, J2, G or E1b1b1. Haplogroups often have a particular geographical origin. Population geneticists study the present-day distribution of
haplogroups in conjunction with information from other disciplines such as archaeology, climatology and linguistics to learn about the history and migratory paths of
our ancient ancestors. Haplogroups are discussed in more detail in the next chapter.

For the purposes of family history research, haplogroups provide another method
of sorting DNA results. If two men have different haplogroups you will know immediately that they cannot be related as they each belong to two different branches of
the human family tree, which diverged thousands of years ago. If they do belong to
the same haplogroup the basic number-matching principles will apply. Men with
very close-matching haplotypes will be related on the paternal line within a genealogical timeframe. If two men share the same haplogroup, but mismatch on a large
number of markers, they will instead share a common ancestor who lived many
thousands of years ago. If you are interested in your deep ancestry or simply wish

to learn more about your haplogroup you should join the appropriate haplogroup project. This will give you the opportunity to compare your results with other men from the same haplogroup and to learn more about your ancient origins. There are now large projects for all the many different haplogroups. All the haplogroup projects are hosted at Family Tree DNA, but test results from most of the other companies can now be added to their database for a small fee.

DNA databases

As we have seen, a Y-chromosome test is of most benefit when you have the opportunity to compare your results within a surname project, geographical project or haplogroup project within your chosen testing company's database. To get more out of your results it can also be an interesting exercise to compare your results in other publicaly available databases with people who have tested with different companies. Such a comparison will be particularly beneficial if you are seeking to find a match for an illegitimate line or you are an adoptee and you have not yet found any meaningful matches in your company's database. This step will also be essential if you have tested with a company that has no facility to host surname projects or only has a very small database. There are a number of free open-access Y-STR databases, some of which will allow you to add your own results for comparison purposes. Although the testing companies all use a different range of markers there is considerable overlap, and it should still be possible to make some useful comparisons.

 Caution needs to be exercised when using any database which allows users to upload their own data, as there is no guarantee that the user has entered his DNA results correctly, especially if the results have been keyed in manually. Some of the databases are sponsored by testing companies and those who have tested with these companies can upload their results automatically without having to re-key all their numbers, but results will not necessarily have been updated to incorporate additional markers or haplogroup refinements. The problem is compounded because, historically, the testing companies used different methods for scoring and reporting the values or alleles for the Y-STR markers. If you took a test with two different companies you would, therefore, be given slightly different results for some markers. A 12 with one company would be reported as a 17 with another company. This does not mean that the companies were providing incorrect results, but is simply a reflection of the different systems used to report results, just as you would get different measurements depending on whether you used the imperial or metric system. Before making any comparisons with results from other testing companies it was previously necessary to convert the non-standard markers to the appropriate values. In 2008, following pressure from the International Society of Genetic Genealogy, the National Institute for Standards and Technology (NIST) in the US proposed a new standardised system for scoring Y-STR

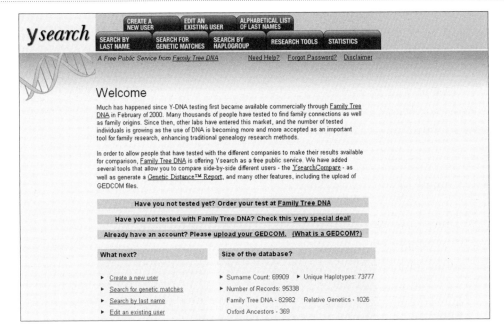

Figure 5　Ysearch is one of a number of public databases collating DNA results from different testing companies. It can be searched by surname or haplogroup.

markers. The NIST standards are gradually being adopted by all the major testing companies, but at the time of writing the process was not yet complete. Most noticeably, FTDNA has not yet upgraded its database. A useful chart of marker standards and comparative values can be found on the Sorenson Molecular Genealogy Foundation website at **www.smgf.org/ychromosome/marker_standards.jspx**. There will inevitably be some discrepancies in the databases, especially if people entered their results before the NIST standards were adopted and did not use the correct conversion values. Haplogroup designations should also be considered with caution if the test was done by a company which does not provide any SNP testing (single-nucleotide polymorphism, see Chapter 3), especially if the haplotype is uncommon.

Ysearch, **www.ysearch.org**
Ysearch, sponsored by Family Tree DNA, is the largest open-access database and it can accommodate results from any testing company. Ysearch contains almost 100,000 Y-DNA results, around 80 per cent of which are from Family Tree DNA customers. The remaining 20 per cent of Ysearch results are from customers of some of the smaller testing companies, some of which do not host surname projects or have now ceased trading. Only around 40 per cent of FTDNA customers choose to upload their results to Ysearch. If you have tested with Family Tree DNA you can upload your results automatically from your personal page. If you have tested with any other company you will have to key in your results manually. You can compare your own

results with other people in the Ysearch database and generate a genetic distance report. You can also search the database by surname or haplogroup. You can include information about your paternal line in your Ysearch entry and you can also upload a GEDCOM file (a special file format used for data sharing by family history software programs – see Table 11) of your pedigree. Other Ysearch users can be contacted through the Ysearch messaging system.

Ybase, **www.ybase.org**
Sponsored by DNA Heritage, Ybase was the first public Y-DNA database. Like Ysearch it will accept Y-DNA results from any testing company. Ybase was taken over by Family Tree DNA when they acquired DNA Heritage in April 2011. At the time of writing the plans for Ybase were not known. There were around 16,000 Y-DNA results in Ybase by the end of 2010, and it is hoped that this valuable resource will not be lost.

The Sorenson Molecular Genealogy Foundation (SMGF), **www.smgf.org**
The SMGF is a non-profit-making organisation dedicated to advancing the field of genetic genealogy by collecting DNA samples and associated genealogical pedigrees from around the world, and publishing the results in an open-access database. The initial goal of the project was to obtain 100,000 DNA samples, which was achieved in 2009. Participants could submit their DNA for research purposes and obtain a free Y-DNA or mtDNA test with the SMGF if they could supply a five-generation pedigree. The test results have now all been made publicly available on the SMGF website. By the end of 2010 the Sorenson database contained Y-DNA results and associated pedigree data from more than 37,000 men throughout the world. A free SMGF account is required to search the database. Searches can be done by surname, but a minimum of seven marker values must be inputted before a search can be performed. Extraction of Y-DNA results from the SMGF database is not particularly difficult and detailed instructions on how to efficiently extract Y-DNA results may be found at **http://www.mennonitedna.com/SMGF_Little_Instructions.html**. The pedigrees can also be viewed with the names of living people omitted, though no contact details are provided. It is, however, not possible to input your own Y-DNA results from another testing company. The SMGF continues to collect DNA samples from around the world, but free tests are now only provided for people with origins in a small number of countries that are under-represented in the database.

GeneTree, **www.genetree.com**
GeneTree, founded in 2007, is the commercial arm of the SMGF. The company sells a limited range of Y-DNA and mtDNA tests and also allows SMGF participants to 'unlock' their results and add them to the GeneTree database for a small fee. Those people who had tested with SMGF were effectively participating in a research project. They were not informed of their results but if their test was processed they could

identify their results from their pedigree details in the Sorenson database, though their genetic profiles were not presented in a meaningful format that could be used elsewhere. By unlocking their results and making them available through GeneTree they are able to utilise all the additional tools and features associated with a commercial testing company. Anyone buying a GeneTree kit can also opt to participate in the SMGF research by signing the consent form when purchasing the test. GeneTree also permits customers from other testing companies to add their results manually to their database free of charge. It is first of all necessary to set up an account and create a basic profile page. An outline of your family tree can also be created though there is no GEDCOM upload facility. Once you have created an account the Y-DNA database can be searched by surname. If you input your Y-DNA results you can search the database for genetic matches. Searches can be performed for exact matches, 85 per cent matches or 75 per cent matches. An estimate of the number of generations to the most recent common ancestor is given. SMGF participants are also included in the database and the associated pedigrees can be viewed, though their names and profiles are protected unless they elect to 'unlock' their results. Many of the people in the GeneTree database have only been tested on a small number of markers and the matches are not likely to be significant. Also, a very large proportion of their customers are in the US.

The Y-Chromosome Haplotype Reference Database, **www.yhrd.org**
YHRD is a repository for Y-chromosome haplotypes from global population studies. The database was designed for use by forensic geneticists but is also of interest to genetic genealogists. By the end of 2010 there were over 90,000 haplotypes in the database from 710 population studies representing 106 countries. The haplotypes are submitted by scientific researchers and results are only added to the database when a paper has been accepted for publication. The haplotypes are all low resolution, ranging from 7–17 markers. The database is of most value in providing geographical context to your test results, especially if your paternal line is from a country that is under-represented in the commercial databases.

Ancestry.com DNA, **www.dnaancestry.com**
Customers of other testing companies are allowed to upload their DNA results to the Ancestry.com DNA database. It is first of all necessary to set up a free Ancestry.com account with a username and password. The results from Ancestry.com customers are automatically included in the database, but results from other testing companies have to be entered manually. There is unfortunately no provision for advanced haplogroup assignments. Judging by the results that I have entered into the Ancestry.com database and the list of matches obtained, I estimate that probably around 30 or 40 per cent of the database consists of customers from other testing companies and especially from Family Tree DNA. Once your results are in the Ancestry.com database you can also join the DNA groups. The groups can be made public or private. Anyone who

is interested in a surname can join one of the groups, regardless of whether or not they have taken a DNA test, and the headline numbers for the Ancestry.com groups are, therefore, very misleading. If you have uploaded a family tree to Ancestry.com you can also 'attach' your DNA results to your tree. Y-DNA results are automatically 'propagated' along your direct paternal line in your Ancestry.com tree.

Getting help

I have discussed in general terms the basic principles of Y-DNA testing and tried to cover all the most obvious scenarios, but there will inevitably be situations which I have not covered and there will also be occasions when you might want a little bit of help or some extra advice. In the first instance, if you are in a project it is always worth raising any questions you might have with your project administrator. Even if they are not able to answer your questions, they will often be able to consult with their fellow administrators and point you in the right direction. A surname project administrator will have a good overview of all the results contained within the surname project. The haplogroup project managers are usually very knowledgeable on the origins and distributions of their haplogroups, and should be able to answer questions about deep ancestry. If you have any concerns about your results or have any technical questions you can get in touch with the testing company. There is much valuable information and advice on the International Society of Genetic Genealogy website and wiki. Finally, there are numerous mailing lists and forums where you can ask questions and get advice. Genetic genealogists have accumulated over a decade's worth of experience and there is rarely a question that goes unanswered. Details of all these resources can be found in the Appendices.

References
1   Laslett, Peter and Oosterveen, Karla, 'Long-Term Trends in Bastardy in England: A Study of the Illegitimacy Figures in the Parish Registers and in the Reports of the Registrar General, 1561–1960', *Population Studies*, Vol. 27 (1973), pp. 255–86.
2   'Live births in England and Wales by characteristics of mother, 2009', Office for National Statistics (21 October 2010). **www.statistics.gov.uk/pdfdir/birth1010.pdf**
3   Redmonds, George, *Surnames and Genealogy: A New Approach*. (FFHS Publications, 2002), pp. 17–26.
4   Hooper, M.D., 'Aliases – a discriminant function'. **http://genuki.cs.ncl.ac.uk/DEV/DevonMisc/AliasesDiscriminant.html**
5   Brown, Mike, 'Some Devon surname aliases'. **http://genuki.cs.ncl.ac.uk/DEV/DevonMisc/Aliases.html**
6   UK Deed Polls Service. **www.ukdps.co.uk**

7   Khan, Razib, 'The paternity myth: the rarity of cuckoldry', Gene Expression blog (20 June 2010). **http://blogs.discovermagazine.com/gnxp/2010/06/ the-paternity-myth-the-rarity-of-cuckoldry**

8   King, Turi E., and Jobling, Mark A., 'What's in a name? Y chromosomes, surnames and the genetic genealogy revolution', *Trends in Genetics*, Vol. 25 (2009), pp. 351–60.

9   Pomery, Chris, 'The advantages of a dual DNA/documentary approach to reconstruct the family trees of a surname', *Journal of Genetic Genealogy*, Vol. 5, No. 2 (Fall/Autumn 2009).

10 Pomery, Chris, 'Defining a methodology to reconstruct the family trees of a surname within a DNA/documentary dual approach project', *Journal of Genetic Genealogy*, Vol. 6, No. 1 (Fall/Autumn 2010).

11 Domesday Book Online. **www.domesdaybook.co.uk**

3

Before surnames:
haplogroups and deep ancestry

Most family historians are able to name all of their parents, grandparents, great-grandparents and perhaps most of their great-great-grandparents too. With a little bit of luck, and a lot of dedicated research, it is often possible to trace some of those lines several generations further back into the 1600s or even the 1500s. If any of those lines intersect with the aristocracy or royalty the pedigree can usually be taken back several more centuries, perhaps going back to William the Conqueror or King Harold. From William the Conqueror it is then just a few more steps back to the eighth century and Charlemagne, King of the Franks, the ancestor of most European monarchs. Sooner or later, however, the written records start to run out for everyone. This is where the genetic records can help to fill in the gaps. The Y-chromosome of every man alive today is a living history record. Preserved in the Y-chromosome are traces of the DNA not just of our more recent ancestors, the ones whose names are inscribed in parish registers and civil registration records, but also the DNA of our distant paternal-line ancestors who lived thousands and thousands of years ago, but who left no written record of their existence.

We have already seen in the previous chapter how a particular type of Y-chromosome marker, known as a short tandem repeat, is used to determine whether or not two men share a common ancestor within a genealogical timeframe. To decipher our deep ancestry, scientists study different types of markers in the Y-chromosome known as single-nucleotide polymorphisms (SNPs – pronounced snips – for short). Nucleotides, or bases, are the basic building blocks of our DNA: the As, Cs, Gs and Ts, which combine in pairs to make up our entire genome. There are around 58 million of these base pairs in the Y-chromosome. The Y-chromosome is passed on intact from father to son, but every now and then a mistake occurs in the copying process, like a transcription error, which results in a change – a polymorphism – in the DNA sequence; with perhaps a T replaced by an A, or a C becoming a G. These changes occur at random and are very rare. Once the mutation has occurred it becomes fixed. In scientific terms this is known as a unique-event polymorphism

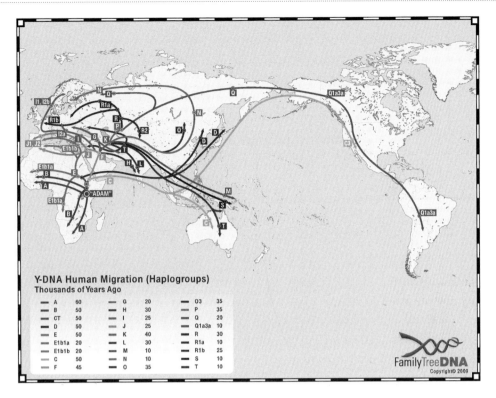

Y-DNA Human Migration (Haplogroups)
Thousands of Years Ago

A	60	G	20	O3	35
B	50	H	30	P	35
CT	50	I	25	Q	20
D	50	J	25	Q1a3a	10
E	50	K	40	R	30
E1b1a	20	L	30	R1a	10
E1b1b	20	M	10	R1b	25
C	50	N	10	S	10
F	45	O	35	T	10

FamilyTreeDNA
Copyright© 2009

Figure 6 A map showing the migratory pathways of the descendants of Y-chromosomal Adam.

(UEP). The man in whom the mutation first appeared passes it on to his sons and all their descendants several thousand years later will also carry the same SNP. Over time, more SNPs accumulate, but the earlier SNPs are still preserved. The Y-chromosome therefore contains a cumulative record of all the SNPs that have ever occurred in a man's paternal line.

By studying SNPs in the Y-chromosomes of the present-day population it is possible to construct a genetic tree of mankind. SNPs are used to identify the branches and sub-branches on this tree. Each branch of the tree is known as a haplogroup. The Y-SNP tree can ultimately be traced back to just one man who is the common ancestor of all men alive today. He is known as Y-chromosomal Adam. We do not know his precise birth date, but it is estimated that he lived around 142,000 years ago and was probably born in Africa. Y-Adam was not the first man who ever lived, or the only man alive at that time. He is simply the only man whose lineage has been preserved in the Y-chromosomes of the present-day population.

Y-chromosome haplogroups are identified by letters of the alphabet and are currently labelled from A through to T. Haplogroups often have origins in specific geographical areas and some are today still confined to particular regions. Haplogroups A and B are the oldest two haplogroups and are mostly found in Africa.

Haplogroup C represents the first human migration out of Africa, following a coastal route through the southern Arabian Peninsula, India, Sri Lanka and into Southeast Asia. Haplogroup F, a sibling clade to haplogroup C, is the ancestral haplogroup of all the major European haplogroups. It is defined by a marker known as M89, which today is found in more than 90 per cent of non-African men. The alphabetical haplogroups are further refined into subclades using an alternating alphanumeric system to denote each newly found SNP. You will, therefore, see haplogroups with complicated names such as R1b1a2, R1a1, E1b1b1, I1 and I2b1. In regions where a population has been geographically isolated for some time, subhaplogroups can develop which are exclusive to that population. The C4 subclade is, for example, found only among aboriginal Australians, whereas Q1a3a is almost exclusively associated with Native American populations.

By studying the chronological record of the Y-chromosome and the present-day distribution of the various haplogroups and their subclades, it is, therefore, possible by inference to gain a unique insight into the ancient history and migratory paths of our distant paternal ancestors. By looking at the genetic diversity within each haplogroup, population geneticists can estimate the age of the haplogroup by working out the time to the most recent common ancestor (TMRCA). The date is only a rough approximation and the progenitor of the haplogroup could have lived many thousands of years earlier or later. TMRCA calculations necessarily have wide margins of error as they are based on assumptions about underlying mutation rates, effective population sizes and the length of a generation, and these measures are highly variable and difficult to quantify accurately. If, for instance, a population undergoes a rapid growth in a short time span, more mutations will occur over 100 years than will be seen in a population which remains static over the same period.

Mutation rates are calculated over a given number of generations, but the length of a generation has not necessarily stayed the same over thousands of years. Today men often marry and have children in their 30s, whereas in Victorian times most men married in their 20s. In ancient times when life expectancy was low, men probably fathered children in their teens. Archaeologists and population geneticists have not agreed upon a standard generation interval. Some studies will allow for twenty or twenty-five years per generation. Anecdotal evidence from genealogists suggests that thirty or thirty-five years is a more realistic assumption for the last 500 years. A generation interval of twenty-five years takes us back 10,000 years over 500 generations, but a thirty-five-year interval would push the TMRCA back to 17,500 years.

Ideally, Y-chromosome evidence should be obtained from ancient specimens. However DNA degrades rapidly over time and the Y-chromosome rarely survives in sufficient quantities for analysis. In the few cases where Y-chromosome DNA has been successfully extracted, the specimen has usually, by chance, been buried in a particularly favourable environment such as in a cave or frozen underneath a layer of ice or snow. As the technology improves and amplification techniques are refined the success rates will no doubt improve. For all these reasons, DNA data in population genetics is best used in conjunction with evidence from other disciplines, such as archaeology, linguistics, climatology and geology, so that dates can be calibrated against known events.

While the methodology for dating the origins of the various haplogroups remains imprecise, our knowledge of the structure, or phylogeny, of the Y-chromosome tree has advanced considerably in the last decade. A chart defining the nomenclature of the Y-SNP tree was first published in 2002 by an international group of scientists from the Y-Chromosome Consortium. In 2005 a team of volunteers from the International Society of Genetic Genealogy assumed responsibility for updating the Y-SNP tree. The first ISOGG Y-SNP tree was published online in April 2006 and an updated version has since been published on an annual basis, with additions and corrections made throughout the year as appropriate. The tree can be found at **www.isogg.org/tree**.

The nomenclature of the main haplogroups has undergone several changes in that time, notably in 2008 with the addition of haplogroups S (formerly K5) and T (formerly K2). The names of the subclades have also undergone many changes in the last few years as new SNPs have been discovered in between existing SNPs, thus altering the relative positions on the tree. The SNP discovery process is not yet complete and further updates are anticipated in the years to come, until such a time as the Y-chromosome has been fully sequenced and deciphered for thousands of men throughout the world. The theories of the origins and distribution of the haplogroups and their subclades are still very much open to debate. Many more samples from around the world need to be tested at a high resolution before the picture can be fully understood.

Haplogroup predictions

As we have seen, haplogroups are defined by a special type of marker known as a SNP (a single-nucleotide polymorphism). However, when you order a Y-DNA test from a commercial testing company the laboratory does not test any SNPs but instead provides you with a *prediction* of your haplogroup based upon your Y-STR (short tandem repeat) markers – the string of numbers that makes up your haplotype. The company and public databases are now sufficiently large that in most cases a haplogroup can be predicted with a high degree of confidence. Two men with identical or closely matching haplotypes would normally be expected to belong to the same haplogroup. Problems can arise if your haplotype is somewhat unusual and you have few, if any, matches in the company's database. In such a situation it may be necessary to order a SNP test, which is sometimes described as a 'haplogroup backbone test', to get confirmation of the haplogroup.

Unfortunately, not all companies offer SNP testing and a small percentage of customers of these companies do find that when they retest elsewhere the haplogroup prediction they were given was wrong. I came across one person who had been tested with two different companies, both of whom incorrectly predicted that he belonged to haplogroup G. A haplogroup backbone test was eventually done at a third company and it was finally discovered that he belonged to haplogroup F. Haplogroup F is very rare in Britain, and only a handful of men of British origin have tested positive for this haplogroup to date. If you are at all interested in your haplogroup designation and your deep ancestry you will, therefore, need to ensure that you test with a company that provides a facility for SNP testing. With most companies a haplogroup test will need to be ordered as an extra. Family Tree DNA is currently the only company which provides a free haplogroup backbone test if they are not able to predict the haplogroup with 100 per cent confidence.

The testing companies use their own proprietary algorithms for predicting haplogroups, some of which are better than others. Two free haplogroup prediction tools are available on the internet which can also be used to double-check your haplogroup prediction. Whit Athey's haplogroup predictor can be found online at **www.hprg.com/hapest5/index.html**. Marker values have to be submitted manually either in numerical order or FTDNA order. Alternatively, the numbers can be copied and pasted from a project results page in text format with separators, for automatic conversion. The predictions are usually reasonably reliable and are generally more accurate than the predictions provided by some of the smaller commercial testing companies. Jim Cullen has designed a haplogroup predictor that complements Whit Athey's tool and is particularly suited for predicting the various subclades of haplogroup I. Jim Cullen's haplogroup predictor can be found at **http://members.bex.net/jtcullen515/haplotest.htm**.

Deep clade tests

The level of haplogroup prediction varies from haplogroup to haplogroup, and also from company to company. As the databases grow in size and haplogroups can be predicted with greater confidence, the prediction can also sometimes be changed or upgraded. Haplogroup R1b1a2 (formerly known as R1b1b2) is now easily predicted, but in earlier years only haplogroup R1b could be predicted with confidence. Other haplogroups cannot be predicted with the same level of refinement. If you are haplogroup J, for example, you might only be predicted as a J, J1 or J2, whereas Fs and Gs might not have any refinement to their prediction at all. The predictions do sometimes change in the light of new research, and the company's database will be upgraded to reflect the latest developments. With the discovery of hundreds of new SNPs in the last few years it is now possible to identify many

Figure 7 A certificate showing the results of a haplogroup R1b deep clade test on the author's father.

different sub-branches of the base haplogroups, and tests are available on a commercial basis to test for the various SNPs that define these subclades. These tests are usually known as deep clade tests, subclade tests or paternal roots tests. A panel of haplogroup-specific SNPs is usually offered, but sometimes SNPs can be ordered à la carte on an individual basis. SNP testing is usually only available to existing customers who have already taken a standard Y-STR test with the company. Not all companies provide these advanced tests, so if it is something that is of interest it is best to check the company's offerings before testing to avoid the need to be retested elsewhere at a later date. Family Tree DNA offers the largest range of subclade and SNP tests on the market. The company is actively involved in the research process and is responsible for the discovery of many new SNPs. The company also hosts all the major haplogroup projects and a growing range of subclade projects, all of which are run by volunteer genetic genealogists.

A subclade test will, therefore, provide increased resolution of your placement on the Y-SNP tree. Every time a new SNP is discovered a new branch of the haplogroup tree is formed. Each branch represents a new lineage or subclade within the haplogroup. Some of these subclades will be found to cluster in specific countries or regions and, consequently, by knowing your subclade you will also get better geographical resolution. The base haplogroups date back for thousands and thousands of years, whereas some of the subclades only arose a few thousand years ago. In time it should, therefore, be possible to correlate subclades with findings from the archaeological record and other historical evidence. As so many of the SNP markers that define the subclades have only been discovered very recently, little is currently known about the history of the various subclades, and few of them have as yet been incorporated in scientific research studies. The greatest knowledge of these subclades is usually to be found within the subclade projects run by the amateur genetic genealogists. As a result, it can be quite exciting to be involved in these projects and to be part of the discovery process!

Subclade tests are available for all the major haplogroups found in Europe, but a subclade test is more beneficial within some haplogroups than others. In some haplogroups the subclade can often be predicted from the Y-STR markers, whereas in other haplogroups there is a dearth of subclade-defining SNPs. The deep clade test is particularly useful for men in haplogroup R1b1a2, where a number of major subclades have been discovered. Haplogroup R1b1a2 is the most common haplogroup in Europe and it spread very rapidly across the continent in a relatively short space of time. Consequently, the haplotypes are often very similar, making it very difficult to predict the subclade from the STR markers. Two men who belong in different subclades will not be related within a genealogical timeframe, so a subclade test can sometimes help to distinguish between two men with closely matching haplotypes. If you are interested in deep clade testing it is best to join the appropriate

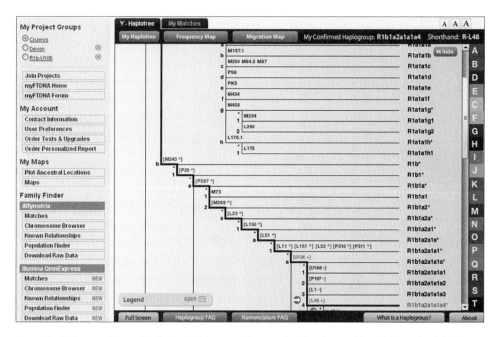

Figure 8   A diagram from a Family Tree DNA personal page, showing the position of the author's father on the haplogroup R Y-DNA haplogroup tree following the results of a SNP test.

haplogroup project and check with the project administrator to seek advice on which tests to order.

As the Y-SNP tree is constantly being updated and revised, if you do order a deep clade test you will find that the nomenclature will change from time to time. The name of my father's subclade has, for example, changed numerous times in the space of the last few years and has been known variously as R1b1c9, R1b1b2g, R1b1b2a1a4 and R1b1b2a1a1d. At the time of writing, his subclade is known as R1b1a2a1a1a4, but this will no doubt change again in the years to come. These ever-changing strings of letters and numbers are very difficult to memorise and a new 'shorthand' system of naming is often used instead. With this approach the name of the most 'downstream', or recent SNP, is used in conjunction with the base haplogroup name. Using the shorthand system my father's subclade is known as R1b-L48. L48 is the name of the SNP which defines his lineage within haplogroup R1b. This name will remain constant regardless of any revisions that are made in the higher reaches of the R1b1a2 tree until such time as new SNPs are discovered below L48.

Walk through the Y

Despite the advances in whole genome sequencing technology in the last decade, the Y-chromosome has proved to be particularly difficult to decipher because of the fact that it is densely packed and has a highly repetitive structure. The Y-chromosome contains around 58 million base pairs – the building blocks of DNA – but only around half of the Y-chromosome has been properly sequenced and there are many errors in the published sequences. The Human Genome Project did not even attempt to determine the complex repeat patterns found on the long arm of the Y-chromosome in the largest 'heterochromatic region' – the non-functional part of the chromosome which contains no genes. It is probable that full Y-chromosome sequencing will eventually be a standard DNA test for the genealogist, but such a test is unlikely to be available or affordable in the near future. With vast stretches of the Y-chromosome remaining a mystery there are still potentially many more Y-SNPs to be found, which will eventually provide much greater resolution of the Y-SNP tree. There is also the tantalising prospect that some SNPs will be discovered that are specific to distinct surname lineages. The Y-chromosome has very few genes and is consequently of less interest to academic researchers who are studying the human genome to find genetic associations with particular diseases and traits. Much of the research into the Y-chromosome is therefore being done by commercial companies in response to demands from their customers who are constantly on the lookout for additional SNPs to further define their particular haplogroup subclades.

Family Tree DNA in Houston is pioneering a project known as Walk through the Y (WTY), with the aim of discovering new subclade-defining SNPs. The WTY test targets the more interesting regions of the Y-chromosome, which can be more easily sequenced and are more likely to yield results. The coverage of the WTY test has significantly increased over time. The original plan was to test 100,000 base pairs with a guarantee of only 50,000 successfully tested. By the beginning of 2011 WTY tests were routinely covering almost 200,000 base pairs. The test currently costs US$750. The WTY test is usually co-ordinated within haplogroup projects. Several people volunteer for the WTY test within each haplogroup and their sequences are compared to see if any new SNPs can be identified. The test is either self-funded or paid for with donations from the haplogroup project members. The latest results from the WTY programme were presented at the Family Tree DNA group administrators' conference at the end of October 2010. By this time, 178 people had participated in the project and 137 previously undocumented Y-SNP markers had been found. Many of the newly found SNPs define major clades within the various haplogroups, whereas others have turned out to be private SNPs confined to family groups. Full details of the Walk through the Y programme and all the associated WTY projects can be found in the ISOGG Wiki at **www.isogg.org/wiki/Walk_Through_the_Y**.

Haplogroup origins and distributions

Once you have your haplogroup designation you will most probably want to learn more about your particular haplogroup. The companies provide information on their websites, together with maps showing the migratory paths of the haplogroups. You will also usually receive a certificate and a map in the post. I have included links to some useful websites (see Appendix A), which contain information on the various haplogroups. The books in the deep ancestry section in the bibliography will also provide further insight. However, much of the published information is now very out of date, as it was based on low-resolution tests and the research was done before many of the new SNPs had been discovered. Haplogroup research is ongoing and the stories of the haplogroups are constantly being revised as further DNA samples from around the world are tested and new scientific papers are published. To keep up to date with the latest research on your haplogroup it is a good idea to join the relevant haplogroup project. There are now also many projects for the various haplogroup subclades, which you can join if you have been SNP tested for the appropriate subclade-defining SNP. The haplogroup and subclade projects often have associated mailing lists where members can discuss the latest theories of the origins of their haplogroup. You can also keep up with the latest news by following some of the genetics and anthropology blogs that are listed in Appendix A.

Although the origins of the haplogroups are still being researched, we do now have a good picture of the distribution of the haplogroups in the present-day population. Men of British origin belong to a limited number of haplogroups. Haplogroup

The U198 / S29 Project - Y-DNA Classic Chart

* Haplogroups in green have been confirmed by SNP testing. Haplogroups in red have been predicted by Family Tree DNA based on <u>unambiguous</u> results in the individual's personal [...] the Haplogroup. If a "-" is in the HAPLO field then we feel that the comparative results are not clear and unambiguous and if the kit holder wants to know their SNP with 100% confidenc[...]

To read more about how to understand this chart please visit the FAQ here

Markers: Y-DNA12 ▾   Page Size: 500   ☑ Show All Columns

Kit Number	Name	Country	Haplogroup	DYS393	DYS390	DYS19	DYS391	DYS385	DYS426	DYS388	DYS439	DYS389I	DYS392	DYS389II	DYS458	DYS459	DYS455	DYS454	DYS447	DYS437	DYS448	DYS449	DYS464
"14 14 group"																							
47928	Allison	Scotland	R1b1a2a1a1a1	14	23	14	10	11-14	12	12	12	13	13	29	17	9-10	11	11	25	15	19	29	14-15-17-18
49733	Meek	Unknown Origin	R1b1a2	14	23	14	10	11-14	12	12	13	13	13	29	16	9-10	11	11	25	15	19	30	14-14-17-18
31283	Meek	Unknown Origin	R1b1a2	14	23	14	11	11-14	12	12	12	13	13	29	16	9-10	11	11	25	15	19	30	14-14-17-18
116413	Stuart	United Kingdom	R1b1a2a1a1a1	14	23	14	11	11-14	12	12	12	13	13	29	17	8-9	11	11	25	15	19	29	14-15-18-18
31588	Meeks	Unknown Origin	R1b1a2	14	23	14	11	11-14	12	12	13	13	13	28	16	9-10	11	11	25	15	19	30	14-14-17-18
74145	Meeks	Unknown Origin	R1b1a2	14	23	14	11	11-14	12	12	13	13	13	29	16	9-10	11	11	25	15	19	30	14-14-17-18
6576	Meek	Unknown Origin	R1b1a2a1a1a1	14	23	14	11	11-14	12	12	13	13	13	29	16	9-10	11	11	25	15	19	30	14-14-17-19
124430	Gibson	Scotland	R1b1a2a1a1a1	14	23	14	11	11-14	12	12	13	13	13	29	17	9-10	11	11	25	15	19	29	14-15-17-18
57678	Finton	Unknown Origin	R1b1a2a1a1a1	14	23	14	11	12-14	12	12	13	13	13	29	16	9-10	11	11	25	15	20	30	14-15-17-18
107471	Sikes	England	R1b1	14	23	15	11	11-14	12	12	12	13	14	29	18	8-9	11	11	25	15	19	29	14-15-17-18
N67868	Sykes	United Kingdom	R1b1a2	14	23	15	11	11-14	12	12	13	13	14	29									
70776	Rhodes	England	R1b1a2a1a1a1	14	23	15	11	11-14	12	12	13	13	13	29	17	8-9	11	11	25	15	19	30	14-15-17-17
69635	Sikes	England	R1b1a2a1a1a1	14	23	15	11	11-14	12	12	14	13	15	29	18	8-9	11	11	25	15	19	28	14-15-17-18
88049	Cakebread	United Kingdom	R1b1	14	23	15	11	11-15	12	12	13	13	14	29									
61445	Sykes	England	R1b1a2a1a1a1	14	23	15	12	11-14	12	12	13	13	14	29	18	8-9	11	11	25	15	19	28	14-15-17-18
56743	Cakebread	England	R1b1a2	14	23	16	11	11-15	12	12	13	13	14	29	17	8-9	11	11	25	15	19	28	14-15-17-17
"Regular type r"																							
178163	Lynn	Unknown Origin	R1b1a2	12	23	14	11	11-12	12	12	12	13	13	29	17	8-10	11	11	25	15	19	29	15-15-17-19
142654	Woodward	Unknown Origin	R1b1a2	12	23	14	11	11-12	12	12	13	13	13	29	17	8-10	11	11	25	15	19	29	15-16-17-19
112836	Lynn	Scotland	R1b1a2a1a1a1	12	23	14	11	11-12	12	12	12	13	13	29	17	8-10	11	11	25	15	19	29	15-16-17-19
107264	Carlile	England	R1b1a2a1a1a1	13	22	14	10	11-14	12	12	12	13	13	29	17	9-10	11	11	25	15	19	32	15-15-17-18
48449	Hayward	England	R1b1a2a1a1a1	13	23	14	10	11-14	12	12	11	13	13	29	17	9-10	11	11	25	15	19	31	15-15-17-18
E10814	Andres	Germany	R1b1a2a1a1a1	13	23	14	10	11-14	12	12	12	13	13	28	17	9-10	11	11	25	15	19	29	15-15-17-18

Figure 9   A haplogroup project provides an opportunity to compare Y-DNA results with your closest genetic cousins beyond your immediate surname relations. The screenshot above shows results from the haplogroup U198/S29 project. U198, a small subclade of haplogroup R1b, is found mostly in the British Isles. All men in this project share a common ancestor who probably lived around 2,000–3,000 years ago. The men in this project have tested positive for the U198 SNP (also known as S29).

R1b1a2 is the predominant haplogroup in Europe and is found in at least 60 per cent of men in Great Britain, and over 80 per cent of men in Ireland. Haplogroup I1 is the next most common haplogroup in Britain and is often considered as a marker for Viking and Anglo-Saxon invaders. Haplogroup R1a occurs in low frequencies in the British Isles, but is more prevalent in the north of England and Scotland, and is associated with a Norse or Viking origin. The other haplogroups that are found in the British Isles are E1b1b, G, J2, I2a and I2b. Haplogroups T and Q are sometimes also seen. A few men from haplogroup F have been found in England, particularly in the south west. A few examples of the African haplogroup A were reported in a number of men in Yorkshire of typical European appearance with a rare English surname, which could be traced back to at least the late eighteenth century.[1] As more men have their Y-chromosome tested we can expect to see a few more unusual results. It is already clear that the genetic composition of the people of the British Isles is complex, and no haplogroup is found to be exclusively associated with the Normans, Vikings, Anglo-Saxons, Romans, Celts or Picts.

Two interesting new academic projects are in the pipeline, which should help to shed further light on the genetic origins of the British. The People of the British Isles project, led by Sir Walter Bodmer from the University of Oxford and funded by the Wellcome Trust, has collected DNA samples from over 4,000 people living in rural areas whose four grandparents were all born in the same region. The project is using a mixture of Y-chromosome and autosomal DNA. The first results from the project are due to be published in 2011 and the resultant data will be freely available once the analysis has been completed.[2] The Roots of the British project, co-ordinated by a multidisciplinary team from the University of Leicester, will explore the histories, genetics and peopling of Britain from 1000 BC to AD 1000. Two strands of the project will focus on genetics: 'Surnames and the Y-chromosome' will explore the genetic legacy of the Vikings and its impact in different regions of Britain; 'Genetics and early British population history' will use existing and new Y-chromosome datasets from modern populations to illuminate British population history and migration. The project commenced in January 2011 and will run for five years.[3]

References

1   King, Turi E., Parkin, Emma J., Swinfield, G. et al., 'Africans in Yorkshire? – the deepest-rooting clade of the Y phylogeny within an English genealogy', *European Journal of Human Genetics*, Vol. 15, No. 3 (March 2007), pp. 288–93. **www.ncbi. nlm.nih.gov/pubmed/17245408**

2   People of the British Isles project. **www.peopleofthebritishisles.org**

3   Roots of the British project. **www2.le.ac.uk/projects/roots-of-the-british**

4

The maternal line: mitochondrial DNA tests

A mitochondrial DNA test is the mirror image of a Y-chromosome DNA test. Y-DNA tracks the male line and is passed down from father to son. Mitochondrial DNA (mtDNA) follows the female line. It therefore tells us about the genetic ancestry of our mother, our mother's mother, our mother's mother's mother and so on back in time for thousands of years. There is, however, one crucial difference, which is of particular relevance to the family historian. A mother passes her mitochondrial DNA on both to her sons and her daughters, and so an mtDNA test can be taken either by a man or a woman, though only women can pass their mitochondrial DNA on to the next generation.

Mitochondrial DNA is found inside mitochondria, curious small structures the size of bacteria, which are present inside all the cells in our bodies. Mitochondria are located inside the cell membrane but outside the nucleus – the core of the cell that contains all the chromosomes. Mitochondria are the power plants in our body, which generate energy from the food we eat so that our organs can function correctly. Each cell in our body can contain thousands of mitochondria. Unlike our chromosomes, which are linear in shape, mtDNA is a circular structure, a legacy from ancient times when mitochondria were free-living bacteria. The circle is divided into two parts: the control region and the coding region. The control region controls the way mtDNA copies itself during cell division. It is not responsible for producing proteins, and any changes that occur in the control region have little effect on the performance of the mitochondria, so mutations can accumulate harmlessly over time. As the control region is the most changeable part of the mitochondrial molecule it is often known as the hypervariable region, or HVR. The coding region is the functional part of the mitochondrial genome, containing all thirty-seven mitochondrial genes. Mutations occur at a much slower rate in the coding region.

Mutations in mtDNA occur more frequently than the SNPs used to define the Y-DNA haplogroups, but less frequently than the Y-STR markers used in surname projects to establish whether or not two men are related within a genealogical timeframe. Mitochondrial DNA is, therefore, a less precise tool for confirming or disproving relationships. It will confirm that two people are related on the maternal line but the timeframe will be much wider. The common ancestor could have lived 200 years ago or over 2,000 years ago. The situation is also exacerbated by the fact that the surname usually changes with each new generation, making it much more difficult to trace the female line back more than a few generations. I can, for example, only trace my own maternal line back to the early 1800s. My most distant known ancestor on the maternal line, Mary Ann Butler, was born about 1815 in Purton, Wiltshire, the daughter of James Butler, a labourer. To take the line back further I would have to invest a large amount of time reconstructing family trees for the surname Butler in Wiltshire to ensure that I had identified the correct parents. If I were then able to find the marriage and identify the maiden name of Mary Ann's mother, the whole process would have to start all over again with a different surname. As a result, it is not surprising that few people take the time and trouble to trace their maternal line much further back than the late 1700s, unless they are particularly lucky and have a succession of unusual surnames, with all their female ancestors remaining in the same parish. Consequently, even if you do have a match with someone, you only stand a reasonable chance of finding the genealogical connection within the last few hundred years.

Unlike Y-DNA tests, which look at specific markers in different places on the Y-chromosome, an mtDNA test sequences a consecutive stretch of DNA. Two people with identical mtDNA sequences are more closely related than two people who have a one-letter difference. If there are lots of differences in the sequences the common ancestor will be much more distant and possibly on another branch of the matrilineal tree altogether. The resolution and accuracy of an mtDNA test depends on the number of bases that are sequenced. There are 16,569 bases or nucleotides in the entire mitochondrial genome. As mutations occur more frequently in the hypervariable region, understandably the first mtDNA tests that became available focused exclusively on this region. The most basic mtDNA test is an HVR1 test. HVR1 covers the bases numbered from 16001 to 16569. The HVR1 test is a low-resolution test and will often result in a large number of matches, most of which will not be within a genealogical timeframe. It can, therefore, be used to prove that two people are *not* related if their results do not match, but an exact match will not be proof of a recent genealogical connection. The standard mtDNA test that is now offered by most testing companies is a combined HVR1 and HVR2 test, which sequences the entire hypervariable region. Some companies subdivide HVR2 into two different regions known as HVR2 and HVR3, and the number of bases included in HVR2 and HVR3 can vary from company to company. A combined HVR1 and HVR2 test will reduce the number of matches and bring down the TMRCA (time to the most recent common ancestor), but there is still more than a 50 per cent chance that the match will be too far back to make a connection.

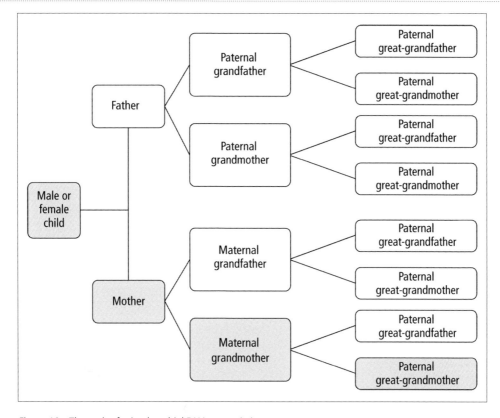

Figure 10   The path of mitochondrial DNA transmission.

The HVR1 and HVR2 tests were the only two tests that were available commercially to the family historian until 2005, when Family Tree DNA introduced
the full genomic sequence (FGS) test on a commercial basis. As the name suggests,
the FGS test sequences all 16,569 base pairs in the mitochondrial genome. The test
is also sometimes referred to as the full mitochondrial sequence test, or the 'mega'.
The introductory price in 2005 was $895 (£568). A few pioneering genetic genealo-
gists took the opportunity to have their full mitochondrial genome sequenced at
that time, but for the average family historian the cost of the test was prohibitive. In
the last few years the cost of sequencing has dropped considerably and by the end
of 2010 an FGS test could be purchased for $299 (£190). With reduced prices the
number of people purchasing the test increased dramatically, and by the end of 2010
there were over 13,000 FGS results in the Family Tree DNA database. The American
company GeneBase announced in May 2009 that it would accept orders for full
sequence mtDNA tests on special request, though at the time of writing the test is
only advertised on its website as an upgrade option for existing customers. An FGS
test will improve the resolution of your matches. The mutation rates are still provisional and have not yet been published, but Family Tree indicates that if two people
have an exact FGS match with no differences in their sequences, there is a 50 per cent

chance that they will share a common ancestor within five generations or in the last 125 years. There is a 90 per cent probability that they will share a common ancestor within sixteen generations or the last 400 years. This does still mean that there is a 10 per cent chance that the common ancestor will have lived more than 400 years ago. The three types of mtDNA test and the probabilities of sharing a common ancestor if two sequences match are summarised in Table 5.

mtDNA test	Bases covered	Probability*
HVR1	16001 to 16569	An exact match indicates a 50 per cent chance of sharing a common maternal ancestor within fifty-two generations or 1,300 years
HVR1 + HVR2	00001 to 00574 16001 to 16569	An exact match indicates a 50 per cent chance of sharing a common maternal ancestor within twenty-eight generations or 700 years
Full sequence test	All 16569 bases	An exact match indicates a 50 per cent chance of sharing a common maternal ancestor within the last five generations or about 125 years. There is a 90 per cent probability of sharing a common ancestor within sixteen generations or 400 years

*A generation is assumed to be twenty-five years for the purposes of these calculations.
Source: Family Tree DNA

Table 5   *Probabilities of sharing a common maternal ancestor with an exact mtDNA match.*

An FGS test is still relatively expensive in comparison to the standard mtDNA tests. For most people, with the current pricing, the best introduction to mtDNA testing will be the combined HVR1 and HVR2 test. An upgrade can be ordered at a later date if necessary, though it is a little cheaper if the FGS test is ordered at the outset. For the family historian an FGS test should be considered as a long-term investment for matching purposes, as the chances of finding a random match are slim while the database is still in its infancy, although once you have taken a full sequence test you will never need to have your mtDNA tested again. In due course, and perhaps within the next five years as the cost of sequencing continues to fall, the FGS test will no doubt become the mtDNA test of choice.

Testing a hypothesis

As we have already seen, a DNA test on its own does not reveal very much information that is of use to the family historian and it is the comparison of results which is of most value. With a Y-DNA test we can compare the results with other people who share the same surname, or another variant spelling, and establish which lines are connected. This approach will, however, not work with the matrilineal line as the surname changes with each new generation. Furthermore, as mtDNA mutates at a much slower rate than Y-STR markers, many people will have several hundred matches even with the combined HVR1 and HVR2 test. Some of your matches might be related to you within the last few hundred years, whereas others will share a common ancestor several thousand years ago. You could spend a lot of time writing to all your matches to see if you can find a link in the paper trail, but in most cases this will be a fruitless task unless you both happen to have ancestors who were living in the same area at the same time. As more people take the FGS test, the problem of the surfeit of matches will be reduced, but even if your match did occur at some point in the last 400 years it will quite possibly be very difficult to find the link. If you are thinking of using an mtDNA test for family history purposes it is, therefore, usually best to have a hypothesis in mind.

With a Y-DNA test you can test the hypothesis that two men who share the same name are related. It does not matter if you have not been able to establish a connection in the paper trail. Even if there is a match it is still possible that the records, which might prove the connection, have not survived. Nevertheless, the match or lack thereof will still be informative and will help to build up an overall picture of the surname and the number of surviving lineages. To prove a hypothesis on the maternal line the contrary situation applies and you will need to have found the possible link in the paper trail *before* you are able to test the hypothesis. One possible scenario could be where you have been unable to find a baptism for your female ancestor. Census records might indicate that she was born in a specific parish but you have searched in that parish and all the neighbouring parishes and no record can be found. At the same time you might have located the potential parents and siblings. This is where the next difficulty arises, because to prove the hypothesis you will then need to trace one or more of the female siblings' lines to the present day to locate the appropriate candidate for testing. With the online availability of census records and birth, marriage and death indexes this is a viable proposition if the descendants have remained in the UK and provided there are not too many common surnames, but it is much more of a challenge if a descendant has emigrated.

A mitochondrial DNA test also serves as a deep ancestry test because, as with a Y-DNA test, you are given a haplogroup designation. The mtDNA haplogroups will be discussed later in this chapter, but for family history purposes this means that an mtDNA test can also be used to prove or disprove a different type of hypothesis, regardless of whether or not a paper trail can be found. There are often family legends that a particular ancestor who lived overseas married a local woman and that there is, therefore, some exotic blood in the ancestral line. An example might be someone with ancestors who lived in British India. There might perhaps be a suspicion of a marriage with a local Indian woman. Haplogroups are often specific to particular regions and an mtDNA test taken by the appropriate matrilineal descendant might thus reveal the presence of a typical Asian haplogroup such as haplogroup M. The mtDNA test can be used in the same way by an American who has a possibility of Native American ancestry. There are five mtDNA haplogroups associated with Native American ancestry – haplogroups A, B, C, D and X, though only some branches of X are exclusively found in the New World. The presence of one of these five haplogroups would therefore provide positive proof of the family legend.

Projects

There are usually discounts for Y-DNA tests ordered through surname projects, but the same discounts do not apply to mtDNA tests and it makes no difference whether you order a test individually or through a project. Projects can, however, still be a very useful way of collating mtDNA test results and finding genetic cousins. A surname project will in most cases not be appropriate as the majority of surname projects are only interested in Y-DNA results. A minority of surname projects will, however, collect mtDNA test results for anyone bearing the surname at any point in their maternal line and display them on their project websites, and it is always worth checking the surname project websites to see if your results might be accepted. If you are interested in taking an mtDNA test but do not have a particular hypothesis in mind it can be helpful to see your mtDNA results within the context of a geographical project, as the matches who will be of most interest to you will be those people who can trace their maternal line to the same part of the country as you. Most of the geographical projects accept both Y-DNA and mtDNA results, but there are a few projects that focus specifically on mitochondrial DNA, such as the Cornwall and the Birmingham mtDNA projects. There are projects for many different countries as well as a growing number of projects for specific English counties or regions, including my own project for the county of Devon. A list of the major western European geographical projects is included in Appendix C. Once you have received your results you can also join the appropriate mtDNA haplogroup project. All the main geographical and haplogroup projects can be found at Family Tree DNA, though some projects with external websites will accept results from other testing companies.

Understanding your mtDNA results

Mitochondrial DNA test results can seem very bewildering at first, especially if you are already familiar with Y-DNA tests, as they are presented in a very different format. The results of my own full sequence mtDNA test can be observed in Figure 11. As can be seen, my results consist of a string of apparently meaningless numbers and letters like 16172C and 16179T. The letters A, T, C and G stand for the four chemical bases adenine, thymine, cytosine and guanine, which form the building blocks of our DNA. There are 16,589 of these letters or bases in human mitochondrial DNA. The bases are given numbers starting from number 1 and going up to 16,589, and the letter that is found at each base is then reported. If I am a 16172C it means, therefore, that I have a C at base number 16172. As we all have mostly the same letters on most of the bases in our mitochondrial DNA, there is little sense in reporting the results for every single one of those 16,589 bases. Our sequence is instead compared to a reference sequence and results are given only for those bases which differ, though some companies will also provide details of your entire sequence for your interest. The sequence used for these comparisons is known as the Cambridge Reference Sequence (CRS). The CRS was the first full mitochondrial genome to be sequenced. The analysis was carried out back in 1981 by a team of scientists at Cambridge University on a placenta donated by a local woman who has remained anonymous. There is nothing special or significant about the CRS or the woman who donated her mitochondrial DNA, other than the fact that her mitochondrial DNA was the first in the world to be sequenced and published. Quite by chance, however, it subsequently transpired that she belongs to haplogroup H, the most common mitochondrial haplogroup in Europe. As the mtDNA tree was

Figure 11   The author's certificate showing the results of a full sequence mitochondrial DNA test.

further refined the CRS was allocated to a branch, or subclade, of haplogroup H known as H2a2a. The CRS was reanalysed in 1999 and a few minor corrections were made. Mitochondrial DNA sequences are now usually compared against the revised Cambridge Reference Sequence (rCRS). Your mtDNA haplotype is the collection of results you receive listing all your differences from this sequence.

Most of the differences from the CRS will be substitutions. For example, for base 16172 I have a letter C whereas the CRS has a letter T in this position. Sometimes as part of the copying process extra letters can be inserted into the sequence or, conversely, a letter might be missed out altogether. These are known as insertions and deletions. I have some insertions in my sequence in HVR2 at bases 315 and 523. For base 315 my results appear as 315.1C. This means I have one additional letter C on this base in comparison with the CRS. At base 523 I have a 523.1C and a 523.1A. This indicates that I have two extra letters − a C and an A − at this position that are not present in the CRS. A deletion is represented by a minus sign. If someone is reported as 424- this shows that they do not have a letter at this location in their sequence. Sometimes two letters will be found instead of the usual one on a single base and the result will appear, for example, as 16093C/T. The technical term for this phenomenon is a heteroplasmy. The process is not fully understood, but appears to be a transitional phase where a mutation is about to happen. Sometimes the heteroplasmy is passed on for several generations. In some cases the base will revert to the original letter in a future generation and in other cases the replacement letter will eventually appear.

This might all sound terribly complicated but in reality there is no need to be concerned with all the individual letters for each base and whether or not you have any insertions, deletions or heteroplasmies. As with Y-DNA, it is a matchmaking game and what you are hoping to find is a match with someone else who has an identical sequence to you. Heteroplasmies are usually discounted for matching purposes. The testing companies will take care of the matching process for you and provide you with a list of all your matches at the various testing levels. It will then be up to you to contact your matches to see if you can find the genealogical connection. Depending on the testing company used, you will either be given the name and email address of your matches or you will be invited to contact your matches through the company's own messaging system. Most companies will provide a profile page where you can list your surname interests and in some cases upload a GEDCOM file. The number of matches can vary considerably from one person to the next. Those people who are in haplogroup H, the most common European haplogroup, usually tend to have the most matches. At one extreme, I have some project members in haplogroup H who have over 8,000 matches with the HVR1 test and over 1,000 matches with the combined HVR1 and HVR2 test. In contrast, other people do not have a single match, even with the basic HVR1 test. My own haplogroup U4 haplotype is one of the rare sequences that is currently unique in the FTDNA database and I am still waiting for my first HVR1 match. If you do have a common haplotype and are interested in finding genealogical connections then it would be worth upgrading to the full genomic sequence test to refine the number of matches. There are, therefore, considerable advantages in testing with a company that offers the FGS test in case an upgrade is necessary.

Mutations in the coding region can very occasionally be associated with medical disorders, though Family Tree DNA will not reveal any medical information when they provide you with your results. These mutations can either be acquired or inherited. According to a paper published by the Human Genetics Commission, approximately 1 in 125 live births and 1 in 10,000 adults in the United Kingdom are affected by mitochondrial disorders with symptoms ranging from mild to severe. Symptoms can include muscular weakness, visual problems, hearing problems, learning disabilities, diabetes, heart disease, liver disease and kidney disease. The Mitomap website, **www.mitomap.org**, maintains a database of all mtDNA mutations found in published and unpublished sources, including those potentially linked to medical disorders. Bear in mind that many of the associations listed are based on a single case report, often with a small sample size. These associations are, therefore, provisional and would need to be replicated in other studies. Very few of the associations listed have been confirmed in large-scale studies and only a few thousand full mtDNA sequences have been published in the scientific literature to date. Anyone wishing to learn more about the meaning of their mutations can order a customised report from ISOGG member and author Dr Ann Turner for a small fee. Details will usually be available from your mtDNA haplogroup project manager or from the members of the ISOGG Newbie mailing list.

Haplogroups

In the same way that a man's Y-chromosome is a living history record that can be used to trace the paternal line back for thousands of years, mitochondrial DNA provides a window into the past on the maternal line. We saw in the previous chapter how all the men alive today can ultimately trace their genetic ancestry back to one man, known as Y-chromosomal Adam, who lived in Africa some time between 80,000 and 130,000 years ago. The mitochondrial DNA of the present-day population can be used in the same way to trace the female line back in time. Our maternal lines all eventually converge on one woman who is aptly known as Mitochondrial Eve. She also lived in Africa but many thousands of years before Y-Adam was born. Mitochondrial Eve probably lived between 180,000 and 200,000 years ago. She was not the first woman and was not the only woman alive at the time, but is simply the only woman whose mitochondrial DNA has been preserved until the present day through a continuous succession of daughters.

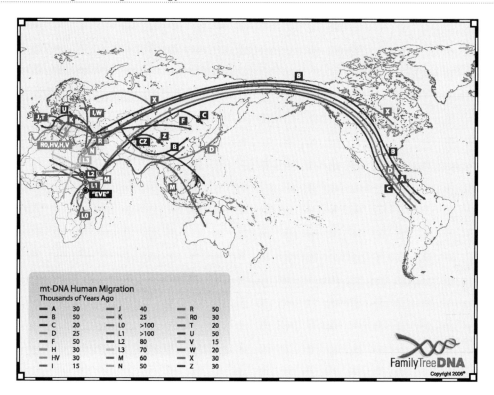

mt-DNA Human Migration
Thousands of Years Ago

A	30	J	40	R	50		
B	50	K	25	RO	30		
C	20	LO	>100	T	20		
D	25	L1	>100	U	50		
F	50	L2	80	V	15		
H	30	L3	70	W	20		
HV	30	M	60	X	30		
I	15	N	50	Z	30		

Figure 12   A map showing the migratory pathways of the descendants of Mitochondrial Eve.

The mitochondrial DNA tree is divided into twenty-six branches, or haplogroups, which are labelled with letters of the alphabet from A through to Z. Each haplogroup has numerous branches, or subclades, which in turn have further branches and sub-branches. The mtDNA haplogroups use the same alternative letter and number system as the Y-DNA haplogroups to define all the subclades. My own mitochondrial DNA, for example, puts me in a subclade known as U4c1a1b. The mtDNA haplogroups often have origins in particular regions and the knowledge of your haplogroup will, therefore, provide an indication of your deep ancestral origins on your maternal line. Confusingly, the mtDNA haplogroups do not correspond with the Y-DNA haplogroups, either by geographical region or in the order in which they are named. The Y-DNA haplogroups begin with haplogroups A and B, the oldest Y-DNA haplogroups. Conversely, the mtDNA haplogroups were labelled in the order of their discovery. The first mtDNA haplogroups to be discovered were found in the Native American population, and haplogroups A, B, C and D are all indicative of Native American ancestry. Haplogroup L is the oldest mtDNA haplogroup. It has six subclades labelled Lo through to L6, each of which has numerous subdivisions. Haplogroup L and its subclades are mostly found in Africa and in people of African origin.

In 2001 Professor Bryan Sykes from Oxford University published the popular book *The Seven Daughters of Eve* in which he showed that 95 per cent of people of European origin could trace their genetic ancestors on the maternal line to one of seven clan mothers. The clan mothers were given names to demonstrate that they were once real women, and Sykes wrote an imaginative biography of each woman's life. The clan mothers corresponded to the major European mitochondrial DNA haplogroups. In the intervening years new 'daughters' have been discovered but the original concept of a small number of founding mothers remains valid. The names provide a useful device to personalise the haplogroups and to remember their names. The original seven daughters are shown below with the corresponding haplogroup names:

Helena	Haplogroup H
Jasmine	Haplogroup J
Katrine	Haplogroup K
Tara	Haplogroup T
Ursula	Haplogroup U5
Velda	Haplogroup V
Xenia	Haplogroup X

Table 6 The Seven Daughters of Eve.

As with Y-DNA test results it is quite often possible to predict a haplogroup from a haplotype – the results you get from your mtDNA test, which indicate your differences from the Cambridge Reference Sequence. Haplogroups can, however, only be confirmed by SNP testing. The SNPs that define the various mtDNA haplogroups can be found both in the control region (the hypervariable region) and the coding region, though the majority of haplogroup-defining SNPs are in the coding region. Family Tree DNA and a few other companies include a selection of coding region SNPs in the cost of an HVR1 and HVR1+HVR2 test to provide confirmation of the haplogroup. If SNP testing is not included with your test then the haplogroup will be predicted and there is a possibility that you will be given the wrong haplogroup designation, especially if you have only ordered a basic HVR1 test. The International Society of Genetic Genealogy maintains a comparison chart showing the various companies which provide mtDNA tests, the prices and the services offered, including SNP testing. The chart can be found at **www.isogg.org/mtdnachart.htm**. With the basic HVR1 and HVR1+HVR2 tests the haplogroup is usually predicted to one of the base haplogroups such as H, U4 or U5. If you take a full sequence test you will be given a more refined haplogroup designation such as U5a1 or K1a1a. The structure or phylogeny of the mtDNA tree is still being worked out and if you take a full sequence test you can expect to see your haplogroup updated from time to time, as and when new studies are published.

There are eleven mtDNA haplogroups which are usually seen in the British Isles, of which haplogroup H is by far and away the most common, being found in perhaps 40 or 50 per cent of the population. It is also the most common mtDNA haplogroup in Europe. The other main mtDNA haplogroups which will typically be encountered in the British Isles are haplogroups I, J, T, V, W, X, U2, U3, U4 and U5. Very occasionally other rarer haplogroups will be found. In my Devon DNA project I have one participant who is haplogroup HV, the mother clade of haplogroups H and V. Another project member has a maternal line from Ireland and belongs to mtDNA haplogroup R1a, which is rarely seen and about which very little seems to be known. (The mitochondrial haplogroup R1a has no connection with the Y-DNA haplogroup of the same name, which is associated with Viking ancestry.)

If the female line does not originate in the British Isles a more diverse range of haplogroups will be found, but even then there can be some surprises. Princess Maria Semeonovna Sviatopolk-Mirski is descended from a line of Polish and Russian nobility with roots in Belarus. Her family were exiled in the Second World War and their ancestral home, Mir Castle in Belarus, came under the control of the Nazis. Princess Maria moved to the UK as a child and now lives in London. She came along to the family history show *Who Do You Think You Are? Live* at Olympia in February 2010, where she had her mitochondrial DNA tested. Princess Maria's maternal line can be traced back to Smolensk in Russia, where her maternal grandmother, Nadezhda Vassilievna Engelhardt, was born in 1879, the daughter of Nadezhda Nikolaevna Tchapline. Princess Maria's DNA results show that she is not in any of the major European haplogroups and instead belongs to the very rare and ancient haplogroup known as ROa, a small branch of haplogroup RO, which was previously known as haplogroup pre-HV1. The parent haplogroup RO is found at its highest frequency in Arabia. ROa was possibly one of the original mtDNA haplogroups in Europe, predating the introduction of farming. Princess Maria has no matches in the Family Tree DNA database, and the company informed us that they only had 350 samples from this haplogroup in their entire database, which at that time had over 110,000 samples in total. In this particular case the mtDNA test did not reveal very much about Princess Maria's maternal origins, but she was fascinated to learn that she belonged to such a rare haplogroup and is very proud of her unique mtDNA signature. In time, as more people are tested, we will learn more about the origins and distribution of mtDNA haplogroup ROa.

For British people of immigrant ancestry, a mitochondrial DNA test can sometimes provide valuable information about the geographical origins of the maternal line, even in the absence of any documentary records. It can be particularly difficult, for example, to trace Jewish ancestors on the female line, as traditionally women went to live in the home villages (*shtetls*) of their husbands, which could be many miles away in another country. As Jewish people tended to marry within their own community, there are some haplogroups and subclades that are associated with Jewish ancestry, which can sometimes help to pinpoint the country or region of origin. Haplogroup N1b is, for instance, seen almost exclusively in Jews and is possibly associated with Sephardic Jews of Middle Eastern or North African origin. The other European haplogroups, and especially K and H, are also found in Jewish people, with some subclades, such as K1a1b1a, K1a9 and K2a2a, confined almost exclusively to Jews.

Databases

To get more value out of your mitochondrial DNA test it can be helpful to compare your results in other databases, especially if you have tested with a company which only has a small database. There are a number of free mtDNA databases, most of which will allow you to upload your own results and search for genetic matches. All of the public databases, apart from GenBank, will only accept HVR1 and HVR2 results.

The databases of the Sorenson Molecular Genealogy Foundation, GeneTree and Ancestry.com were discussed in Chapter 2. These organisations have equivalent mtDNA databases which work in much the same way as their Y-DNA databases. With the SMGF mtDNA database you can either search by surname or input your mtDNA results and search for genetic matches, though you cannot add your mtDNA results to the database. By the end of 2010 the SMGF database contained mtDNA results from more than 73,000 people throughout the world, though with a significant percentage from America. GeneTree incorporates mtDNA results from SMGF and from GeneTree customers. As with the Y-DNA results, SMGF participants who have not 'unlocked' their results have protected profile pages, though the pedigrees can still be viewed. There is also a very useful mtDNA surname search. When I tried searching for my maternal surnames I received mostly hits from people in the US, but there were a handful of results from SMGF participants in England, Canada and Australia. Mitochondrial DNA results can also be added to the Ancestry.com DNA database, where you can search for genetic matches. As with Ancestry.com's Y-DNA database, there is a considerable overlap with the Family Tree DNA database.

Mitosearch, www.mitosearch.org
Mitosearch, sponsored by Family Tree DNA, is the largest public mtDNA database and will accept mtDNA results from any testing company. The database can be searched by haplogroup with searches refined to geographical regions if desired. Family Tree DNA customers can upload their results automatically from their personal pages, whereas results from other companies have to be inputted manually. It

is also possible to upload an outline GEDCOM file of the maternal line, though surprisingly few people choose to do so. Frustratingly, there is no ability to search by surname. Before using the service to check for genetic matches it is first of all necessary to create a user ID and password.

GenBank, **www.ncbi.nlm.nih.gov/genbank**

GenBank is an open-access database of DNA sequences provided by the National Center for Biotechnology Information in the United States. It contains sequences not just from humans, but from over 100,000 distinct organisms. The majority of sequences are provided by laboratories and sequencing centres as an accompaniment to scientific publications. Scientific researchers who are studying mitochondrial DNA now routinely sequence mtDNA in their studies and the resultant sequences are uploaded to GenBank. An increasing number of private individuals, most of whom are Family Tree DNA customers, are now also adding their full sequence mtDNA results to GenBank. By the end of 2010 there were around 8,000 mtDNA sequences in GenBank, including a substantial number uploaded by FTDNA customers. Once sequences have been made publicly available on GenBank they can be used by other scientific researchers in their studies to improve knowledge of mtDNA mutation rates, or to identify new branches of the mtDNA tree. The most up-to-date version of the mtDNA tree is published on the Phylotree website, **www.phylotree.org**, and is maintained by Mannis van Oven, a researcher at the University Medical Center in Rotterdam in the Netherlands. An mtDNA researcher by the name of Ian Logan provides details on his website at **www.ianlogan.co.uk** for uploading full sequence mtDNA results to GenBank, and he will also help with the upload if required. On his website he also maintains full details of all the mtDNA sequences on GenBank organised by haplogroup with corresponding lists of mutations.

Ancient DNA

There is an additional layer of analysis which is often possible with mitochondrial DNA, which is rarely a viable proposition with Y-DNA results. Each cell in our body can contain thousands of mitochondria and there is perhaps a thousand times more mtDNA in the average cell than all the other types of DNA combined. For this reason, when DNA is extracted from ancient remains, it is usually only the mitochondrial DNA that survives in sufficient quantities to be sequenced. For the amateur genetic genealogist it can be an interesting exercise to compare mtDNA results with the ancient and famous historical DNA samples that have been sequenced. One of the best known examples is Cheddar Man, whose skeletal remains were found in a cave at Cheddar Gorge in Somerset in 1903. Carbon dating revealed that he lived around 9,000 years ago, 3,000 years before farming reached Britain. Ninety-four years after the discovery of Cheddar Man, scientists were able to extract mitochondrial DNA from his tooth, and the first hypervariable region was sequenced revealing that he belonged to haplogroup U5. Haplogroup U5 has since been found in other ancient specimens in other European countries. It is one of the haplogroups thought to be representative of the first hunter–gather populations to settle in Europe, but is still found in around 10 per cent of modern-day Europeans.

More recently, in 1991, the mummified body of a man was found preserved in a glacier on the border between Austria and Italy. He was named Ötzi the Iceman after the Ötztal Alps where his body was discovered, and it was estimated that he lived about 5,300 years ago. Two attempts were made to sequence part of his mtDNA and then, in 2010 with advances in DNA technology, scientists were successfully able to sequence his entire mitochondrial genome. He was found to belong to haplogroup K1, one of the major European haplogroups. Haplogroup K1 is divided into three subclades in the present-day population: K1a, K1b and K1c. Ötzi's mutations placed him in a previously undiscovered branch of haplogroup K1, which has been labelled in Ötzi's honour as K1ö. His lineage has quite possibly died out leaving no living descendants, or it may simply be that no one from his lineage has yet been tested. The knowledge that one has a distant connection with Cheddar Man or Ötzi the Iceman is of no practical benefit, but it can still be very interesting to learn about our ancient cousins, and especially so if we share the same haplogroup.

Historical mysteries

Mitochondrial DNA can also be used to solve historical mysteries from more recent times. In these situations the mtDNA of a presumed maternal relative is also tested to provide positive identification of the remains. One of the better known cases involved the identification of a young boy known as the Titanic baby. Six days after the *Titanic* sank on 15 April 1912 on its maiden voyage from Southampton to New York, a baby boy was found dead floating in the Atlantic Ocean. The baby could not be identified and he was buried in a grave in Halifax, Nova Scotia, which was poignantly dedicated to the 'unknown child'. In 2001 researchers in Canada were given permission to exhume the body. From passenger lists and other records they established that the baby could only be one of four children. In 2002 the baby was identified as a 13-month-old Finnish boy by the name of Eino Panula, after preliminary DNA tests on a matrilineal relative appeared to provide confirmation of his identity. Doubts remained, however, as the dental evidence suggested that the boy was nearer 2 years old. Advances in DNA technology allowed the research-ers to review the case and conduct further DNA tests in 2007, and it was finally established that the lost child was not the Finnish boy after all but another one of the four children, a 19-month-old English boy by the name of Sidney Leslie Goodwin, who was travelling on the *Titanic* with the rest of his family to start a new life in America. An HVR1 mtDNA test was carried out on the baby and on a sample provided by a maternal relative of the Goodwins who was living in the US. The two samples matched, thus confirming his identity.

Mitochondrial DNA was also used to solve the mystery of the Romanovs, the last Russian Imperial family, who were executed on 18 July 1918. In 1991 nine sets of skeletal remains were excavated from a mass grave near Ekaterinburg, Russia, which were believed to be the remains of the Romanovs. Circumstantial evidence suggested that the bodies were probably those of Tsar Nicholas II, his wife the Tsarina Alexandra and three of their daughters, along with their physician and three servants. A comparison of mitochondrial DNA from living Romanov relatives, including Prince Philip, the Duke of Edinburgh, who is related on the maternal line to Tsarina Alexandra, provided confirmation of their identities. However, two of the Tsar's

Famous DNA

DNA Haplotypes (DNA signatures) for famous, or infamous, homo sapiens*

Mitochondrial DNA - mtDNA

The Romanovs - The Last Russian Royal Family

In July 1991, nine bodies were exhumed from a shallow grave just outside Ekaterinburg, Russia. Circumstantial evidence, along with mitochondrial DNA sequencing and matches, gave strong evidence to the remains being those of the Romanovs, the last Russian Royals who were executed on July 18, 1918. The following sequences for Tsar Nicholas II, his cousin, Count Nicholai Trubetskoy, Tsarina Alexandra, and Prince Philip, the Duke of Edinburgh, are taken from Bryan Sykes book, "*The Seven Daughters of Eve*."

Name	Haplo	mtDNA Sequence	
Tsar Nicholas Romanov	T	16126C, **16169**Y, 16294T, 16296T	73G, 263G, 315.1C
Count Trubetskoy	T	16126C, **16169**Y, 16294T, 16296T	73G, 263G, 315.1C

The Tsar's sequence contains a new mutation at position 169, a state referred to as *heteroplasmy* - the existence of more than one mitochondrial type in the cells of an individual, i.e., the presence of both normal and mutant mtDNA in a single individual. The remains of his brother, Grand Duke of Russia, Georgii Romanov were exhumed, and the results were identical to the Tsar's, including the

Figure 13   The International Society of Genetic Genealogy's 'famous DNA' page records the mtDNA sequences for the Romanovs, Marie Antoinette, Prince Philip and the Cheddar Man.

children were absent from the mass grave. Their bodies were eventually discovered in 2007 in an area of rough burnt ground near Ekaterinburg. DNA tests carried out in 2008 confirmed that the two bodies were indeed those of the two missing children Alexei and Maria. For the latter case Y-DNA testing was also used to confirm the relationship between Alexei and his father.

These are just a few examples of historical mysteries that have been solved by DNA testing, and there will no doubt be many other cases in the future. If you are interested in comparing your mtDNA results with those of famous or historical figures, the International Society of Genetic Genealogy maintains a famous DNA section on its website with the published haplogroups and haplotypes where known.

5

Cousins reunited: autosomal DNA tests

Y-chromosome DNA tests and mitochondrial DNA tests can be very useful tools as an aid to family history research, but these tests have a very limited application as they only tell us about two distinct lines of our family tree. The Y-chromosome test traces the direct paternal line and mitochondrial DNA tracks the direct maternal line, which correspond to the two outermost lines on a family tree diagram. These tests, therefore, tell us nothing about all the lines in the middle of our family tree. As we trace our lines back in time the number of ancestors doubles with each generation. We therefore have eight great-grandparents, sixteen great-great-grandparents and thirty-two great-great-great-grandparents. If you are a male, a combined Y-DNA and mtDNA test will only help with the ancestry of two of those thirty-two ancestors. If you are a female you can only learn about one of those thirty-two ancestors – unless you have a living male relative such as your father, brother or uncle who can act as a proxy. One solution is to test further proxy relatives who represent the other lines in your tree. If you wish to trace your maternal grandfather's surname, you might have a cousin with that surname who could take a Y-DNA test. If you are interested in the surname of a particular great-great-great-grandparent you could try and trace the surname line forwards on another branch in the hope of finding a living name-bearer who could test on your behalf. Inevitably, there will be some cases where the line has become extinct or where no living male relative with the appropriate surname can easily be found. Fortunately, a new autosomal DNA test is now available which fills in the gaps and helps us to find genetic cousins on all our ancestral lines.

As of the end of 2010 there were two companies which offered this new test: 23andMe and Family Tree DNA, both of which are in the United States. The 23andMe test includes a feature referred to as the Relative Finder. The Family Tree DNA equivalent is called the Family Finder. To understand how the test works we need to understand a few basics about the inheritance of autosomal DNA. Humans have twenty-three pairs of chromosomes, which consist of twenty-two pairs of auto-somes and one pair of sex chromosomes – the Y-chromosome and the X-chromosome.

A male receives an X-chromosome from his mother and a Y-chromosome from his father, whereas a female has two X-chromosomes, one from each parent. Autosomal chromosomes are inherited from both parents. The matching autosomes from each parent are shuffled up during the process of recombination and, as a result, we receive a random mixture of roughly 50 per cent of our autosomal DNA from each parent. In turn, our parents have received 50 per cent of their DNA from their own parents. We therefore inherit approximately 25 per cent of our DNA from each of our four grandparents and 12.5 per cent of our DNA from our great-grandparents. The further back in time we go the smaller the percentage of DNA we will receive from our distant ancestors. DNA combines at random and the actual percentage of DNA we inherit from our ancestors varies. We do not necessarily inherit precisely 25 per cent of our DNA from each grandparent, but will sometimes inherit more from one grandparent than another. We will still have traces of the DNA from most, if not all, of our great-great-great-great-grandparents, but for each generation you go back in time beyond our fourth great-grandparents the probability of carrying DNA from a specific ancestor falls considerably. Table 7 shows the average amount of DNA we share with our close relatives.

The following figures show the average percentage of autosomal DNA shared with close relatives. The actual percentage can vary and will sometimes be higher and sometimes lower. Source: ISOGG Wiki

Relation	Percentage
mother, father and siblings	50
grandfathers, grandmothers, aunts, uncles, half-siblings, double first cousins	25
first cousins	12.5
first cousins once removed	6.25
second cousins, first cousins twice removed	3.125
third cousins	0.781
fourth cousins	0.195
fifth cousins	0.0488
sixth cousins	0.0122
seventh cousins (circa 92,000 base pairs)	0.00305
eighth cousins (circa 23,000 base pairs)	0.000763

Table 7   How much autosomal DNA do we share with our relatives?

The FTDNA Family Finder test and 23andMe's Relative Finder feature look at hundreds of thousands of base pairs – the building blocks of DNA – across the entire human genome. The positions chosen are places where variants are known to occur. These variants, known as single-nucleotide polymorphisms (SNPs, pronounced *snips* for short) are autosomally inherited. One nucleotide, or 'letter', of each base pair is inherited from the mother and one from the father. You share many of the same SNPs with your siblings, grandparents, aunts, uncles and cousins, but will share fewer SNPs with your more distant cousins. The number of SNPs you share with another person can, therefore, be used to tell how closely related you are to another person. These autosomal SNPs are not passed on from parent to child singly, but in large blocks. Each chromosome in the child therefore contains a combination of large DNA segments from each parent. With each new generation these segments are broken up into smaller pieces as part of the random process of recombination, and they gradually reduce in size until they are no longer detectable. You will thus have large blocks of DNA handed down intact from all four of your grandparents, but smaller segments from your great-grandparents and even smaller segments from your great-great-grandparents. The number of shared DNA segments, the size of those segments and the number of matching SNPs can then be used in combination to predict the closeness of the relationship between two people. Complicated mathematical calculations are involved, but fortunately the testing companies do the number crunching for us using their own proprietary algorithms. When you get your results you will be presented with a list of your matches and the predicted relationship. You will then be able to contact your matches and see if you can work out how you are related.

While the Family Finder and Relative Finder tests are sensitive enough to detect shared segments of DNA for most third cousins, some fourth cousins will test and not have a match. In contrast, because of the random way in which the blocks are inherited, you might have a match with a sixth cousin or even more distantly related cousins such as seventh to twelfth cousins. The new autosomal tests can predict genealogical relationships reliably up to the second cousin level, but beyond the fourth cousin level the precise genealogical relationship is difficult to predict unless multiple related people are tested. It is recommended, wherever possible, to test the oldest generation in your family to maximise your chances of finding matches with your more distant cousins. If your parents are alive you should aim to test both of your parents. If only one parent is living you can test the surviving parent, your siblings and yourself. In this way you will have a better chance of working out on which side of the family your matches occur. If you have no surviving parents you can take the test yourself and get your siblings and your cousins on each side of your family to test as well.

DNA tests are very good at telling us that two people are related. They are, however, not so good at predicting precisely where that relationship occurs and they will not identify the name of the common ancestor. The same limitations apply to autosomal DNA tests. You will be given predicted relationships for your matches, such as third, fourth or fifth cousin, but you will also be given a relationship range. A predicted fourth cousin could, for example, potentially be anywhere between a third to a seventh cousin, whereas a predicted fifth cousin could be anything from a third to a tenth cousin. The reason for the wide relationship range is because of the random way in which DNA is inherited. The blocks of DNA are not passed on in standard sizes. Large blocks can sometimes persist by chance in deeper relations but can get broken up into smaller segments in more recent cousins. The predictions will also appear to be closer than they actually are if you have any close-cousin marriages in your ancestry. If a husband and wife are first cousins, a child from the marriage will have six great-grandparents instead of eight, and will, therefore, inherit proportionately more DNA from the two double great-grandparents who appear on both sides of the tree. The effect of cousin marriages will vary depending on how recently they occurred and how many such marriages appear in the person's ancestry. Cousin marriages are historically more prevalent in some cultures than others. Ashkenazi Jews, for example, traditionally married within their own community, and marriages between first and second cousins occurred very frequently. Even in the UK today over 50 per cent of British Pakistanis marry their first cousins.

As with any other type of DNA test, an autosomal DNA test should, therefore, be used as a tool in conjunction with the traditional documentary research. To get the best out of the test you will need to research all your lines for as many generations as possible to maximise the chances of finding the link in the paper trail with your newly found genetic cousins. You must also hope, of course, that the people you match will have done the equivalent research too. The process of tracing all your lines back for multiple generations is not an easy task. I found it to be quite a sobering experience when I examined the progress I had made on my own tree. Over the course of the last nine years I have actively researched all of my ancestral lines, though I have tended to focus on some surnames more than others. I have a few lines that can be traced back to the 1600s and, of these, a handful of lines go right back to the 1200s. I have had less success on other lines. My great-great-grandfather George Tidbury, born in 1856 in Sydmonton, Hampshire, was illegitimate and I have not been able to find any reference to his father. My great-grandfather James Lymer Ratty has defied all attempts to trace his ancestry. He was supposedly born about 1859 in Bermondsey or St Luke's in London, but no birth registration nor baptismal record can be found and he is also absent from the 1861 census. I suspect he was illegitimate and that a fictional father's name was given on his two marriage certificates. Fortunately, he was living with his grandmother at the time of the 1871 census, which has enabled me to trace his Ratty line, but the other line is at a complete dead-end. As a result of these gaps, I am only able to name fourteen of my sixteen great-great-grandparents, twenty-five of my thirty-two great-great-great-grandparents and just twenty-two of my sixty-four great-great-great-great-grandparents. Anecdotal evidence from other family historians suggests that they too have had similar difficulties in researching all their lines for more than three or four generations, though I have come across some people who have at least successfully traced all thirty-two of their great-great-great-grandparents. However, most people will probably, like me, have a few gaps in their tree, so if you do get a match with a potential fourth or fifth cousin, it could potentially be very difficult to find the actual connection in the paper trail unless you find that you have a rare surname in common.

The X-chromosome

Autosomal DNA is inherited randomly from both parents, which, in the absence of any shared surnames, makes it difficult to establish where you share a common ancestor with your match. A match on the X-chromosome can help to refine the match because of the special way in which the X-chromosome is inherited, which thus narrows down the number of ancestors who could have contributed their DNA. A man receives a Y-chromosome from his father and an X-chromosome from his mother. A match on the X-chromosome can, therefore, only have come from

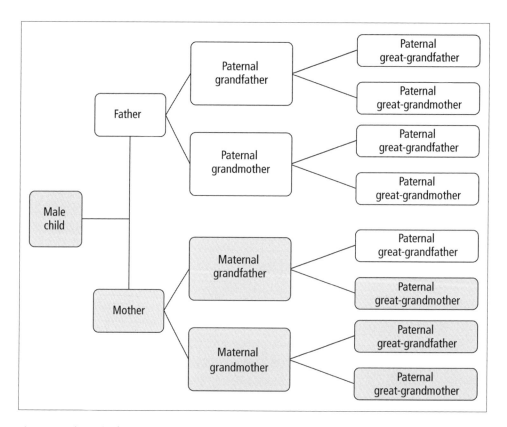

Figure 14   The path of X-chromosome inheritance in a male.

his mother's side of the family. The X-chromosome from his mother can either be the X he inherited from his mother's father, the X he inherited from his mother's mother or, more usually, a combination of the two. As such, a man can potentially inherit X-chromosome DNA from both his maternal grandmother and his maternal grandfather. The situation is complicated, however, because he could inherit 50 per cent from each maternal grandparent or he could receive 0 per cent from one maternal grandparent and 100 per cent from the other. Going back one further generation, a male can potentially inherit X-chromosome DNA from just three of his great-grandparents, as can be seen in Figure 14. A female has two X-chromosomes, one from each of her parents, and she can thus inherit X-chromosome DNA from a wider range of ancestors. She can potentially inherit X-chromosome DNA from three of her four grandparents and five of her eight great-grandparents, as can be seen in Figure 15.

Ann Turner has prepared a useful text file, which lists the Ahnentafel numbers of the ancestors who could potentially contribute X-chromosome DNA. This can be found at: **http://dnacousins.com/AHN_X.TXT**. Ahnentafel numbers can be generated by most family history programs. Jim Turner has provided a range of printable X-chromosome charts, which can be filled in manually to identify the ancestors who

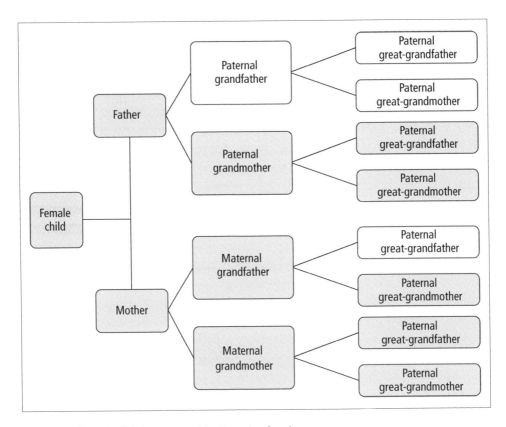

Figure 15   The path of X-chromosome inheritance in a female.

contributed to an X-chromosome match. His charts can be found at **http://freepages .genealogy.rootsweb.ancestry.com/~hulseberg/DNA/xinheritance.html**. These charts also show the amount of autosomal DNA that can be inherited from each contributing ancestor. A pie chart on Blaine Bettinger's website at **www. thegeneticgenealogist.com/2009/01/12/more-x-chromosome-charts** also nicely illustrates how males can inherit the X-chromosome, and a chart for females may be found at **www.thegeneticgenealogist.com/2008/12/21/unlocking- the-genealogical-secrets-of-the-x-chromosome**.

How many cousins?

We have seen how the new generation of autosomal tests work in theory, but how can they be used to help with your family history research? If you have already been researching your family history for some time you will probably already be in con- tact with quite a number of your second, third and fourth cousins, and you will quite possibly have been able to identify many more by name in your family tree. I am now fairly confident, for example, that I have identified all of the descend- ants of my eight great-grandparents. I have a total of fifty-seven first cousins, first cousins once removed and second cousins who are related to me through my great- grandparents. If I go back one more generation, the task of identifying all my cousins then becomes much more complicated and with each subsequent generation the difficulties increase. I have done a tally of the number of cousins I have been able to identify in my genealogical research to date and the results are shown in Table 8. For simplicity I have excluded everyone beyond the once removed level. One can prob- ably expect the numbers at least to double with each new generation. It is clear that I still have many more distant cousins who are as yet unidentified. In practice, the numbers are likely to increase exponentially because families were much larger in the nineteenth century, and most people will probably have several thousand relatives at the fifth cousin level and beyond.

The process of tracking and documenting all these thousands of cousins would be a task of monumental proportions and quite probably a sterile exercise. Most family historians are more interested in exploring the lives of their ancestors and tracing their trees as far back in time as possible, rather than exploring the descendants of their more recent collateral relatives. In the process many people acquire an interest in a particular surname or surnames. I have, for example, done extensive research on my maiden name Cruwys, which has now developed into a one-name study. I record all references to the surname and trace all Cruwys trees forwards to the present day. I simply do not have the time or the inclination to perform a similar exercise for all the other surnames that appear in my tree. Instead, I hope to make connections with other people researching those surnames in the hope that they will be able to contribute to my research on the earlier generations. If they share their research with me then I will only record one or two generations on from our common ancestor rather than every single descendant in the line. To make these connections with other researchers, family historians were previously reliant on the traditional genealogical networks, and to make the connection you need some surnames to work with.

first cousins	3
first cousins once removed	21
second cousins	33
second cousins once removed	77
third cousins	13
third cousins once removed	90
fourth cousins	73
fourth cousins once removed	89
fifth cousins	17
fifth cousins once removed	31

Table 8   Number of cousins identified by the author by traditional genealogical research.

The FTDNA Family Finder test and the 23andMe Relative Finder feature now provide an alternative method of making these connections, which does not rely on surnames or on a completed paper trail. The hope is that by taking such a test you will find a genetic cousin who is related to you on one of the lines that you have been not able to research. Such a situation might apply if you have an illegitimate line or there is an adoption in your tree. Alternatively, your research might have reached a brick wall because one of your ancestors had a particularly common surname. In my own tree, for instance, I have a William Hunter who was born *c.*1798 in Scotland. Although he appears in both the 1851 and 1861 censuses, he only tells us that he was born in Scotland and does not reveal the parish or even the county where he was born. There are rather a lot of William Hunters on the Scotland's People website who were born around the same time as my William, and it would be a huge undertaking to trace and eliminate each one. As he is my only Scottish ancestor I am, therefore, hoping that one day a DNA match will provide me with the breakthrough that I need on this line. As the Family Finder and 23andMe tests have only been available for a couple of years it will inevitably take some time for the databases to grow in size to reach critical mass so that such research problems can be solved. There will invariably still be some ancestral lines that will be impossible to trace despite all our best efforts.

How many matches?

To get an idea of what people might eventually expect from the new autosomal DNA tests we can look at the current situation of the databases, the number of matches that people are getting and the experiences of the early users. 23andMe's Relative Finder feature was released in October 2009 and was provided as a free, opt-in extra to the company's personal genomics health test. By the end of 2010 23andMe had around 60,000 people in their database, though not all of their customers choose to participate in the Relative Finder programme. Anecdotal evidence from other genetic genealogists suggests that, as of the end of 2010, people of northern European origin are getting matches with between 140 and 600 people with the 23andMe Relative Finder test. Those at the higher end of the range are mostly Americans with lots of early Colonial American ancestry. Ashkenazi Jews, who tended to marry within their own community and who also have large families, will often have in excess of 1,000 matches.

Family Tree DNA's Family Finder test was launched in February 2010 but, because it is an addition to their product range, the test has to be purchased separately. No figures are currently available for size of the Family Finder database, but a reasonable estimate is that the number of people who have done this test by the end of 2010 is 5,000–10,000. It has, therefore, not yet caught up with the size of the 23andMe Relative Finder database, but is growing rapidly. Anecdotal evidence suggests that people are getting anything between 20 and 100 matches with the Family Finder test, with a minority of people, mainly those of Ashkenazi Jewish ancestry or early Colonial American ancestry, having in excess of 200 or 300 matches.

It is clear that, even in the early days of these tests, most people of European origin are finding that they have quite a large number of matches and the numbers can be expected to grow rapidly in the coming years. It is very reassuring to learn that we have so many genetic cousins, but a match will not mean very much unless it is possible to find a genealogical connection. The majority of matches that people are getting are with fifth cousins and more distant cousins. In most cases, unless you share an ancestral surname in common, or at the very least have ancestors living in the same geographical location, it will not be practical to pursue the match as there will be little chance of finding the connection. Inevitably, as both the testing companies are based in America, a large proportion of your matches will probably be with Americans. Many of the Americans who have tested have ancestry going back for many generations in America but, despite their best efforts, will not have any idea where in the UK any of their lines originated, and there will thus be little hope of finding a link. Comparatively fewer people from the UK, Australia and Canada have taken the tests so although you might have what seems at first like a daunting list of matches, in reality only a handful of matches will be worth pursuing. Even if you have a match with a fifth or distant cousin from the same country as you, it can still be quite a challenge finding a connection, as there will inevitably be gaps in your family trees and the match could easily be on a line that you have not yet had time to research, or on a line on which you are completely stuck. As such, the most fruitful matches will be with your closer genetic cousins who are predicted to be third or fourth cousins or more recent cousins. In some cases a match will simply provide verification of your existing paper trail, but in other cases a close match could potentially provide a breakthrough on a previously intractable line. In these early days anyone taking a Family Finder or 23andMe test and hoping to find random matches of genealogical benefit is likely to have a low success rate, but the odds will undoubtedly improve in the years to come as more people get tested.

Testing a hypothesis

In the short term the new autosomal tests are best used for proving or disproving a particular hypothesis, and there are many scenarios where these tests could be useful. If during the course of your research, for example, you discover that your great-grandfather reputedly had a child out of wedlock, then you could test yourself and a descendant of the illegitimate line and see if you both have the expected amount of shared DNA. A Y-chromosome test could, of course, also prove or disprove such a hypothesis, but only if both living relatives are descended in the direct paternal line from the great-grandfather. Often in such situations there are no living males to take a Y-DNA test. The advantage of the autosomal tests is that it criss-crosses through all the generations, irrespective of gender, and any living descendant can, therefore, take the test regardless of their line of descent.

An autosomal test can also be used to provide an additional level of verification in conjunction with a Y-chromosome or mitochondrial DNA test. If you are researching a recent illegitimate line, a Y-chromosome test could potentially provide a match with another surname, which might provide a clue to the father's identity. If the matching surname can also be found in the parish in question then the chances of the match being significant will increase, but how can you be sure? If a 'suspect' can be identified it should then be possible to find a living relative to take an autosomal DNA test, which will give a prediction of the likely relationship.

If you are using an autosomal DNA test to prove a hypothesis it is important to bear in mind the limitations of the test. It is a very accurate tool for confirming close relationships, but the chances of success diminish with each additional generation because of the random way in which DNA is inherited. Two second cousins will almost always share enough DNA to be predicted as a match, whereas 90 per cent of third cousins will have a matching DNA segment. This does mean, however, that 10 per cent of third cousins will not have a matching DNA segment even if they are known to be related. Only around 50 per cent of fourth cousins will share enough DNA for it to be detected. Consequently, a matching DNA segment will confirm the hypothesis, but a lack of a matching DNA segment is not proof that there is no relationship. If a matching DNA segment is not found then further tests can be done on other cousins to verify the relationship. Table 9 shows the probabilities of a matching DNA segment being found between two people at various levels of cousinship with the two different tests. The companies use different algorithms and match criteria which combine to produce slightly different probabilities.

Relationship	Family Finder Percentage	Relative Finder Percentage
first cousin or closer		~ 100
second cousins or closer	> 99	> 99
third cousins	> 90	~ 90
fourth cousins	> 50	~ 45
fifth cousins	> 10	~ 15
sixth cousins and more distant	Remote (typically less than 2)	< 5

Source: Family Tree DNA and 23andMe

Table 9   Chances of finding at least one matching DNA segment with the Family Tree DNA Family Finder test and the 23andMe Relative Finder feature

23andMe's Relative Finder feature

The 23andMe Relative Finder and FTDNA Family Finder tests broadly work in the same way, but they each have a number of different features and there are advantages and disadvantages for both tests. The Relative Finder service is one component of the personal genomics service offered by the California-based company 23andMe. When the Relative Finder feature was first launched in October 2009, 23andMe was using a chip that tested around 600,000 SNPs. The majority of the SNPs were autosomal, but about 3,000 mitochondrial DNA SNPs were also included, along with 13,786 SNPs on the X-chromosome and, for males, 1,800 SNPs on the Y-chromosome. At this time it was possible to purchase separate 'Ancestry' and 'Health' tests or, for an additional sum, a 'Complete Edition', combining both the ancestry and health components. A new chip was launched at the end of November 2010 offering around 1 million SNPs for the same price as the previous Complete Edition, but at the same time the option of ordering a standalone Health test or Ancestry test was discontinued. From the end of 2010 onwards, 23andMe has experimented with a number of different pricing models. The test has been offered for a lower sum with a commitment to a small monthly subscription to the Personal Genome Service or at a higher price without a subscription. The company has also held a number of sales when the test has been offered at a generous discount. Many genealogists have taken advantage of these sales to learn more about their health and to see how the Relative Finder feature works.

The health component of the 23andMe test does not generally provide a medical diagnosis, but instead looks at the various SNPs in your genome and provides you with your relative risk of contracting a particular condition or exhibiting a specific trait. Many of the SNPs chosen are on genes that are thought to have a possible link with a particular disorder. The predictions are based on scientific studies known as genome-wide association studies, which examine SNPs in large populations and try to establish if a particular disease or trait is associated with a specific SNP. All such, studies have to be considered with a good deal of caution as they are not predictive but only suggest a possibility of an increased risk. Very few conditions are attributable entirely to genetics; environment and lifestyle will also play their part. In many cases your family history will be the most reliable predictor. Even if the results show that you are at moderately increased risk for a particular disease, there is no guarantee that you will actually develop it. Conversely, some people can have a low relative risk for a disease, but might already be suffering from that condition or might develop it at

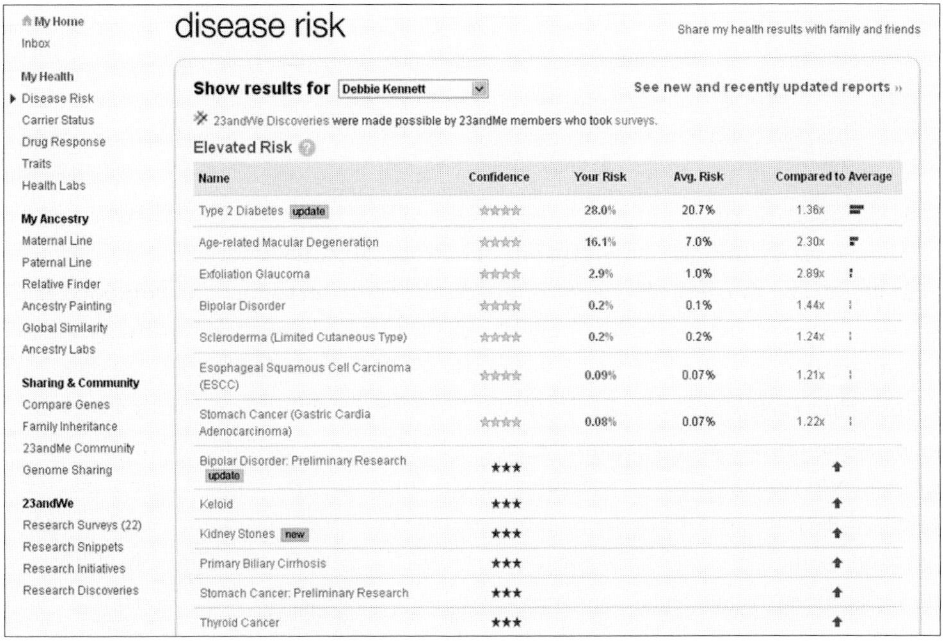

Figure 16 The 23andMe test provides reports on possible genetic associations with various traits and diseases. The report above shows an extract from the author's disease risk results. Most diseases have a mixture of genetic and environmental causes. An increased genetic risk is not an indication that someone will develop a specific disease. Similarly, someone with a decreased genetic risk might still have the disease in question or develop it later in life. Family history will usually be the most reliable predictor.

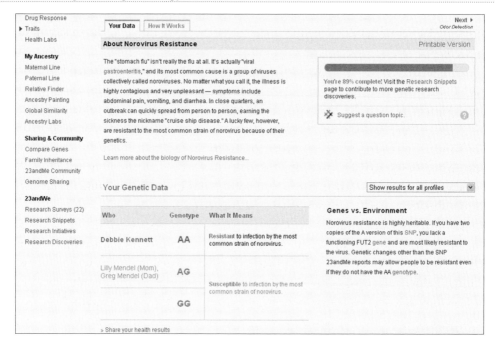

Figure 17   A page from the author's 23andMe report, showing that she has a genotype that makes her resistant to norovirus, a viral form of gastroenteritis often encountered on cruise ships. She shares this genotype with around 20 per cent of people of European or African ancestry.

some point in the future. The scientific studies can themselves provide contradictory results. For example, longevity is one of the traits covered by the test. I have a CC genotype on one SNP which, according to one study, gives me substantially higher odds of living to 100. On another SNP I have the TT genotype which only gives me typical odds of living to 95.

The 23andMe test currently provides results for over ninety disease risks and over forty traits. The diseases cover a very broad spectrum and include diabetes, rheumatoid arthritis, Parkinson's disease, obesity, psoriasis and various types of cancer, as well as a number of rare and obscure diseases that will be unfamiliar to most people. The traits include hair curl, earwax type, pain sensitivity, freckling, eye colour, bitter taste perception, muscle performance and norovirus resistance. In addition to the results for disease risk and traits, the test also provides information on the carrier status for a number of heritable conditions and your predicted response to various drugs. Carrier status information is provided for over twenty conditions including cystic fibrosis, haemochromatosis and selected breast cancer mutations. Drug response information is given for a number of drugs including caffeine metabolism, heroin addiction, warfarin sensitivity and response to hepatitis C treatment. I discovered, for instance, that I am a fast metaboliser of caffeine, which is perhaps not surprising as I consume vast amounts of tea every day! I have an increased risk of heroin addiction, though I am unlikely ever to be tempted to sample the drug. I also learned that I have a slightly increased sensitivity to warfarin. In the event that I ever need to take this drug my general practitioner will be able to modify the dosage accordingly.

23andMe provides excellent resources on their website and very detailed explanations of all the diseases and traits covered by the test. Your results are also updated on a regular basis in the light of new scientific studies, and so the value of the test will grow over time as scientists discover more about the contribution of genetics to disease – though it will probably be necessary to maintain a subscription to have continued access to these updates. The 23andMe test should always be used in conjunction with your family history and if your results give you any cause for concern you should always consult your general practitioner.

For the mitochondrial DNA and Y-chromosome DNA part of the analysis, you will be given a haplogroup designation, which will help you to learn more about your deep ancestry on your direct maternal and paternal lines. You will not, however, be able to compare your Y-DNA and mtDNA results with people who have tested with other companies or use your results in any Y-DNA or mtDNA projects. Surname projects use the faster-mutating Y-STR markers, which 23andMe does not test, so you will not have any 'numbers' to compare with other people. The standard genealogical mtDNA tests look at specific regions within the mitochondrial genome and the results are compared against the Cambridge Reference Sequence. 23andMe analyses a mixture of mtDNA SNPs but does not sequence the entire hypervariable region. 23andMe mtDNA results are, therefore, not compatible with the mtDNA results received from genetic genealogy companies. Consequently, the Y-DNA and mtDNA components of the 23andMe test can only be used for deep ancestry purposes.

The 23andMe Relative Finder service was a spin-off from the health test. It was launched in October 2009 and was the first such test available on the market. Relative Finder is an opt-in service, which is included with the personal genome test. If you choose to participate in the Relative Finder programme you will be presented with a list of your potential relatives along with the predicted relationship, the suggested range (for example, fourth to tenth cousin), the percentage of DNA shared and the number of shared segments. The names of your matches are not shown and you will instead see the gender of your matches and their haplogroups. Customers can optionally fill in a profile page, providing details of the surnames they are researching, their country of residence and any additional information they think might be of interest. Profiles can either be made public or can be restricted to your contacts. If 23andMe customers have filled in their profile details, you will see in your list of matches the number of surnames entered in their profile, though not the actual names, and their country of residence. In practice, very few people provide these details. The only way to find out more about your matches is, therefore, to make contact through the 23andMe messaging system. If the person accepts contact you will be able to see their full profile and you will have the opportunity

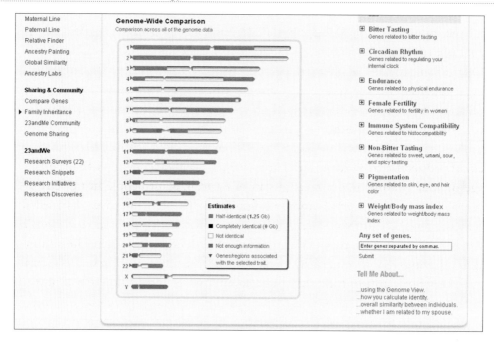

Figure 18 A 23andMe demo family inheritance chart, showing a comparison of the genomes of a grandfather (Fred Mendel) and his grandson (Alan Mendel). Note the random nature in which the autosomal blocks of DNA are inherited. The grandson has none of his grandfather's DNA on chromosomes 10 and 16, but has large blocks of DNA in common on other chromosomes.

to compare your family trees to see if you can work out how you are related. Once you have established contact you can invite your match to 'compare genomes' with you. This will allow you to see a diagram showing the matching segments on the relevant chromosomes (see Figure 18).

23andMe only allows you to send contact invitations to five people a day, so if you do have a lot of matches and wish to make contact with them all it could take some time. However, as the majority of people who have tested with 23andMe signed up for the health test, only a small proportion will respond to contact requests. I tested with 23andMe in April 2010. By the end of the year I had 175 matches. I contacted all of them but only twenty-four of those matches accepted contact. Five people declined contact and the remainder did not reply. The discussions in the 23andMe Forums suggest that most people are getting similar response rates. The average seems to be about 30 per cent, though some people are more successful than others. Of my matches who provided details of their country of residence – including some of those who declined contact – thirty-two were living in America, two in Australia, two in Canada, one in France and one in the United Kingdom. To date I have not been able to find a genealogical connection with any of my matches. My match from the UK is a Parkinson's disease patient who tested for health reasons and has only just started to research her family history. My own figures are probably a reflection of the composition of the 23andMe database and I would guess that well in excess of 90 per cent of 23andMe customers are in the US. My genetic genealogy friends in America have had some success and have found some useful matches with the Relative Finder test. For those of us in the UK, however, the chances of finding a random meaning-ful match are currently very slim, though the situation will no doubt improve in the long run and as more people get tested.

The 23andMe test also includes some features which will provide information about your ethnic admixture. The Ancestry Painting feature tells you what percent-age of your genome is European, Asian or African. Most people in the UK will probably be of 100 per cent European origin, so this feature is not particularly helpful unless you suspect that you have some particularly exotic ancestry in your tree. The Ancestry Finder feature provides hints of your likely country of origin. The informa-tion is based on surveys taken by 23andMe customers who were asked to indicate the country of birth of their four grandparents. If you already know that all your ancestors were born in the British Isles this feature is again not likely to be of much significance, but could be of interest if you have gaps in your tree and suspect that you have lines originating in other countries.

If you wish to find out more about the 23andMe test you can sign up for a free demo account. This will also allow you to search the database to see if anyone has already been tested who is researching one of your surnames. Bear in mind that only a small percentage of people actually fill out their profile pages and list their ancestral surnames, though the people who do so are likely to be the most active genealogists. The Relative Finder feature might not yet have much application for family history researchers in the UK but the health component is very interesting. The test is also an excellent educational tool. There is nothing like having access to your own genome to help you to understand genetics!

Family Tree DNA's Family Finder test

The Family Finder test, launched in February 2010, is Family Tree DNA's answer to 23andMe's Relative Finder feature. It is a genealogical test without any of the health reports which are a key component of the 23andMe test. When the Family Finder test was first launched it used 563,800 autosomal DNA SNPs. The platform was upgraded in February 2011 and the test now looks at around 710,000 autosomal DNA SNPs. The test does not include any mtDNA or Y-DNA SNPs. FTDNA instead offers spe-cialised Y-DNA and mtDNA tests, which can be purchased separately.

When you receive your Family Finder results you will be given a list of your potential genetic cousins. The names of your matches are provided along with a con-tact email address, the suggested and predicted relationships, the length of the longest block of matching DNA and the number of shared centiMorgans (a measurement of

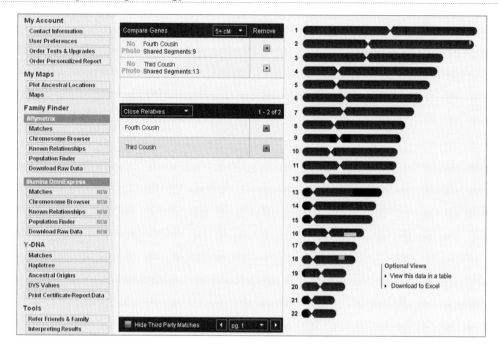

Figure 19   The Family Tree DNA 'Family Finder' chromosome browser showing matches with a predicted third and fourth cousin, with names obscured for privacy. The third cousin has one sizeable shared segment of DNA on chromosome 16. The fourth cousin has a smaller shared segment on chromosome 18 and a small fragment on chromosome 2.

matching DNA segments). FTDNA customers can fill in a list of their ancestral surnames and upload a basic GEDCOM file with details of the people in their ancestral lines. If a GEDCOM file has been provided by your matches you will be able to view diagrams of their family trees, though only around 10 per cent of FTDNA customers currently upload a GEDCOM file. If your match has filled in his or her ancestral surnames then these names will also be shown in the list and details of their location will often be included too. Surprisingly, only around half of FTDNA customers choose to fill in their ancestral surnames. If the surnames have been provided, any surnames that you have in common are highlighted in a bold typeface. A chromosome browser is also provided so that you can see the location of the segments you share with your matches. You can also compare the genomes of up to three of your matches at a time.

Both my mother and father have taken the Family Finder test. As of the end of 2010 my mum had forty-nine matches, all of which were at the fifth to distant cousin level, which FTDNA classifies as 'speculative' matches. Unless both matches have detailed genealogies, it is unlikely that a connection will be found with a speculative match. My dad had thirty-four matches, including one predicted third cousin and one predicted fourth cousin. These were, however, both in America and we were unable to find the connection. The remainder of his matches were all in the speculative range. Although the country of residence is not currently given it is clear from the names and locations provided in the list of ancestral surnames that the majority of my parents' matches are in the US. FTDNA does have a much more geographically diverse database than 23andMe because of their association with the Genographic Project (see Appendix B) and also because of the huge range of surname and geographical projects they host from around the world. As the company specialises in genetic genealogy tests their customers are also more likely to be genealogists, who will be interested in corresponding and sharing details of their family history in order to find the connection in the paper trail. If you are interested in taking an autosomal DNA test for family history purposes then the Family Finder test will for most people be the best option in the long run, but it will take time for the database to grow in size.

The Family Finder test also includes an admixture component known as Population Finder. This feature, which is currently still in beta-testing, compares your DNA with selected reference populations from around the world. For most British people the results are not as yet very meaningful, as the only British reference population is from the Orkney Islands. However, if you suspect that you have some non-European ancestry, then the results could potentially be more revealing. The reference populations used to make the predictions are taken from published sources. As more research is published further reference populations will be added and more refined admixture predictions should then be possible.

The Family Finder test does not yet report results for the X-chromosome, but FTDNA is looking into the possibility of developing a dedicated X-chromosome browser. A platform is also being developed to allow for the upload of 23andMe results.

DIY projects

A number of enterprising genetic genealogists have established projects to explore various aspects of autosomal DNA testing. Some projects will collect autosomal DNA results from all the descendants of a specific ancestor, or ancestral couple, to verify existing lines and provide clues for undocumented links. Larry Vick, for example, has established a large project to explore the genetic heritage of the descendants of his immigrant ancestor Joseph Vick who settled in Virginia, US, in 1670. Other projects are collecting autosomal DNA results from people with ancestry from a particular country or region such as the Bahamas, Portugal or Newfoundland. These projects are all still in their infancy but could potentially yield some very interesting results. There are also a number of more technical projects that require you to submit your raw data for analysis. Some of these projects will provide you with an alternative admixture interpretation. Adriano Squecco's Y-Chromosome Genome Comparison Project is collecting the raw Y-chromosome data from men who have taken the 23andMe test. The results are compared in a spreadsheet to see if any new Y-SNPs can be identified. This project has led to the discovery of a number of new subclade-defining SNPs, which are now available commercially through Ethnoancestry and Family Tree DNA. Up-to-date lists of all the various autosomal DNA projects can be found on the following pages in the ISOGG Wiki:

www.isogg.org/wiki/23andMe_project
www.isogg.org/wiki/Family_Finder_project
www.isogg.org/wiki/Admixture_tests

More advanced users can also experiment by using third-party programs to manipulate and analyse their raw data. A free program called Promethease can, for example, be used to create a report with additional health and trait information. David Pike, a pioneering genetic genealogist in Canada, has developed a utility which analyses a raw data file and looks for runs of homozygous segments, which would indicate the presence of cousin marriages in your ancestry. Homozygous SNPs are base pairs which have two identical letters in the DNA code, such as TT or CC. An up-to-date list of autosomal DNA tools can be found in the ISOGG Wiki at **www.isogg.org/ wiki/Autosomal_DNA_tools**.

The future

As the autosomal DNA tests are still in the early stages of development we can expect to see further refinements in due course. As the cost of sequencing comes down more SNPs will be added providing higher resolution matches. Your list of matches will, therefore, be revised from time to time and new features will occasionally be added to the tests. The admixture analyses are still very basic because autosomal DNA has only been examined in a small number of reference populations. As more studies are published we can expect to get better geographical resolution from the test results. In the meantime, genetic genealogists are still exploring the tests and finding out how to use them to their best advantage. More experienced users who have tested a large number of people within a family have already discovered that it is possible to 'phase' the results, in order to establish whether particular DNA segments have been inherited from the father or the mother. David Pike has embarked on an ambitious project to reconstruct the autosomal DNA of his paternal grandparents by testing their seven surviving children. Larger databases with accompanying detailed genealogies will eventually give us a better understanding of the inheritance patterns of autosomal DNA and the effect of close-cousin marriages on relationship predictions. The full possibilities of the X-chromosome have not yet been explored. With so many new discoveries still to be made, the next decade is likely to be very exciting indeed!

6

Setting up and running a DNA project

In the previous chapters we have looked at the three different DNA tests which are used as an aid to genealogical research, together with the range of surname, geographical and haplogroup projects which are actively collecting and interpreting DNA results. In the early days most people who were interested in investigating their surname through DNA testing had no choice but to set up their own DNA project. A decade later we have reached the stage where most people who are considering taking a Y-chromosome DNA test will probably find that their surname, or a closely related variant spelling, is already included in a surname project. By the end of 2010 Family Tree DNA, the company that hosts the majority of projects, had more than 6,200 different DNA projects. A surname project will typically focus not just on one surname, but also on all the associated spellings. There is no limit to the number of variant spellings that can be included in a DNA project and the choice is at the discretion of the project administrator. Some projects will only include a handful of surnames in their studies whereas others will incorporate a long list of fifty or more related spellings. If your surname is somewhat more unusual then it is possible that a project will not yet have been established, though the name could still be included in one of the many geographical projects. A geographical project can provide a good entrée to the world of DNA testing, and if you are only interested in testing a few people to prove or disprove a particular hypothesis it will not be necessary to set up a separate surname project.

Many people do, however, become particularly interested in a particular surname and will want to explore the surname in depth through their own DNA project. There are already pre-existing projects for nearly all the high-frequency surnames. Consequently, anyone setting up a new project is likely to be focusing on a less common surname and the work will probably not be too onerous. A certain amount of commitment is required as you will need to communicate with your project members on a regular basis and respond to email enquiries from potential participants. A project can be run passively simply by registering a surname and waiting for people

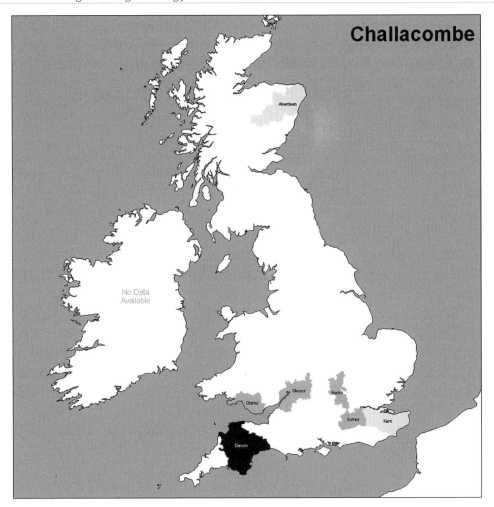

Figure 20   Before setting up a surname project it is a useful exercise to map the distribution of the surname to get an idea of the size of the task in hand. This map of the rare surname Challacombe, based on data from the 1881 censuses for England, Wales and Scotland, shows a distinct clustering effect. The presence of the surname in the south-east of England, Wales, Gloucestershire and Aberdeen is probably accounted for by recent migrations in the search for work. The map was generated using the Surname Atlas CD-Rom from Archer Software.

to join the project, but if you wish to see the project grow more quickly you will need to take a more pro-active approach to recruitment. Another way to get involved in project management is to serve as a co-administrator on an existing project. This will give you an insight into the running of a project and will in time give you the confidence to take on the challenge of your own project. Projects for high-frequency surnames usually have several administrators who each take on a different role within the project.

Before setting up a DNA project it is worth spending some time considering what you are hoping to achieve, what the scope of your project will be and which variant spellings you would like to include. Project administrators sometimes find that they have to adapt as the project progresses and their project members get matches with other variant spellings that they had not anticipated. It is often the case that a seemingly rare surname is a late-forming variant of a more common surname. For low-frequency surnames it is usually best to adopt a global approach and accept everyone with the surname, regardless of origin, from the outset. If the surname is very common, the project will be more manageable if it is restricted to a particular country or county, unless you can collaborate with a team of researchers in different countries. It is a useful exercise to search the census indexes on one of the commercial websites, such as Ancestry.com or Findmypast, to get a feel for the size and distribution of your surname. If you find, for example, that there are thousands of people with your surname in the American

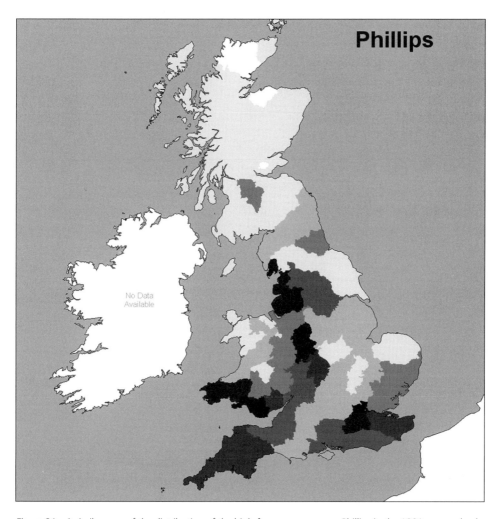

Figure 21   A similar map of the distribution of the high-frequency surname Phillips in the 1881 census clearly shows that the surname has multiple origins but has hot spots in South Wales, Lancashire, Staffordshire and London. The map was generated using the Surname Atlas CD-Rom from Archer Software.

censuses then it will be more sensible to restrict the project to the UK, and perhaps only accept people from the US in your project who have lines with proven connections to the UK. There are a number of surname mapping websites, which are listed in Appendix D, and these will also help you to gauge the distribution of the surname. Some surnames will be found to cluster in one specific region and will clearly have a single origin (see Figure 20). More common surnames will tend to be spread out throughout the country, with many different clusters indicating a multiple origin (see Figure 21). A multiple-origin surname will produce many more genetic families than a surname of single origin. People often intuitively expect all the DNA results for a rare surname to match, but even the rarest surnames will inevitably produce a few distinct genetic clusters and I am not aware of any surname project with a complete set of matching DNA results.

Another question to consider is how much family history research you are prepared to take on. As we have already seen, DNA testing works best when it is used in conjunction with traditional documentary research. Therefore in order to be able to interpret the results correctly some knowledge of the trees is required. If a rare surname is being studied it will often be possible for the project administrator to reconstruct all the trees for the surname to establish how many different lines there are and to identify potential candidates for testing. Such an approach is, however, not a practical proposition for more common surnames, but you will probably still want to encourage your project members to submit pedigrees. At the very least you should encourage them to supply outline details of their direct paternal line, which you can publish on your project website if space is provided. Pedigree information is best obtained before people join the project or immediately after they have joined. For extra-large projects the project administrator might not have the time to collect pedigree information and will merely be responsible for collating results into genetic clusters of matching DNA results. The project members will then be left to communicate with each other and make their own connections. The project administrator should still encourage participants to supply information about the name, date and location of their most distant known ancestor.

Choosing a testing company

A list of the main DNA testing companies is provided in Appendix B. Only two of these companies, Family Tree DNA and Ancestry.com, currently provide project management tools and an easy-to-use facility to create your own DNA project website. The websites do not require any specialist expertise and can easily be compiled and updated by anyone who has basic word-processing skills. If you are prepared to set up your own DNA project website then in theory any company can be used, but this will require a lot more effort and technical knowledge. In some cases the choice of company will be dictated by the surnames that are already represented in the company's database. It is thus a good idea, as a first step, to check the two company databases to see if anyone else with your surname has already been tested. Even if there is no project for the surname people might have tested instead with a geographical project or simply ordered a test out of curiosity. The company will usually happily contact the testers on your behalf and encourage them to join your project. Alternatively, you might find that the results have been uploaded into one of the public Y-DNA databases and you will be able to contact the candidates yourself. Note that the public listings in the Family Tree DNA database will only give an indication of the number of people with the surname in the database. Some of these testers could be females who have taken an mtDNA test or an autosomal DNA test.

There are a number of factors to consider when choosing a company to host a surname project. A few of the more important points to bear in mind are provided below:

Cost Are discounts offered for tests ordered through projects? Is a refund available if a kit is ordered but not used? Can payments be accepted by credit card and PayPal? Is there a facility to collect donations from sponsors to pay for tests for key participants? Remember that the cost is just one factor to consider. Prices can go up or down and the company that offers the cheapest tests at any given time is not necessarily the best option in the long term.

Range of tests How many Y-STR markers are tested? Is it possible to upgrade at a later date to order extra markers? Does the company provide SNP tests to confirm haplogroup assignments? How many different SNPs are tested? Is the company actively involved in the SNP discovery process? Can new SNPs be ordered as and when they are discovered? Does the company offer mitochondrial DNA tests and autosomal DNA tests? Are SNP tests provided free of charge for accurate mtDNA haplogroup assignments? Is it possible to upgrade to a full sequence mtDNA test?

Project management tools What tools does the company provide to help you manage your project? Is there a courtesy website? How are the results displayed? Are there any proprietary tools to help you to compare results and sort project members into subgroups? Is there a facility to download project results in a spreadsheet for further analysis? Does the company have a bulk email system? Can the administrator keep track of the tests online?

Participant tools What facilities are provided for the participants to help them to understand their results? Do they receive email notifications of matches? Can a GEDCOM file or family tree be added to the member's profile? Do they receive certificates?

Projects Can project members join other surname projects? Does the company offer geographical and/or haplogroup projects?

Size of the database How large is the company's database and how fast is it growing? A large database is particularly important when searching for matches with different surnames in cases of illegitimacy or adoption.

Sample storage Does the company provide a facility to store DNA samples so that upgrades can be ordered when new tests become available?

Customer service Do staff respond in a timely fashion to email enquiries? Does the company have specialist staff who can provide advice in the event of an unusual or unexpected result? Is the company responsive to the suggestions of its customers and project administrators?

Scientific research Is the company involved in the scientific research process? Do they have any scientific advisers or a scientific advisory board? Is the testing done in-house or does the company resell kits from another laboratory?

The International Society of Genetic Genealogy provides a number of charts on its website which will enable you to compare the tests and project-management facilities provided by the main testing companies. It is worth reviewing the companies' websites and looking at a few sample surname projects of different sizes to see which features you like and will find the most useful. The best people to ask are your fellow surname project administrators, and you can solicit their views on the various mailing lists and forums, which are listed in Appendix A.

Marketing your project

After deciding on a testing company the next stage is to register your surname and the associated variants with your company of choice. There is no charge to set up a DNA project and a project can be established with zero participants until such time as you are ready to start recruiting. It is worth investing some time at the outset to produce an appealing website for your project with some information about the surname and the objectives of the project. Do not be put off if you have never created a website before. The facilities provided are very easy to use and a website can be created with just a few clicks of the mouse. It can help to look at other project websites to get ideas on presentation and content. Once the project website has been up and running for a few weeks it will start to appear in search engine results. To increase the chances of your site being found you should also try and advertise the project as widely as possible. To this end many of the resources discussed in Part II of this book can be used, such as mailing lists, message boards and social networking websites. Search engine rankings are based partly on the number of incoming links, so the more places you can publish the URL of your website the higher up the rankings your website will appear.

Many people with your surname will probably not have considered taking a DNA test. For these people to find you it will be necessary to create an online presence on as many genealogical websites as possible, again using the resources in the second part of this book. A blog can be an especially effective way of publicising your surname research and is very easy to set up (see Chapter 10). I have found that most of the people who have tested in my surname project contacted me first to enquire about their family history research, and I was then able to persuade them to participate in the project. Once you have the first couple of people in the project the recruit-ment process also becomes much easier as there is much more incentive for people to test once you have begun to build up a body of results for comparison purposes. If you have already been researching your family history for some time you might well already have identified a number of potential candidates from your pre-existing contacts. The best prospects are likely to be other genealogists who will already have an interest in the surname, and will, therefore, be more amenable to the idea of taking a DNA test as they will understand the benefits. Do not overlook the role of female researchers. Often it is the female in the family who is the most active genealogist. Even if she is not able to take a test herself she will probably be able to persuade her husband, father or brother to participate in your project. The resources in Part II can be trawled in an attempt to find further likely prospects, supplemented with searches in the online telephone directories. Other contacts will be found by searching the electoral register on one of the commercial websites such as **www.192.com**.

Managing a project

The amount of work involved in running a project will depend very much on the frequency of the surname. The main tasks will be dealing with enquiries, interpret-ing the results when they come in and grouping the participants in their respective genetic clusters or families. As the project grows in size you will want to keep your project members up to date with the latest news by sending out occasional emails or perhaps even a more detailed report on the findings of the project. The companies generally provide a lot of useful information on their websites and in some cases provide specialist tools to help with the interpretation process. The more respon-sive companies will be happy to answer questions by email, and will refer technical questions to a specialist. Your fellow project administrators will, however, probably be your best resource. Some administrators are now able to draw upon a decade of

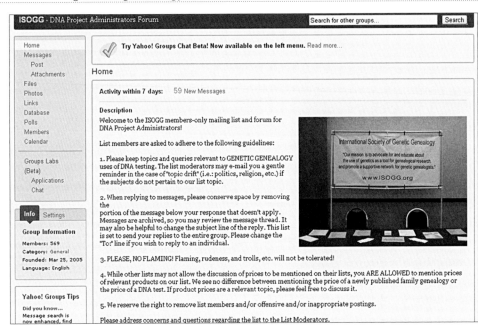

Figure 22   The International Society of Genetic Genealogy (ISOGG) is a volunteer-run organisation which provides a number of useful resources for project administrators including a dedicated mailing list. Membership of ISOGG is free of charge.

experience across a broad range of projects and however obscure your question there will usually be someone who knows the answer. There are a number of DNA mailing lists and forums listed in Appendix A. The list that I have found most beneficial is the ISOGG project administrators' mailing list on Yahoo.

Geographical and haplogroup projects

I have focused primarily in this chapter on surname projects as, for most people, this will be their first exposure to project administration. Many project administrators find that they become hooked on DNA testing and often become involved in the management of other projects too. The haplogroup projects are now in many cases very large and usually have several project administrators. If you become interested in deep ancestry or a specific haplogroup you might consider helping to run a haplogroup project as a co-administrator. Geographical projects can be a natural extension of a surname project, especially if you have a single-origin surname that clusters in a specific geographical area. There are already a number of projects for English counties and regions, including my own project for Devon, but there is still scope for further regional projects for other counties or for specific towns or villages, perhaps as an accompaniment to a one-place study.

The long term

In the first part of this book we have looked in detail at the DNA testing process and the different types of tests on the market. We have also reviewed the various types of DNA projects being run by genetic genealogists and discussed the process of setting up and managing a project of your own. A DNA test is effectively a long-term investment which becomes more meaningful over time as the databases grow in size, giving you more people to compare your results with and hopefully more matches. A DNA test will never provide all the answers to our genealogical questions and will always work best when used in conjunction with traditional documentary research, but it can often be a very powerful tool which can sometimes provide vital breakthroughs and reveal connections that cannot be found in the paper records alone. I hope that after reading this section you will be sufficiently inspired to get tested yourself, if you have not already done so. The process becomes much more interesting when it is your own DNA that is being analysed and the results can be placed in the context of your own family history research. Once you have discovered for yourself the value of DNA testing you will want to get in touch with other people researching your surname and encourage them to test as well. You might have a particular genealogical mystery that can be solved through mitochondrial DNA testing or autosomal testing, and the hunt will be on to find the appropriate candidate to take the test. The second part of this book explains how you can use both traditional and new networking techniques to make those all-important connections.

II

THE SOCIAL NETWORKING REVOLUTION

Introduction

Social networking is one of the buzz terms of the last decade which is more often associated with teenagers interacting on Facebook and MySpace than with family history research, but whether we use the phrase or not, social networking is something that every genealogist does quite naturally. The *Oxford English Dictionary* describes social networking as 'the use or establishment of social networks or connections' or 'the use of websites which enable users to interact with one another, find and contact people with common interests'. Finding and connecting with people with common surname interests is a key component of family history research, and the family history websites that enable us to make those connections are our social networks. This section of the book looks at the many different ways to make contact with other researchers and to track down your distant cousins. The techniques used will apply both for family history research and for tracing potential candidates for DNA testing to participate in a DNA project. We will look at traditional networking methods using conventional genealogical resources as well as the mainstream social networking websites such as Facebook and Twitter, which are becoming increasingly useful for the family historian. We will discuss new social media resources such as blogs, wikis and photo-sharing websites which can be used to share your research online, and the collaborative tools that are beginning to transform the research process.

It is ironic that although the internet has made some aspects of research much easier, it has also had the knock-on effect of making traditional resources less useful, as people become more concerned with privacy issues. Telephone directories are freely available online but many people now choose to remain ex-directory, while some do without a landline altogether and rely solely on a mobile phone. The UK electoral register can be searched online for a fee, but since the facility to opt-out from the published version was introduced in 2002 an increasing number of people have chosen to do so. However, many of those who have decided to make their telephone number ex-directory and who have opted out of the electoral register will still have a presence online on one of the many social networking websites.

I will discuss the various types of social media that can be used by the genealogist in detail in the following chapters, but there are a few general points to consider, which apply equally to all these resources. Social networking websites provide an exciting new way to communicate instantly with friends and family all over the world, but the platforms that host these communications are still very much in their infancy. Many of the sites that we now take for granted did not even exist ten years ago, and some of the most popular sites have only been established in the last five years. The design of social media websites is constantly evolving with new features added and settings readjusted, though not always necessarily in the best interests of the user. If a website provides services free of charge the cost of providing that service has to be funded by advertising. In order to target advertising efficiently it is, therefore, in the companies' interests to gather as much data as possible about their users. Many of the sites are hosted in America where data protection laws are less strict than in Europe. The US government has announced that it intends to take a more proactive role in monitoring online privacy and has set up a new taskforce to help turn recommendations into policy, but it will take time for these actions to bear fruit. With any website or computer database there is always a risk that mistakes will be made and user data will be unwittingly made available, and there have been a number of well-publicised privacy breaches in recent years.

The problem is not confined to social media websites. Commercial organisations such as Google have been affected, as have government organisations and high street banks. In my view the benefits of using social media websites far outweigh the disadvantages, but these services need to be used responsibly as anything that is published online could potentially come back to haunt you. The amount of personal information that is published online is very much an individual choice. Some people are happy to publish their email address, postal address and telephone number so that anyone can contact them by whatever means they prefer. At the other extreme, there are genealogists who will sign up to a mailing list but never contribute because they do not even wish to have their email address in the public domain. Most people will probably fall somewhere between the two extremes. Whatever your views, it is advisable to think carefully before publishing any personal details online, whether on a public website, on a members' only website or to a limited circle of friends on a social networking website. When signing up for a new service you do not need to answer every single question and there is no compulsion to provide the correct information for your date of birth, if asked, or your residence. Social networking websites have varying levels of privacy controls. Sometimes the default settings are designed to encourage you to reveal more information than is necessarily wise. Make sure you check all the available settings to ensure that you are comfortable with the information revealed in your public profile. The settings should be reviewed on a regular basis and especially when a site has undergone a major redesign.

Preserving our digital inheritance

The availability of the internet and the popularity of the new social media have revolutionised our methods of communication. Letters and diaries have been replaced by blogs and emails, with mundane details of everyday life published in status updates on social networking websites. The preservation of this information consequently presents a new challenge. If you have been researching your family history online for any length of time you will rapidly acquire a large number of accounts with a variety of different passwords. You will inevitably subscribe to a few genealogy websites, join a couple of mailing lists, set up accounts with some of the free social networking services and perhaps upload a family tree and photos to one or more websites. You will probably have had your DNA tested and will belong to a number of different DNA projects. All these accounts are easily manageable by one person, but can become a big problem after someone's death. No protocols have yet been established for the management of social networking profiles and DNA accounts after a person's demise. The next of kin can usually be given access to an account if they can provide documentary proof of their relationship but to do so they will need to know of the account's existence in the first place. To avoid these problems, it is preferable to make plans in advance for the preservation or otherwise of your online presence. Whatever you decide, the simplest solution is to leave written instructions in your will and to leave the details with your close relatives so that they know how to access your various accounts. Inevitably a number of enterprising websites have been set up, with apt names such as Deathswitch, Legacy Locker, My Webwill, iDeparted and the GreatGoodbye, which promise to deal with your digital assets after your death. Some will even send out posthumous emails and videos! The risk of using such services, however, is that there is no guarantee that any of the companies will still be around at the time of your demise.

The importance of preserving our internet heritage is increasingly being recognised by public bodies and charitable organisations and there is a good chance that much of what is published on the internet will be preserved, at least in part. The British Library is now archiving a growing selection of UK websites and blogs in its web archive, including my own blog. The Internet Archive, a non-profit making organisation in San Francisco, began archiving websites back in 1996 and the collection became public in 2001 with the development of its Wayback Machine. The US Library of Congress has been archiving all tweets on Twitter from March 2006 onwards, though no search facility is yet available.

The focus of the second part of this book is on online resources, and I have assumed that anyone who is motivated to read the book will have internet access. It is worth remembering that not everyone is online and that the internet will not always be able to provide all the answers. The Office for National Statistics issued a report on internet usage in the UK in August 2010. It was revealed that over 10 million adults in the UK (21 per cent of the adult population) had never been online. The majority (60 per cent) of those, aged 65 and over, had never used the internet. There were also marked regional variations with 87 per cent of adults in London using the internet but only 71 per cent in the North East. The websites discussed here will have a valuable role to play in putting you in contact with other researchers and providing the means to collaborate on your research, but there will still be occasions when it is necessary to turn to pen and paper.

Links

www.thedigitalbeyond.com A blog about your digital existence and what happens to it after your death

http://mashable.com/2010/10/11/social-media-after-death Social media after death

www.webarchive.org.uk The British Library's UK web archive

www.archive.org The WayBack Machine Internet Archive

www.loc.gov/today/pr/2010/10-081.html Twitter donates tweet archive to US Library of Congress

7

Traditional genealogical networking methods

Family history societies

Family history societies have traditionally played a vital role in providing a plat-form for genealogists to connect with other interested researchers. The Society of Genealogists, founded in 1911, was the first genealogical society in the UK. Family history societies for various counties started to become established in the 1970s. In 1974 family history societies were linked together through the Federation of Family History Societies, an umbrella organisation which now acts as a representative for over 160 societies from around the world. In the internet era, family history societies continue to have an important role to play and are a good way of making contact with other researchers who share similar interests. Each society publishes its own journal, which is usually sent out to members on a quarterly basis. More impor-tantly, the societies maintain lists of members' surname interests. These are usually published in the society's journal or in a supplement. Increasingly, family history societies are making members' interests available online on their websites. In some cases the website lists are a replacement for the written listings. Society membership fees are usually very modest and it is, therefore, worth joining all the family history societies for your areas of interest. Once you have joined a society you will then be able to submit your members' interests for publication. Some societies encourage members to submit lengthier queries or to write letters asking for help with their research. I have found that some of my most valuable contacts have come from enquiries or articles published in family history society journals, and many of these have come from experienced researchers with a wealth of knowledge who are not on the internet. It is also worth checking the online register of the Guild of One-Name Studies to see if any of your surnames of interest have been registered. Guild members will have often built up a network of contacts for their particular surname of interest over the years.

Figure 23   By joining your local family history society you will have the chance to connect with other researchers with interests in the same region. The Federation of Family History Societies maintains a listing of all member societies in the UK and around the world.

Links

www.ffhs.org.uk Federation of Family History Societies

www.one-name.org Guild of One-Name Studies

www.sog.org.uk Society of Genealogists

www.cyndislist.com/societies Cyndi's List societies page

www.fgs.org/societyhall Federation of Genealogical Societies Society Hall (USA)

http://genuki.org.uk/big/Societies.html Genuki societies page

Surname listings

The first comprehensive worldwide surname listing was a booklet known as the *Genealogical Research Directory* (GRD). This was first published in 1981 and was published annually for twenty-seven years until 2007. In later years it was also available on CD. At its peak the GRD featured over 70,000 research queries. In the pre-internet era the arrival of the latest edition of the GRD was the highlight of the genealogical calendar. With the increasing prevalence of free online surname listings the venture was no longer commercially viable. Back issues can still be found in local studies libraries or family history society libraries. There is no single online replacement for the GRD. There is instead a proliferation of surname listing websites, some of which are more useful than others. The dedicated researcher will spend time listing his or her surnames on all the available sites.

RootsWeb surname list, **http://rsl.rootsweb.ancestry.com**.
The RootsWeb Surname List (RSL) is probably the largest online register of sur-name interests. It is a free service provided by the RootsWeb community. It is claimed that names are added at the rate of 700 a day. In order to list your surnames you will need to create an account with a username (known as a 'name tag') and a password. It is also possible to include in your entry your website(s). There are over a million names listed in the directory but no check is kept on the validity of email addresses and it can sometimes be frustrating contacting people on this list as many of the emails will bounce.

Graham Jaunay's online name listings, **www.onlinenames.net.au**
Graham Jaunay's website of online surname listings was set up in 1997 and provides a free central location to register your surname interests. The site was upgraded in June 2011 and now offers a number of new features. The database was previously organised on a country-by-country basis, and it was necessary to renew your surname interests every year or every two years to avoid the problem of email addresses becoming out of date. The separate country databases have now all been merged into one large database. Users are able to update their own details on a regular basis by logging in with their email address and password.

UK genealogy interests directory, **www.ukgid.com**
Free registration is required to list your surnames but the surnames already submit-ted can be browsed without registering. No statistics are provided on the number of surnames and contributors.

UK surnames, **www.uk-surnames.com**
This site has around 60,000 surnames submitted by over 8,000 contributors. Free registration is required to list your surnames, to access more detailed searches and to contact other researchers. The surnames can be browsed alphabetically by county without registration. Entries submitted from bouncing email addresses are periodi-cally removed.

Surname site, **http://surnamesite.com/surnames.htm**
This site is easy to use and search. There is no need to register to perform searches or to add surnames. As the surnames listed are mostly in America, the site will be of more use to researchers wishing to trace relatives in the US.

SCGS surname wall, **www.scgsgenealogy.com/SurnameWall.htm**
The Southern California Genealogical Society maintains a virtual surname wall.
Listings are encouraged not just from California and the US but from other countries too. The names of the submitters are not shown and all contacts have to go
through the SCGS.

Message boards and forums

Message boards and forums provide a simple and effective way of posting genealogical interests. All the boards and forums operate in a similar way. A public website is
provided where interested researchers can post messages, which can be viewed by
anyone visiting the site. Most boards will require you to set up an account in order to
post a message or reply to a previous posting. Message boards can be somewhat cumbersome to monitor, and it can be difficult to check for replies to your postings on
multiple boards. Some boards will notify you by email when you receive a reply or
when a message is posted in response to a particular topic or 'thread'. In some cases
you can subscribe to a board's RSS feed (online news reader) so that you can monitor
threads of interest in your RSS reader (see Chapter 10). Family history societies, local
history groups, genealogy software programs and commercial organisations often
provide forums on their websites. Before posting a message on a board or a forum it
is a good idea, first of all, to familiarise yourself with the site, get a feel for the content of the postings and read the appropriate community guidelines or forum FAQs
(frequently asked questions). Message boards are best suited to short communications
and are not a suitable vehicle for lengthy discussions. Keep your messages short and
to the point, and include appropriate keywords so that your messages can easily be
found in the archives. The boards will have an international readership so make sure
you provide full location details to avoid confusion. Once you have made contact
with a fellow researcher you will probably want to exchange information off-board
by email. The main genealogy forums are discussed below. This is not intended to
be a comprehensive listing but focuses instead on the boards that are of most value,
organised in descending order of usefulness.

Ancestry.com/RootsWeb boards, **http://boards.ancestry.co.uk; http://
boards.rootsweb.com**
The Ancestry.com and RootsWeb message boards are the most visited and most
extensive genealogical message system on the internet, with over 161,000 boards
by the end of 2010. The Ancestry.com and RootsWeb boards are mirror sites but
with slight differences in functionality. You can find specific boards by searching by
keyword or by scrolling through the alphabetical lists of surnames and the categories.
The messages are publicly viewable and searchable but you will need to set up a free

account with either Ancestry.com or RootsWeb to reply to a posting. With both Ancestry.com and RootsWeb you are encouraged to set up a profile page where you can provide a list of your research interests and links to your websites. If you change your email address make sure you update your profile. One of the best features about these boards is that the messages are permanently archived. Sometimes you will get a response to an enquiry several years after you posted the original message. With both boards you can compile a list of favourite boards, categories, authors and threads. If you access the boards via the home page URLs shown opposite, your favourites will all be listed at the top of the page. When you subscribe to a board you can opt to receive an email alert every time a new message is posted to the board. Alternatively if you do not want to subscribe to the whole board you can opt to receive an email notification when someone replies to a 'thread' (a topic) to which you have contributed. With both boards it is possible to include an attachment with your reply. You can contact other users either through the Ancestry.com or RootsWeb messaging system. Registration was not required prior to December 2006 and if the person has not taken out a RootsWeb or Ancestry.com account you will be given a link to an encrypted image of their email address. The older the message the more likely it is that any reply you send will bounce.

If you visit the boards on Ancestry.com you can opt to subscribe to the RSS feed to monitor updates in your RSS reader. Favourite message boards can also be added to Ancestry.com profile pages for easy access.

Rootschat, **www.rootschat.com**

Rootschat was set up in December 2003 and has developed into a very lively and friendly community with a constant stream of postings throughout the day on a variety of topics. Rootschat describes itself as an 'easy to use messaging forum for everyone researching their family history roots or local history'. The focus is on the British Isles, but there are boards for many other countries such as South Africa, Australia and New Zealand. Registration is required to make postings and to take advantage of the advanced search facility. Members benefit from a free profile and can also add their interests to the surname interests table. If you contribute to a discussion you can opt to follow the thread and receive an email notification whenever someone replies. Private messages can also be sent to other users via the Rootschat messaging system.

Curious Fox, **www.curiousfox.com**

Curious Fox is a forum based on localities in the UK and Ireland. There is a two-tier system: a free registration is required to use the site but a small fee is payable to benefit from the full features. With a free account you can only send messages to those people with paid accounts, whereas subscribers can send messages to all registered users. Posts by non-subscribers must not include email addresses, links or any other

Board name	Topics	Posts	Last post
Beginners			
Beginners Everyone has to start somewhere, so why not start here. Post your genealogy questions on how to search your family history and post your local history questions here! Also, if you can think of things to help a budding local history or family history beginner, then please post your tips here! See also **Help Pages: Guidelines to Posting**	8755	71690	**Today** at 13:01:32 in Re: Monetary values in d... by JenB
How to Use RootsChat If you have questions on how to use RootsChat, look in the ⚲Help Pages For instance: **FAQs, Tips an Hints** or in the **Index to Help-Pages** If you can't find the answers in the Help-Pages, then try here ...	980	8473	**Wednesday 30 March 11 07:18 BST (UK)** in Re: Where's my PM outbox... by majm
▼ **Old Photographs, Recognition, Handwriting Deciphering**			
Photograph Restoration & Dating. Would you like a treasured photograph restored or dated ? *Moderator: PrueM* *Child Boards: Resources, Tips, Tutorials*	20230	224646	**Today** at 12:56:36 in Re: Restoration and dati... by SUSANHORTON
Deciphering & Recognition Help Need help deciphering old handwriting on wills, certificates and other FH documents ? Want to know where a place is on your old photos ?? Post your queries here ..	3112	29786	**Today** at 12:57:40 in Re: 1601 Will – Silver w... by bristolloggerheads
▼ **General**			
The Common Room Join in and discuss more general genealogy and local history things here. If you can't think of what category, country or county your message should come under, then perhaps you could put your message here! *Child Boards: The Lighter Side, Totally Off Topic Bit*	16550	191122	**Today** at 12:59:56 in Re: Medical advice, hear... by LizzieW
Technical Help Need some technical help with using your computer, or using the internet? *Child Boards: FH Programs, Organisation, Presentation, Surname Interest Table, Webspace*	4903	44505	**Today** at 12:37:08 in Re: It's driving me mad ... by LizzieW
Useful Links Links to other local history or genealogy websites of interest	518	1126	**Wednesday 30 March 11 13:30 BST (UK)** in Burns Monument Centre, K... by gibbied

Figure 24   Rootschat is a popular free messaging forum with a variety of boards covering family history topics with a specific focus on the British Isles.

information that circumvents the Curious Fox messaging system, though subscribers are allowed to include URLs in their posts.

British Genealogy Forums, **www.british-genealogy.com/forums**
These forums were originally set up by Rod Neep, the founder of Archive CD Books, but they have now been taken over by a commercial genealogy organisation. There are boards for the various counties in England, Scotland, Wales and Ireland, as well as a variety of boards devoted to different occupations and a wide range of history topics. The site is marred by a strict links policy which prohibits links to personal websites, family history society websites and commercial genealogy websites, thus providing little incentive to use the boards and making it very difficult to provide any useful advice. The archives are publicly searchable, but registration is required to make postings and to use the search facility. The interface is also somewhat difficult to navigate, though an RSS feed is provided to monitor threads of interest.

Family history journal forums
Most of the mainstream UK family history journals have forums on their websites, some of which are more active than others. You can discuss features in the magazine or post more general genealogical enquiries:
Family Tree Magazine forum, **www.familyhistoryforum.co.uk**

Who Do You Think You Are? magazine, **www.bbcwhodoyouthinkyouaremagazine. com/forum**
Your Family History forum, **www.your-familyhistory.com/forum**
Your Family Tree forum, **www.yourfamilytreemag.co.uk/yft-forum**

Genforum, **http://genforum.genealogy.com**
Genforum is the message board service provided by the American genealogy company Genealogy.com. It has boards for localities and surnames, but understandably has a particular focus on the US. The boards have basic functionality and you can opt to receive an email notification if someone replies to your posting. Genealogy.com merged with Ancestry.com in 2009. The boards have not been developed since then and do not appear to be very well used, but might be worth a visit if you are trying to make contact with researchers in America.

Mailing lists

Mailing lists are one of the most effective ways of contacting other family historians, for discussing topics of interest with like-minded researchers and for keeping up with all the latest developments in the world of genealogy. A mailing list is a group email system hosted on an external computer. To join a mailing list you must first of all 'subscribe' to the list. Once your subscription is accepted you are added to the group list and you will receive all emails which are sent to the group email address. As the messages are delivered to your inbox, mailing lists are a much more convenient method of following discussions and keeping in touch than the old-style message boards, where conversations can be very disjointed with replies received months, or even years, after an initial posting. Some lists are very small with just a couple of hundred subscribers, and you will sometimes only receive emails on a very infrequent basis. The more popular lists can have over a thousand subscribers, and you might on some days receive twenty or more emails in a day. Most mailing lists provide the option to receive list mails either as individual emails or as a daily digest, whereby all the messages sent in one day are sent out in a single email. If you subscribe to a busy list a daily digest can be less distracting than a constant stream of emails throughout the day, but the digests can be difficult to skim through easily. Old list messages are usually stored in an online archive, which can in itself be a valuable resource.

Finding a list
The first ever genealogy mailing list, Roots-L, was established back in 1987. With increasing use of the internet, the number of lists has grown exponentially and there are now literally thousands and thousands of genealogy mailing lists devoted to every conceivable topic. There are lists for surnames, geographical locations, family history

software, occupations, obituaries and a variety of military subjects. If you are looking for help with any specific subject, such as research in Sweden or Switzerland,
or resources for mariners or miners, there will invariably be a list devoted to the
topic. There are hundreds of lists for the British Isles alone, divided into counties and
sometimes with lists for individual parishes. Most family history societies will also
have their own mailing list, which will usually be restricted to members, though the
archives might well be publicly searchable. RootsWeb is the largest list host with over
30,000 genealogy mailing lists, but increasingly lists are sprouting up elsewhere, and
particularly on Yahoo Groups. The Yahoo lists have the advantage of an associated
webspace where files connected with the group, such as photos and parish register
transcriptions, can be stored. Yahoo also provides an option to host a closed list with
archives only accessible to group members.

To find a list on RootsWeb, or to search the archives, start with the 'Mailing List
and Archive Search' at **http://lists.rootsweb.ancestry.com**. Alternatively, you can
browse the index at **http://lists.rootsweb.ancestry.com/index**. If you subscribe
to multiple lists it is worth setting up a RootsWeb account so that you can manage all
your lists from one page at **http://myaccount.rootsweb.com**.

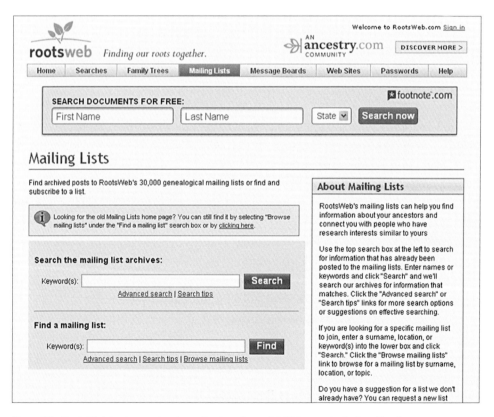

Figure 25   RootsWeb hosts an extensive collection of over 30,000 genealogical mailing lists on every
conceivable subject.

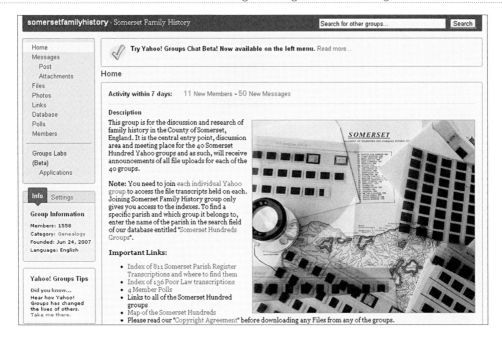

Figure 26   The Somerset mailing list on Yahoo. The Yahoo service provides a facility for a group to share files, photos and links in a collaborative online workspace.

It is more difficult to find the genealogy groups on Yahoo as the company hosts a huge variety of mailing lists dedicated to a wide range of subjects. The lists can be searched by keyword at **http://groups.yahoo.com**. Somerset researchers in particular have embraced the Yahoo format. There is a very active Somerset list at **http://groups.yahoo.com/group/somersetfamilyhistory** and a large number of associated lists for the various Somerset hundreds, each of which hosts parish register transcriptions provided by members. Many of the DNA mailing lists are hosted on Yahoo such as the ISOGG (International Society of Genetic Genealogy) lists and various haplogroup project mailing lists. To subscribe to a Yahoo list you will first of all need to set up a Yahoo account with a username and password. Once this has been done you can manage all your lists and access the archives from one central page at **http://uk.groups.yahoo.com/mygroups**.

A few genealogy groups can also be found on Google groups, which can be searched at **http://groups.google.co.uk**. Genuki maintains an incomplete list of genealogy discussion groups for those with research interests in the British Isles at **www.genuki.org.uk/indexes/MailingLists.html**. Cyndi's List has a page devoted to the subject of mailing lists with links to some useful articles on how to use them at **www.cyndislist.com/mailing-lists**.

Mailing list etiquette

Each mailing list has an administrator who is responsible for the general running of the list, welcoming new subscribers and establishing the list guidelines. If you have problems subscribing or unsubscribing from a list, or have any concerns with the running of the list or the suitability of a topic, you should always contact the list administrator in the first instance. No two lists are alike and each administrator will operate the list in the way that he or she sees fit. Some administrators can be very strict and will ensure that all discussions are kept 'on topic'; others will adopt a more lenient approach and will tolerate the occasional diversion into 'off topic' discussions. Some mailing list administrators will send you an FAQ (frequently asked questions) file when you first subscribe to the list, which will give you a good idea of the sort of topics that are acceptable.

Discussions on religion and politics should be avoided at all costs, as should messages about viruses, spam and chain letters. Advertising and the promotion of commercial services is not permitted on most lists. The subject of DNA testing can be a particularly contentious issue. Some lists will not permit any discussion of the subject at all. Others will permit discussion but will request that you do not mention prices or promote specific companies. You should also ensure that you do not publish copyright material on a mailing list unless you have the permission of the copyright holder. Private email messages should never be reproduced on mailing lists without the sender's permission. It is always a good idea when first subscribing to a list to wait for a while before making a posting so that you can get a feel for the list and the type of messages that are posted. Check the list archives first to see if other postings have been made in the past on your surname of interest or if the question you would like to ask has already been answered.

- Use an informative subject heading and list surnames in capital letters
- Keep your message short and to the point
- Send your message in plain text
- Send thank you emails off-list
- Do not post any copyright material without the permission of the copyright holder
- Do not offer 'look-ups' from copyright material
- Do not discuss religion, politics, viruses, spam and chain letters
- Do not post commercial messages or advertise products or services in which you have a personal interest
- Do not copy or forward another person's private email without permission
- Do not publish personal details or announce your holiday plans in advance

Table 10   Top ten tips for mailing lists.

To get the best response, take time to formulate your posts. It is important to use an informative subject heading. Some mailing list veterans subscribe to multiple lists and often delete emails with unpromising subject lines without even reading them. You want your message to be read by as many people as possible so make sure that the relevant information is included in the title, and especially the surnames. Send your message in plain text. Most lists have limits on the size of individual messages, and if you send a post in html it will increase the file size and your message will probably become trapped by the list's filters. Provide as much information as possible without making the post too lengthy. Write surnames in capital letters. Make sure that you provide full details of locations, especially on general mailing lists. Identical place names often appear in many different countries. You might know for instance that your ancestors are from Launceston in Cornwall but an Australian researcher will assume you are talking about the Launceston in Tasmania! Similarly, Chapman county codes and American state abbreviations can be very confusing for the uninitiated. Make sure too that you provide details of any sources you have already searched so that there is no duplication of effort.

Mailing list subscribers are a cross-section of the population and you will find a mix of personalities and styles, with some people offering more helpful advice than others. As with face-to-face conversations, occasionally mailing list discussions can get heated and develop into what is known as a 'flame war'. In such situations most list administrators will step in and put the culprits on 'moderation' until tempers have cooled. Their posts then have to be approved by the admin before being released. In the worst-case scenario troublemakers can be banned from a list. Fortunately, such incidents are usually very rare. As a courtesy you should always write and thank people off-list for any advice or information they have given you.

Remember that most mailing list archives are publicly searchable. Make sure that you do not publish any personal details in your posts that you do not want in the public domain. It is also advisable not to announce holiday plans in advance on a mailing list.

When replying to list emails, always double-check the reply field to ensure that you are replying to the list or an individual as appropriate. Some lists are set up so that the replies are automatically directed to the list, in which case you will need to amend the details manually to send a private reply to an individual. Other lists encourage replies to individuals and if you wish the whole list to see your reply you will need to manually copy in the list. There can be few genealogists who have not been caught out on a list, sending a reply intended for an individual to an entire mailing list, sometimes with embarrassing consequences! You can manually delete your message from the archives but by this stage everyone on the list will have already received the email.

8

Genealogy
social networking websites

There are a number of specialist genealogy networking websites which enable family historians to connect with their cousins or other researchers who share their surname interests. These websites all offer more functionality than the traditional message boards and mailing lists. Some sites provide the facility to store family trees online and search for matches in the company's database. Most of the sites allow the user to upload photos and videos. Often there will be additional social networking-style features, such as the ability to create a profile page or add 'friends'. Most sites provide a basic service free of charge but will require a small subscription to access additional services, such as the ability to contact other users. The features on offer vary from company to company, and the choice will depend very much on the nature of your research and the likely location of the cousins you are hoping to connect with. To get the best out of these sites you will need to enter details of your family tree or your research interests to maximise your chances of finding those all-important connections. It is very likely that during the course of your research you will make use of several of these websites. I will look in detail here at the most popular sites and those which are most likely to be of relevance to family historians in the UK. I have provided links for a few other similar websites which might also be of interest.

Genes Reunited

Genes Reunited, **www.genesreunited.co.uk**, was probably the first real social networking website for genealogists in the UK, and it transformed the process of making easy contact with distant cousins. It is a sister site of Friends Reunited (see Chapter 9), the website that began the social networking revolution in the UK. The site was set up in November 2002 as Genes Connected and officially launched in May 2003. The name was subsequently changed to Genes Reunited in 2004. Websites such as the RootsWeb WorldConnect project (launched in November 1999) already provided

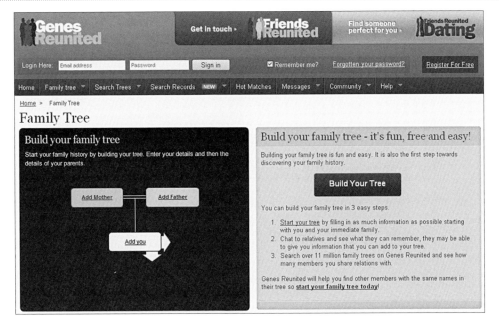

Figure 27 Genes Reunited is the most popular family tree website in the UK with over 11 million members. For a small subscription it provides an easy way to make new contacts and to share your tree online with friends and relatives.

facilities to upload family trees and publish them online, but for many people publication was not an easy process as it relied on the creation of a GEDCOM file, a special file format used for data sharing by family history software programs (see Table 11). Not everyone uses a family history program to store their genealogical data, and especially not those who are just starting out with their research. A further disadvantage of making your tree publicly available online on a website such as WorldConnect is that it is very easy for other researchers to copy your data and republish it, sometimes introducing errors in the process, without ever making contact. Finally, a large majority of the trees on WorldConnect are American, and it can be quite a challenge sifting through the search results to find the few UK trees that might be of interest.

Genes Reunited provided an alternative platform which anyone could use to build their tree online without the need to create a GEDCOM file. The user could provide as little or as much information as they liked, but with the added benefit that the trees were not publicly available and you had total control over who could see your tree. For the more experienced users, trees can be uploaded to Genes Reunited from a GEDCOM file. Your Genes Reunited tree can also be exported as a GEDCOM file to the family history software program of your choice. Trees are hosted free of charge but a modest annual subscription is required to enable you to contact other researchers and to view their trees. Messages are sent through the proprietary Genes Reunited messaging system so that you do not reveal your email address. Once contact has been established you can then share your tree with your newly found relative, with details of living descendants being suppressed if preferred.

Genes Reunited proved so popular that by the end of 2003 it had acquired over 650,000 members. By the end of 2004 membership had grown to over 2 million, with over 25 million names added. By the end of 2010 Genes Reunited boasted over 11 million users, representing over one in four of the adult population of the UK. I joined Genes Reunited back in March 2004 and over the years it has brought me into contact with more relatives than any other site. I made contact through Genes Reunited with a lost second cousin who had immigrated to New Zealand, and re-established contact with the family of my mother's first cousin who immigrated to Australia back in the late 1960s. I have also been in touch with many other more distant cousins, some of whom have provided me with valuable information and sometimes photographs and other documents relating to my tree.

The design of Genes Reunited has changed little over the years, and it is a some-what cumbersome process to update a tree online. The hot matches menu provides you with a list of all your matches, which are listed in descending order of the number of matches you have in common with other Genes Reunited members. The matches are rated according to the accuracy of the match but the system is not very intelligent, and matches principally on names and dates. Place names are taken into account but if,

GEDCOM, an acronym for GEnealogical Data COMmunication, is a method of exchanging genealogical data between different family history software programs and online tree-build-ing websites. The GEDCOM format was developed by the Church of Jesus Christ of Latter-Day Saints as an aid to genealogical research. All the major genealogy software programs support the creation of GEDCOM files. For most programs you will need to export your data into a GEDCOM file. The resultant file can then be imported into an alternative software program or uploaded to the website of your choice. Some genealogy programs work directly with GEDCOM data and files are automatically saved in the GEDCOM format. A GEDCOM file will usually have the file extension '**.ged**'.

The majority of family tree websites allow users to make their trees available online by importing GEDCOM files created with an external family history program. The details of living people are usually privatised before publication. The popular tree-building websites such as Genes Reunited, Geni, Ancestry.com and MyHeritage allow the user to create a GEDCOM file from their family tree data, which can then be exported into a family history program or uploaded to another website.

Although GEDCOM is a standardised format, in practice most genealogy programs have adapted the GEDCOM format for their own purposes by adding extensions, not all of which follow the recommended GEDCOM standard. When importing or exporting data from one program to another some fields such as notes might appear in different loca-tions or might not be handled correctly, and some adjustments will be necessary. Most of the major programs have dedicated mailing lists or forums to help resolve such problems. Despite its limitations GEDCOM is still the easiest and most reliable method of transferring genealogical data.

Table 11   What is a GEDCOM?

for example, one person has entered a place of birth as Kintbury and the other person has entered the place of birth as Kintbury, Berkshire, the match is given a low rating.

Other family tree websites have now been established that provide much slicker and easier-to-use interfaces, but Genes Reunited is likely to remain the most popular family tree website in the UK for many years to come simply because of the sheer size and reach of its database. In March 2010, after clearance from the Competition Commission, the Friends Reunited Group (the parent company of Genes Reunited) was sold to Brightsolid, the company behind Findmypast and the Scotland's People website. The acquisition could potentially give Genes Reunited a much-needed makeover.

Online tree-building websites

A growing number of websites have now followed the example set by Genes Reunited and provide the facility to store family trees online, allow the user to search for matches and make contact with other researchers. The new websites all operate in a very similar way. Trees can be built manually online or you can create a file in your family history program and upload the resultant GEDCOM file. Many of the sites allow you to integrate photographs, census images, video and audio files into your tree. It is usually possible to have your own profile page where you can provide information about yourself and the surnames you are researching. Access to trees can be controlled with varying levels of privacy. Trees can be kept private with access only permitted to trusted relatives and fellow researchers. If desired your tree can be shared for matching purposes with other users of the website. Some sites will allow you to make your tree public. All responsible sites should ensure that you do not publish the details of living people without their permission. A basic tree-hosting service is usually provided free of charge after setting up an account with a username and password. For most sites it will be necessary to pay for a premium subscription to take advantage of extra facilities such as the ability to contact other researchers or to have extra storage space for a bigger family tree or more photos.

A tree-building website can often be good for a beginner who wants a simple way to store the results of his or her research, without investing the time and money in exploring the various commercial family history programs. Your tree can easily be shared with your newly found relatives and because the tree is online you can access it any time from any location such as a record office or library. Once your tree has been uploaded all the people in your tree can be included in the company's database for 'match-making' purposes. You can either actively contact your matches or passively wait for people to contact you. Most companies will send you regular emails informing you of your new matches. You need to think carefully about how much information you wish to upload to these sites. If your tree is on a public website you will inevitably lose a certain amount of control, as there is nothing to stop other researchers or family members copying your data and publishing it elsewhere. If you include too much detail on peripheral lines you might find that these generate more enquiries than you can handle, especially if the lines are particularly prolific or the surnames are especially common. The best compromise is to publish a partial tree, providing sufficient information on key surnames and dates for people to match you but without providing too much detail. You can then share more detailed information and more extensive trees with your close relatives and trusted researchers.

The choice of provider will, to some extent, depend on the nationality of your ancestors and the composition of the companies' databases. If your lines are all in the UK you will want to choose a site that has the largest number of users from the UK. If you have lines from other European countries or you are hoping to make contact with cousins in America or Canada, then one of the more international sites will be more likely to help you to make connections. With a larger database you will have a greater chance of finding a connection with a distant cousin, but the chances of finding a match also depend on the number of relatives that users have entered into their trees. If the companies quote statistics look out both for the number of users and the number of 'profiles' – pages created for individual people in their tree. If the ratio of users to profiles is low, then few people will have entered extensive details of their tree and the site will be less useful for making connections. A site with a large number of users might still be very helpful if you are trying to track down a living person.

The tree-building facilities vary from company to company and the choice of company will also depend on the features provided. It is a good idea to ensure that the company provides the ability to export your data, preferably in a GEDCOM file. As your research progresses you will inevitably find that an online site has its limitations and you will find it easier to manipulate and store the data in a proprietary family history program on your home computer. You might also find that you will not always want to be tied to one company, especially if you have to pay an expensive annual subscription to continue using all the advanced features. Once you have created a family tree on one website, it is then a very easy matter to export the GEDCOM file and upload it to another website of your choice. When you are adept at importing and exporting GEDCOM files you can easily upload a basic GEDCOM file to a number of different sites for maximum exposure.

There is now a bewildering range of companies that provide online tree-hosting and match-making facilities. There will inevitably be a period of transition as the key players become established. A number of smaller family networking websites have already been the subject of acquisitions and mergers in the last few years and there will undoubtedly be further consolidation in the years to come. Other sites have launched and then disappeared completely after a year or so. When new sites are set up the services are usually provided free of charge to the early adopters in an attempt to build up the database. Some companies will offer a free or discounted lifetime membership for a limited period until the website becomes established. It is difficult to predict in advance which websites will eventually become dominant in the next decade. In the meantime it is best to try out a few different sites and see which ones you find the easiest to use, or which provide you with the most matches. Never rely on any one website as a repository for all your family history data and make sure that you back-up your data offline on your home computer, and preferably in other locations as well.

Ancestry.com, **www.ancestry.co.uk**

Ancestry.com launched a tree-building service in July 2006. The site now hosts over 20 million family trees and the company claims to be the 'largest online community dedicated to family history'. A family tree can be created from scratch on the Ancestry.com website by any registered member, either with or without a subscription. If preferred you can upload a tree from your own GEDCOM file. Trees can be made either public or private. Public trees are not, as their name suggests, viewable by members of the public and can only be seen by other Ancestry.com subscribers. The names in your tree will, however, appear in public searches. Private trees can be viewed by invitation only, though the names will again still appear in public search results. For the ultra-cautious there is also an option to exclude your tree from being found in the search index.

Once your tree is in the Ancestry.com database you will be given 'hints' of matches in other trees. The ability to contact matches is restricted to subscribers. Subscribers also benefit from receiving hints in matching historical records in the Ancestry.com collection, such as census images and parish register pages. These records can then be attached to the appropriate person in your tree as a source. If you are considering an Ancestry.com subscription then it can be useful to store your tree on their website, though once your subscription has lapsed you will have to rely on other Ancestry.com members contacting you. However, beware of Ancestry.com's terms and conditions. Once you have uploaded your tree to Ancestry.com you give them permission to 'reproduce, compile, and distribute, all information about non-living individuals in your submitted GEDCOM file'.

At the time of writing, Ancestry.com is beta-testing a new website by the name of Mundia.com, **www.mundia.com**, which provides family tree-building and social networking facilities integrated with the main Ancestry.com global family tree, and with the option to link to a Facebook account. In view of the size of the Ancestry.com database and their marketing power, this site might well be one to watch in the future.

Findmypast, **www.findmypast.co.uk**

Findmypast, the main competitor to Ancestry.com in the UK, launched Family Tree Explorer, a beta-version of its own online family tree-building program, in 2010. At the time of writing the service was not fully functional, but this will possibly be a useful choice if you have a Findmypast subscription and wish to integrate all your family history research on one website.

GeneaNet, **www.geneanet.org**

GeneaNet is a long-running French website that was founded back in December 1996 and is now available in a number of different languages. GeneaNet hosts a large number of original and transcribed records from European sources, particularly from France, and also provides a social networking facility. It is potentially a good choice if you are trying to connect with relatives in France or elsewhere in Europe.

Geni, **www.Geni.com**

Geni is a collaborative family networking site with a number of unique and innovative features. It was launched in January 2007 and is now available in over forty languages. A family tree can be created free of charge but a subscription is required to access most of the facilities. GEDCOM import is restricted to subscribers and the maximum file size permitted is 50,000 individuals. Subscribers can export a GEDCOM file of their entire tree whereas non-subscribers can only export a GEDCOM file of their blood relatives. The Geni interface is attractive and easy to use. The software is in a constant state of development with new features added every few months. As with other online tree-building sites, each person in your tree is given an individual profile page, to which you can also add photos, videos and other files. By January 2011, Geni had around 6 million users who had created over 100 million individual profile pages for their ancestors. Once you have made a connection with relatives on Geni you are encouraged to work together and merge the profiles of your common ancestors. Geni operates in some ways like a wiki (see Chapter 11). Each profile page has a discussion page where issues relating to the profile can be resolved. There is also a revision page where users can keep track of changes made to the profile, though the actual edits cannot presently be seen. Unlike a wiki, Geni profile pages have named managers. Additional managers can be added on request or someone can ask to take over the management of a profile.

The ability to perform surname searches and to look for matches is restricted to subscribers. The match-making algorithms are not very sophisticated and matches are made purely on names, with no account taken of dates or locations. If you have some common surnames in your tree you are likely to get a large number of spurious matches, though you can review these and discard them. As the software is regularly upgraded this issue could well be addressed in future updates. The majority of members appear to be in North America, though bizarrely, according to the Alexa rankings, the site is also particularly popular in Estonia! It could be a useful site if you are hoping to make connections across the pond. I was able to make contact through Geni with a distant cousin in Ontario who provided me with information on a previously unknown branch of my family in Canada.

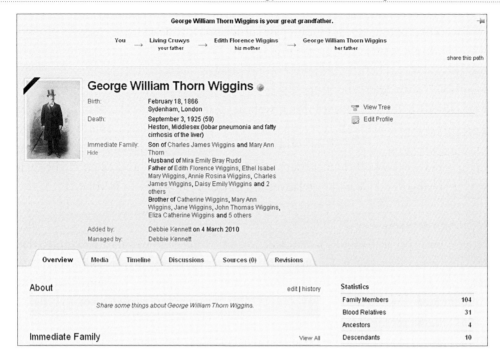

Figure 28 An ancestor profile page from Geni.

The stated aim of Geni is to have one big, shared family tree for the whole world showing how we are all related. The Geni community is actively working together to create profiles and trees for celebrities and historical figures. Popular profiles include those for Barack Obama, Adolf Hitler, John Lennon, Karl Marx, Charlemagne, Princess Diana and William the Conqueror. These profiles can often have several hundred managers. Once a comprehensive, well-sourced page has been created it becomes a 'master profile' with its own curator. Curators are volunteer community administrators who have taken responsibility for particular pages and trees, and have the ability to 'lock' pages in the event of a dispute. The master profile page for 'Jesus of Nazareth, The Christ' has proved particularly controversial with ongoing disagreements as to his parentage, marriage and relationships! If you have a match with a master profile page you are encouraged to merge your record with the master profile. The largest tree in the Geni database, known as the 'big tree', included profiles for over 50 million people by January 2011. It reputedly contains the profiles of many biblical characters going back to Adam and Eve, with often dubious sourcing. The introduction of curators and master profiles should in the long run help to clear up the problems with this tree. In October 2010 Geni introduced 'projects' to the website. A number of projects have now been set up looking at a diverse range of subjects such as the Kings of Wessex, the Plantagenets, the Wives of US Presidents and the Salem Witch Trials.

It will be interesting to see how Geni develops in the coming years. At present it is becoming a very useful resource for the family trees of famous and historical personalities. There are advantages and disadvantages to the collaborative Geni approach for the trees of our less illustrious ancestors, for whom fewer sources will exist. In theory, it makes sense for everyone to collaborate with their research so that everything is stored in one place and efforts are not duplicated. However, the quality of research is very variable. While there are many diligent researchers who meticulously record all their sources and only add people to their tree when they have reliable proof, there are many other people who collect ancestors from the internet without checking sources and who, in the process, introduce many errors into their trees. If you do decide to share your large, well-sourced and carefully researched tree on Geni, you will not want to spend a long time merging your profiles with other users who have error-strewn trees with lots of mistaken connections. There is, however, no compulsion to merge trees or profiles so you could simply ignore those trees and only merge with accurate and reliably sourced profiles created by trusted collaborators. Profile management is possibly a further issue of some concern. Although each profile can have multiple managers, there can only be one overall profile manager. This could be a cause of conflict if there is a profile for an ancestor who has many living descendants on Geni, especially if the person who manages the profile is not the one who has contributed most of the research and does not want to relinquish control. A final cause for concern is that Geni is a commercial company and not everyone will feel happy contributing their data to a profit-making organisation who could potentially capitalise on your freely given and painstaking research.

Despite these reservations Geni does have many excellent features, and the online tree-building software is far superior to all its competitors. The subscription fees are also much more affordable than those for its main online rival, MyHeritage (see below). Geni will be particularly useful for those who are just starting their family history research and wish to have an easy-to-use facility to store their tree online and to share it with other family members. Geni is certainly a site that is well worth trying and is one to watch for the future.

MyHeritage, **www.myheritage.com**

Founded in 2003 in Israel, MyHeritage has since grown to become the second largest commercial genealogy company in the world after Ancestry.com. It is also among the top twenty social networking websites on the internet. By the end of 2010 MyHeritage had over 53 million members from all over the world, with over 3 million members in the UK. The company has in recent years purchased a number of European genealogy-related social media websites with coverage in countries such as Germany, Poland, Denmark, Sweden and Spain, and, therefore, has a very strong European presence. The site is also available in numerous languages and consequently has a very international

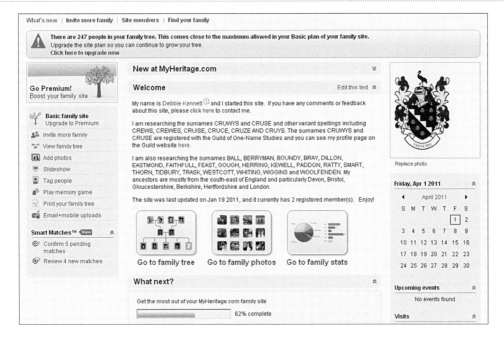

Figure 29   A basic free account at MyHeritage provides a free profile page and a tree-building service to store the details of up to 250 people.

mix of members. The MyHeritage website allows the user to store a family tree online, upload photos and videos, invite family members to share their tree and connect with potential relatives. A basic account can be set up free of charge. This enables the user to create a profile page, a simple website and to store details of up to 250 people in an online family tree together with up to 250 megabytes worth of photographs and videos. Family trees can be built manually or imported from a GEDCOM file. With a basic account you can search for matches and contact other users. MyHeritage uses its own proprietary 'smart matching' software, which provides more accurate matches and grades them in descending order of quality, though most of the functionality is only available with a subscription. With an annual subscription, a premium account provides extra storage and space for a larger family tree with a maximum of 2,500 individuals. A premium plus account gives you unlimited storage and an unlimited family tree. The subscription rates are more expensive than those for rival sites such as Genes Reunited and Geni.

The photo features on MyHeritage are free for all users and are quite fun to use. There is a 'look-a-like meter' that determines which parent a child most resembles, and a 'celebrity morph' which compares facial features with celebrity photos and tells you which celebrity you most resemble. I came up with a 71 per cent match with someone called Marcia Cross, who I had never heard of but subsequently discovered is an American actress in *Desperate Housewives*. I can, however, see very little resemblance between us! MyHeritage also provides the popular genealogy program Family Tree Builder as a free download available in thirty-six different languages.

MyHeritage appears to attract a different range of users from the traditional genealogy networking sites. Many of the members seem to be much younger than the average family historian, but quite a few have only entered limited details, if any, of their family trees. The international membership is, however, a big bonus and the site will be particularly useful if you are looking for living relatives in non-English-speaking countries. I have come up with a number of useful matches on MyHeritage and it has brought me into contact with some close and distant cousins in Australia.

Other tree-building websites

www.ancestralatlas.com A UK-based networking site with a unique mapping function, which connects ancestors and their neighbours by place rather than surname

www.ancestralforest.com A UK-based family tree-building site

www.ancestralhunt.com A new US-based service, in beta-testing at the time of writing, which seeks to provide 'a platform for member genealogists and family historians to place their genealogy and family history records in a geo-spatial and time-based context'

www.ancestorjunction.com A new UK-based site launched in April 2011

www.appletree.com An American family tree-building site in beta-testing at the time of writing

www.arcalife.com A Canadian site with an emphasis on preserving your family history and stories online for future generations

www.familypursuit.com A collaborative, invitation-only private family tree website

www.generationfiles.com A family social network and private archival space

www.genoom.com A Spanish-based English language family social networking platform

www.onegreatfamily.com An American site which claims to be 'the world's largest online family tree' with over 180 million submitted pedigree-linked names. The company uses a proprietary 'handprint' tool which looks for matches with a person and his or her immediate family members. Trees are automatically merged when the same person is found in both trees. Potential matches and conflicting dates are flagged with icons

Tamura Jones's Modern Software Experience website, **www.tamurajones.net**, provides regular news and updates on the various 'social genealogy' websites with often very critical and probing commentary. The website also has a comprehensive list of social genealogy websites, which can be found at **www.tamurajones.net/SocialGenealogySites.xhtml**.

GenealogyWise

GenealogyWise, **www.genealogywise.com**, is a dedicated genealogy social networking website which was launched in the summer of 2009. The site was created by Family Link, a new company launched in 2006 by Paul Allen, the former CEO of Ancestry.com, and several key members of the original Ancestry.com team. The company is based in America in Provo, Utah, and operates a family of websites including World Vital Records. There was much excitement in the genealogy community when the site was first launched and membership grew to 15,000 within the first two months. Since then the growth has slowed markedly and a year after the launch there were around 21,000 members, but with a steady trickle of new members joining every day.

GenealogyWise membership is free of charge and once you have registered you can create your own public profile page where you can list all your surname interests. Members connect with other researchers on GenealogyWise by joining groups. There are groups for surnames, locations, commercial organisations, family history programs, genealogy websites, genealogical societies and various other specialist groups. Each group effectively has its own mini website where members can add comments to the 'wall' or start new discussions in the forum. Once you have joined a group you will receive email notifications every time someone joins the group, makes a comment or starts a new discussion, though you will need to visit the website to read the actual comments made by your visitors.

Figure 30   The GenealogyWise social networking website.

GenealogyWise also gives you the option of adding 'friends'. Your friends' names appear on your profile page and once someone is your friend you have the ability to send them private messages via the GenealogyWise messaging system. If people are not on your list of friends the only way to contact them is to post a public message on their profile page, which will not always be appropriate. The site has not attracted anywhere near the number of users as the other social networking sites covered elsewhere in this chapter, but it does at least have the advantage of being completely free to use. If you do take the trouble to create a surname page you will find that it will appear quite highly in the various search-engine rankings.

GenealogyWise was acquired by the Canadian National Institute for Genealogical Studies in February 2011. The Institute offers a number of web-based courses, including a dedicated course on 'Social media for the wise genealogist'. It remains to be seen what plans they have for the website but their association with GenealogyWise might well breathe new life into the network.

Lost cousins

Lost Cousins, **www.lostcousins.com**, provides the opportunity to connect with other researchers based on common ancestors in the censuses. You can include details of your ancestors and their households in the 1841 and 1881 censuses for England and

Figure 31   Lost Cousins has a unique matching facility based on relatives who were recorded in the censuses.

Wales, the 1881 Canadian census, the 1881 census of Scotland, the 1880 US census and the 1911 Irish census. The more relations you enter the greater your chances of finding a match. The downside, however, is that entering all the census details is a very laborious process and consequently many people do not bother. Basic membership is free but a small subscription is required to contact other members and to access additional facilities. Lost Cousins has grown steadily since its launch in September 2004 and by May 2010 had acquired over 80,000 members in more than fifty countries around the world. A regular newsletter is published which provides much excellent advice and a useful round-up of the latest news from the genealogy world. It is worth joining to receive the newsletter even if you do not find any lost cousins.

9

General
social networking websites

Numerous social networking websites have been established that were not created with the family historian in mind, but which, nevertheless, are often very useful either for connecting with other genealogists or for keeping up with the latest news from the genealogy world. These websites often attract huge numbers of users and can be particularly useful if you are trying to trace a long-lost friend or relative or track down a particular candidate to take a DNA test. Social networking websites can also provide an effective method of publicising a surname study or a DNA project. In this chapter we will take a look at the popular sites that will be of most benefit to the family historian.

Friends Reunited

Friends Reunited, **www.friendsreunited.co.uk**, was an early leader in social networking and the first social networking site to rise to prominence in the UK. The site was founded by a husband-and-wife team, Julie and Steve Pankhurst, working from the back bedroom of their suburban semi in Barnet, North London, and is now the classic internet start-up success story. The aim of the site was to enable old school friends to get in touch with each other. Users could list the schools they attended and create a simple profile page telling other users about themselves. Space was provided to upload old school photos and share memories of favourite teachers. Friends Reunited was officially launched in July 2000 and by the end of the year it had 3,000 registered members. Word spread slowly at first but in 2001 it started to attract media attention and the membership rapidly snowballed as it reached 'critical mass', the point at which every new member was likely to find at least one familiar name. By the end of 2001 more than 2.5 million people had registered with Friends Reunited and it was starting to become a household name.

The site gradually expanded to include workplaces, teams and clubs, streets and the armed forces. Sister sites were launched in Australia, New Zealand and South

Africa. A dating site was launched in 2003 along with the genealogy site Genes Reunited (see Chapter 8). In 2005 Friends Reunited was bought by the broadcaster ITV for the sum of £175 million. By this time the site had over 15 million users. The initial excitement was, however, now beginning to fade and growth began to slow down. Once you had registered with Friends Reunited and made contact with your old friends there was little need to keep returning. There was increasing competition from other social networking sites such as MySpace, Bebo and Facebook, which were much slicker and offered greater levels of customisation. More importantly, the rival sites were free to use whereas Friends Reunited required a small annual subscription. In 2008, in an attempt to regain market share, the subscription fee was dropped. With TV advertising falling, in 2009 ITV put Friends Reunited up for sale and a deal was agreed in August 2009 with Brightsolid, the parent company of Findmypast and Scotland's People, to buy the company at the knockdown price of £25 million. After clearance from the Competition Commission the sale was finalised in March 2010. Brightsolid announced that they were intending to reposition the brand as a specialist genealogy platform.

From the genealogist's point of view, Friends Reunited is still potentially a useful resource. It now has over 20 million members. Although many of its members will have joined other social networking sites like Facebook, not everyone has done so. If, therefore, you are trying to make contact with a specific person and cannot find them elsewhere then it is worth searching on Friends Reunited. You cannot search by

Figure 32   Friends Reunited is a useful website for getting in touch with old school friends, but is also helpful for family history research when trying to make contact with living relatives.

surname alone, but it is possible to search by surname and initial. If you are researching a rare surname, it is quite easy to extract a lot of relevant information about
present-day name-bearers. The site underwent a redesign at the beginning of January
2010 with an attempt to copy some of the Facebook-style features such as friends
and groups, but it is still somewhat difficult to navigate. If you did sign up in the early
years make sure you check the privacy settings on your account so that you are not
revealing any information you do not wish to be made public.

Facebook

Facebook, **www.facebook.com**, is the social media phenomenon of the internet
age. It is by far and away the most popular social networking website in the world
and is jostling with Google for top spot as the website with the highest number of
visitors. Facebook has become increasingly popular with people of all ages in the last
few years, and it is now an essential resource for the family historian.

   Facebook was founded in February 2004 by Mark Zuckerberg, a student at
Harvard University. Membership was initially restricted to students at the university. The new site was so popular that within the first month more than half the
undergraduate population at Harvard were registered on the service. Membership
gradually expanded to include all universities in the United States and Canada.
Schools were added in September 2005, followed by employees of companies such
as Microsoft and Apple. In September 2006 membership was extended to include
everyone worldwide aged 13 and over with an email address. By August 2008 there
were 100 million users. In July 2009 Facebook had 250 million users. In July 2010
Facebook passed the 500 million-user milestone. By this time the UK had the second
highest number of users, second only to the US; with around 26 million people in
the UK on Facebook, representing almost half the UK population. These astonishing
figures make Facebook a very important website for family historians, and especially
for tracking down living people, though Facebook will often require a slightly different approach to standard genealogical networks because of the demographics of
the site. Facebook has traditionally been the preserve of students and teenagers, but
the age gap is beginning to close and between 2009 and 2010 the fastest-growing age
group were those between the ages of 25 and 54. Growing numbers of over 55s are
also joining Facebook, but they still only make up a small percentage of the total user
base. If you are trying to contact a particular person in your family tree or hoping to
track down the last living descendant of a particular lineage to take a DNA test, the
person you are seeking might not necessarily be on Facebook, but you will almost
certainly find their son, daughter or other family member on Facebook instead.

   In addition to providing a facility to contact long-lost friends and relatives,
Facebook is also a very useful way of keeping in touch with your genealogy friends

Figure 33   The fan page for the National Archives on Facebook.

and for making contact with other people sharing similar research interests. I have found that friendships often build up when I initially contact someone who is researching one of my surnames, but once the exchange of information is completed there is less incentive to keep in touch. If you are both on Facebook it is much easier to maintain the contact.

Facebook is free to use and setting up an account is a straightforward process. Once you have registered you are given your own personal webspace, known as a profile page, where you can provide information about yourself and upload photos. Facebook only starts to make sense once you start to link up with your other friends and contacts. If you use one of the popular Internet Service Providers (ISPs) you can use the Friend Finder. You simply input your email address and password and the software will search Facebook to see how many of your friends and relatives in your email address book already have accounts. You can also search for people by name or by email address. You will probably find that quite a number of your existing contacts are already on Facebook. You can then invite them to become your 'friend'. Once your friends have accepted your request you will have access to their profile pages, photographs and news feeds. It is a good idea just to lurk for a while and see how your friends use Facebook, so that you can get an idea as to how it all works.

Facebook is also a handy way of keeping up to date with the latest genealogy news. A growing number of genealogical organisations and companies are using Facebook as a way of communicating with their customers and users, and have set up

Figure 34   A Facebook group for the Kirkman surname.

their own 'fan' pages. Once you have found a page of interest you will need to click on the 'like' button and any updates from the company or organisation will appear in your news feed. The British Library, The National Archives, the Commonwealth War Graves Commission, the Families in British India Society and the Guild of One-Name Studies all have active Facebook fan pages. There are also a number of family history magazines and commercial genealogy companies such as Genes Reunited, Findmypast and Ancestry.com with pages on Facebook.

For genealogists, one of the most useful features on Facebook is the ability to join and create groups. Numerous groups have been set up for various surnames. The groups operate rather like discussion groups, and members can opt to receive email notifications of all the messages that are posted to the group. Members can also share photos and videos with the group. Groups can either be closed, with membership controlled by an administrator and the content restricted to members, or open, so that anyone can join and the group pages are publicly available. It is also possible to have 'secret' groups, which do not show up in searches. If there is no group for the surname you are researching it is very easy to start a group of your own. Some of the family history societies are now starting to set up their own Facebook groups. There are active groups for, amongst others, the Devon, Kent, Nottinghamshire, Hillingdon and Isle of Wight family history societies. Groups can be a good way of getting to know the other members of your society, and will often give you the chance to put a face to a name if members have uploaded a photo to their profile.

Facebook has its own messaging system, which allows you to make contact with other Facebook users, provided they have not opted out. Messages are sent through the Facebook system without revealing the email address of either user. If you are trying to track down a particular person and you know they have a Facebook account you can then send them a message. This approach works best if the person you are looking for has a more unusual name. If you're trying to locate a particular John Smith, for example, the task would be much more difficult. There are over 250,000 John Smiths on Facebook and it would be impossible to establish which John Smith is yours! Facebook emails, messages, chats and texts are integrated together so that all communications are stored in one place.

If you set up a surname group, the messaging system can also be used to invite people to join your group. Care needs to be taken that you do not send out too many messages at once. I know of one user whose account was temporarily suspended after he enthusiastically sent messages to everyone on Facebook with his surname! The messaging system is also particularly useful for keeping in contact with people whose email address has changed or is temporarily unavailable, and it has come to my rescue on more than one occasion. The advantage of sending a message through Facebook is that, so long as the recipient checks their Facebook page on a regular basis, you can guarantee that they will receive your message, whereas emails can sometimes disappear into cyberspace.

There are also numerous applications ('apps') that can be added to your profile page, most of which are quite frivolous and very few of which have any practical use for family historians, though they can be a lot of fun. You can, for example, play all sorts of online games with your friends, send birthday cards and participate in quizzes. You will find that some of your friends become deeply engrossed in games such as Farmville or Mafia Wars on Facebook. If you do not share their enthusiasm for these games make sure you remove these applications from your news feed so that you are not inundated with updates about their barn-building and mafia-hunting activities!

A number of family tree apps have been developed for Facebook such as WeRelate, One Family Tree, My Family Tree and Family Tree, often with seemingly large numbers of users. They all operate in much the same way by asking you to input the names of all your relatives who are on Facebook and to define their relationship to you. In reality most people try out the applications, add a few relatives and discover that the apps are not actually of much use. Most family history apps on Facebook are designed as a way of making money from advertising rather than with the needs of the family historian in mind, and are best avoided.

Facebook can be used as little or often as you like, but a Facebook account is now virtually an essential requirement for any family historian. I find that I have some friends who grasp the concept of Facebook immediately and keep me regularly updated with little snippets of news or interesting links. Other friends sign up, but very rarely seem to check their account. Facebook is, however, much more fun if you do join in and add the occasional comment to your friends' posts or simply click on the 'like' button if they have posted something of interest. Similarly, if you post something yourself it is always gratifying if you receive a response so that you know that at least some of your friends are reading what you have written!

The unprecedented growth of Facebook in such a short space of time has inevitably meant that the company has attracted a huge amount of press attention, particularly over security and privacy issues. Hacking of Facebook accounts to scam people out of money became an issue for a time in 2010, with a number of people paying out significant sums of money to family members who were believed to be in distress, before realising that their accounts had been compromised. Most of these problems related to students on gap-year travels. Facebook has since responded by tightening up its security controls, so that if you log in from an unusual location or with a different device you are asked additional security questions before you can access your account.

A number of Facebook privacy breaches have also been highlighted by the press in the last few years. A privacy breach on Facebook is potentially a very serious threat because of the large number of users worldwide who are affected. In practice, the seriousness of these breaches has been exaggerated, and in most cases the information that was revealed was already public. The publicity did, however, highlight the open nature of the Facebook default privacy settings, which are optimised with the needs of advertisers in mind and not the privacy concerns of individuals. Only a small proportion of Facebook users take the trouble to adjust their privacy settings, and consequently many users are unwittingly revealing more information in public than they perhaps realise. The problem was exacerbated because the Facebook privacy controls were at one time fiendishly complicated to use. To its credit, Facebook took some of the criticism on board and radically overhauled and simplified its privacy controls in May 2010, making them much easier to navigate. Despite these changes, the default settings still encourage users to be more open with their data than is normally advisable. Friend lists, status updates and photo albums are by default made publicly available to everyone. A further problem is that as new features are introduced, the tendency has been to opt everyone in automatically without permission. Various privacy organisations, such as the European Commission's Data Protection Working Party, have raised these issues with Facebook, and it is likely that the privacy policy will evolve in the years to come to address these concerns.

The applications on Facebook are another potential cause for concern. Applications are third-party software programs that use the Facebook platform but are not directly controlled by Facebook. If you decide to add an app to your account you will need to give them permission to access some of your data to allow the app to function. The settings can be adjusted on an individual basis for each application. There have been problems in the past with some applications inadvertently leaking personal data

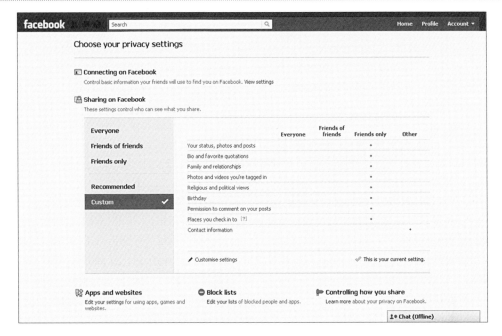

Figure 35 The customisable Facebook privacy settings.

and passing it on to advertisers and data collection agencies. The information was mostly taken from user profiles that were already in the public domain, either deliberately or unintentionally, and the loophole that made this possible has now been closed, but you should exercise caution before installing any apps, and review the settings on a regular basis.

Another issue to consider is what will happen to your account in the event of your death. Facebook now provides the option for an account to be 'memorialised' after death. Sensitive information such as status updates and contacts are removed but the profile is kept as a permanent tribute with access restricted so that only confirmed friends can see the profile or locate it in a search. Alternatively, family members can request the permanent removal of the account. It is now possible to export the data from a Facebook account and this is potentially a good way to archive the account of a family member. The status updates of a long-established and active Facebook user will often serve as an online diary, recording key events in their lives and providing an insight into their interests and pre-occupations.

It should be remembered that privacy issues will affect all websites. Facebook tends to receive all the publicity because of its high-profile status, whereas similar problems on other social networking websites are often overlooked. The benefits of Facebook for the genealogist far outweigh any disadvantages but, as with any public website, you should think carefully about the personal information you make available on the site, whether publicly or to your friends. Facebook's privacy controls are in fact far superior to those offered by most other social networking websites. The settings can be finely tuned and, when used properly, confer a high level of privacy (see Figure 35). You can, for instance, sort your friends into groups such as genealogy friends, school friends, university friends and work friends. Photos and individual status feeds can be set so that they can only be viewed by particular groups. If you do not want all your friends to be overloaded with genealogy news you can confine your family history updates to your genealogy friends. Similarly, if you do not want all your genealogy friends or your work colleagues to see your photo album from your student days you can restrict access to your university friends.

It is essential that you check and adjust your privacy settings when you set up a Facebook account. Make sure too that you adjust the directory settings. These settings determine how your profile appears in public searches. The default settings currently make your location, interests and friend list available in public searches. You might wish to change your settings so that this information is only accessible to your friends. If you prefer, you can choose to remove your profile so that your name does not appear in the public Facebook directory at all. Once you have adjusted your directory settings you can preview your profile to see how it will appear in public searches. It is a good idea to review your privacy settings on a regular basis, and especially when a new feature is introduced. The very interactive nature of Facebook means that whenever there is a change in the settings you will most likely be alerted to it by one of your friends.

A number of external tools such as Profile Watch and Zesty have also been developed that enable you to check your own privacy settings, or those of your children or friends, to warn you about any settings that might be unexpectedly public. Openbook enables you to search public Facebook updates by keyword.

My own experience of Facebook has been very positive. I joined back in January 2008 before it had started to become popular with genealogists. My only reason for joining at that time was to re-establish contact with a cousin in America whom I was hoping to persuade to join my newly established DNA project. His emails were bouncing but a quick internet search revealed that he had a Facebook account. It seemed much easier to contact him via Facebook than to send a letter to America via snail mail! We duly became Facebook friends and he was one of the earliest members of my DNA project. It did not take me long to work out how useful Facebook could be for my family history research, and I quickly set up various surname groups for my one-name study. My Cruwys and Cruse groups have both attracted more than 100 members and have brought me some very useful contacts. I was also particularly pleased that one of my second cousins managed to find me on Facebook after joining my Cruwys group. Through him I have now managed to make contact with a whole branch of my family who are descended from a great-uncle who went to live in Paris just before the First World War. Of all the social networking sites I use, Facebook is the one that has become the most indispensable.

Links

www.allfacebook.com The unofficial Facebook blog

www.checkfacebook.com Facebook statistics

www.socialbakers.com Facebook statistics by country

http://mashable.com/social-media/facebook Facebook news from Mashable

http://techcrunch.com/tag/facebook Facebook news from Techcrunch

Facebook privacy checkers

www.profilewatch.org

http://youropenbook.org

http://zesty.ca/facebook

Some light entertainment courtesy of YouTube

www.youtube.com/watch?v=iROYzrm5SBM Facebook manners

www.youtube.com/watch?v=kFKHaFJzUb4 What Facebook is for

Twitter

The micro-blogging website Twitter, **http://twitter.com**, has become a household name in the last couple of years and is now possibly one of the most influential websites in the world. Unlike most of the other mainstream social networks, which are often the preserve of teenagers and students, Twitter has always been more popular with adults. In the UK, the actor and comedian Stephen Fry and the TV presenter Jonathan Ross were among the enthusiastic early adopters. Twitter's popularity has been fed by the increasing usage of internet-connected smartphones, which enable users to post messages or 'tweets' to Twitter from anywhere in the world. Stephen Fry famously tweeted from his mobile phone when he was stuck in a lift on the 26th floor of the Centre Point building in London in February 2009. He was inundated with responses from his followers who provided jokes and time-killing tips to keep him amused until the engineers came to his rescue. Twitter has also contributed to the rise of 'citizen journalism', whereby members of the public use the site to break major news stories or provide updates on events of international importance. When terrorists launched a co-ordinated series of shooting and bombing attacks in Mumbai, India, in November 2008, Twitter users in the city were instrumental in spreading information on the events as they unfolded. In January 2009, when US Airways flight 1549, piloted by Captain Chesley Sullenberger, made a miraculous safe landing on New York's Hudson River, the news broke first on Twitter. Within minutes of the landing, members of the public who had witnessed the event posted messages to Twitter from their mobile phones. Another eye-witness, Janis Krums, watching from a ferry, snapped a picture on his

Figure 36   Keeping up with the latest news on Twitter.

iPhone and uploaded it to Twitter. Within seconds the photo was being viewed all over the world before the mainstream media had even picked up on the story or sent any photographers to the scene.

Twitter was launched in 2006, and by September 2008 had acquired over 3 million users. Twitter began to grow dramatically in 2009 as a result of the media publicity generated by its celebrity users and its reputation for breaking news stories, but it was in 2010 that Twitter entered the mainstream, ending the year with over 200 million users, over 100 million of whom had been added in the previous twelve months. Within the family history world the early Twitter adopters tended to be bloggers, writers and professional genealogists. Most of the genealogy companies quickly realised the potential of Twitter and began to set up Twitter accounts. With the ever-increasing genealogical presence on Twitter it is now becoming a very useful resource for keeping up with the latest news on family history and genetic genealogy, and for making connections with other genealogists.

Twitter is rather like a giant message board where anyone can post a short text message – known as a tweet – from an internet-connected computer or a phone from anywhere in the world. Naturally no one can possibly monitor the tweets of millions of people, and the knack is, therefore, to find people on Twitter that you already know and those with whom you share common interests. Once you start 'following' people on Twitter their tweets show up in your timeline, where you can view all the tweets in quick succession as they are posted. Tweets are restricted to 140 characters but, crucially, URLs can be included in tweets and this is what makes Twitter such a valuable communication tool. If you follow the right people you will receive links to interesting news stories and the latest blog postings. You will be alerted to new websites or major updates to genealogical databases. If there is a problem with a company website, Twitter is often used to inform users of the issues and when they might be resolved. Companies sometimes announce special offers for their Twitter followers or ask for feedback from their customers. Most of the major genealogy companies such as Ancestry.com, Genes Reunited, Findmypast, MyHeritage and Geni are now on Twitter, as well as many local and national archives including The National Archives and the British Library. Genealogical organisations such as the Society of Genealogists, the Guild of One-Name Studies and some family history societies are now using Twitter, both to communicate with their members and also to reach out to prospective members. The DNA community is particularly active on Twitter. Most of the major testing companies have Twitter accounts along with many of the key bloggers, writers and journalists in the field of personal genomics.

Family historians and genetic genealogists are increasingly using Twitter at conferences, with attendees tweeting from their mobile phones and providing instant updates and commentary on the speakers' talks. To keep all the related conference tweets together, the conference tweeters agree on a 'hashtag', which is a simple way of labelling tweets. A suitable abbreviation for the conference is used, prefaced by the hashtag symbol #. For example, tweets from the Family History Expo in Atlanta, Georgia, in November 2009 used the hashtag '#fhexpo'. A simple search on Twitter for '#fhexpo' then returns all the tweets from the conference.

To get started on Twitter you will need to set up a free account, choose a username and create a profile page. Tweets can either be public or 'protected'. If you choose to protect your tweets they will only be visible to your followers. Twitter works best as a public forum and very few people choose to protect their tweets. If you use Hotmail, Googlemail, Yahoo or LinkedIn you can connect your account and see which of your contacts are already on Twitter. However, the easiest way to find people from the family history world is to use one of the Twitter directories. The most comprehensive directory is probably WeFollow. A search on the keyword 'genealogy' for instance, returns a list of several hundred people who have entered their name in the directory. The list can be sorted either by the number of followers or ranked in order of their influence. Other directories that might be of use include Twitr, Twellow and Listorious. Another good way to find people is to look at the followers' lists of other people who share your interests, or to search the genealogy-specific lists created by other users. Once you have started to follow a few people Twitter will provide you with a list of suggestions of other people to follow using special algorithms to find appropriate matches.

Direct message Often abbreviated to DM. A private tweet between two Twitter users. DMs can only be sent to your followers

Follow To subscribe to the tweets of other Twitter users

Follow Friday Often abbreviated to FF. A Twitter convention whereby users recommend to their followers the people, companies or organisations who post the most interesting tweets. The recommendations are usually, though not always, posted on a Friday

Follower Someone who follows your tweets

Geneatweep A genealogist who uses Twitter

Hashtag The hashtag symbol '#' is a method of tagging tweets by keyword. The keyword is prefaced by the hashtag for ease of searching, e.g. #genealogy or #WDYTYA. Hashtags are often used when several people are tweeting from one event so that all the related tweets can be viewed together

Retweet often abbreviated to RT. A tweet which is forwarded by another user to his or her followers

Tweep A Twitter user, also know as a tweeter or twitterer

Tweet A message posted on Twitter containing a maximum of 140 characters

Twitterverse The world of Twitter

Unfollow To stop following another Twitter user

Table 12   Twitterspeak

Twitter starts to become much more meaningful when you engage with the medium by responding to other people's tweets, sending out your own tweets and building up your own collection of followers. Once people see that you are providing interesting and informative tweets they will be much more likely to follow you. It can seem a little bewildering at first but as you acquire more followers and begin to interact with other tweeters it will all make a lot more sense. You will know that you have arrived when people start to 'retweet' your posts by forwarding them to their own followers, or if they 'mention' you by name in one of their own tweets! If you see interesting tweets from other users you might also like to return the favour by retweeting their posts. It is always courteous too to take the time to thank people for any retweets and mentions.

It can be quite an art writing a message with just 140 characters, but it becomes easier with practice. It is important to focus on the keywords that will get your tweets noticed by your followers. URLs can often take up a large number of characters, but are now automatically truncated when included in a tweet. As an alternative you can use a free URL shortener such as Tinyurl or Bit.ly to give you more space for your message. Many websites and blogs now provide a Twitter button which allows you to post a message to Twitter direct from the website, and the links will often be shortened for you. The timing and frequency of tweets also need to be taken into consideration. If you tweet too often or tweet about too many mundane subjects you will start to lose followers. It is also difficult to build up a following if you rarely tweet. If you tweet in the morning UK time, your American followers will still be in bed and might miss your tweets altogether. In some cases you might, therefore, want to repeat your tweets later in the day.

Twitter is less useful as a people-finding tool, and most Twitter users will probably already be found on other social networking websites such as Facebook or LinkedIn. There is also no easy way to contact people on Twitter. Twitter has a facility for sending direct messages to other users, but a message can only be sent if the person is already following you. Direct messages are also restricted to 140 characters. You can try replying to a person's tweet, but if someone does not receive email notifications of their 'mentions', or has a large number of followers, your reply will probably not be noticed.

Twitter is a very fast-moving site and if you follow a lot of people it can sometimes be difficult to pick out the interesting tweets. One solution is to organise the people you follow into lists such as 'genealogy favourites' or 'genomics' so that the people you follow are filtered by topic. There are also numerous free third-party applications that have been developed that will help you to manage your followers and the people you follow. A directory of Twitter tools is maintained on the Oneforty.com website. The site also has a variety of other apps for every conceivable situation, such as sharing multimedia on Twitter, archiving your tweets and using Twitter on your mobile phone.

Twitter provides its own search engine, but the results are organised chronologically and tweets that are more than about a week old will not show up in their search results. It can, therefore, be very difficult to locate an old tweet or to do a search for all references on Twitter to a particular keyword, such as a surname. Google are in the process of indexing all public tweets right back to the very first tweet on 21 March 2006, but at the time of writing only tweets dating back to February 2010 appear in Google search results. Microsoft are beta-testing a social search at **www.bing.com/social**, which will return hits on all public status updates on both Twitter and Facebook, but it is better for picking up recent tweets. The most useful Twitter search facility is currently provided by Topsy, **http://topsy.com/tweets**. In the Topsy 'advanced menu', tweets can be searched by date and by Twitter username. The US Library of Congress announced in April 2010 that they would preserve all public tweets, but it is not clear if the archive will ever be publicly searchable online.

Twitter probably has the steepest learning curve of all the social networking sites, but it is a valuable communication tool and is well worth the investment of time, though it might not be to everyone's taste.

Links
http://blog.twitter.com The Twitter blog
http://twitpic.com Twitpic photo sharing
http://twitter.pbworks.com The Twitter fan wiki

http://mashable.com/guidebook/twitter Twitter guide from Mashable
http://mashable.com/social-media/twitter News on Twitter from Mashable
http://oneforty.com A directory of Twitter tools and apps
http://techcrunch.com/tag/twitter News on Twitter from Techcrunch
www.socialbakers.com/twitter Twitter statistics
www.youtube.com/watch?v=LJr8uAqQCBM& What is Twitter for? (a bit of fun!)

Twitter directories
http://listorious.com
http://twitr.org
www.twellow.com
http://wefollow.com

Twitter search engines
www.bing.com/social
http://topsy.com/tweets

Link shorteners
http://bit.ly
http://goo.gl
http://tinyurl.com

LinkedIn

LinkedIn, **www.linkedin.com**, is a business-oriented social networking site which is mainly used by professional people to network and find jobs. It was launched in 2003 and has grown slowly but steadily in the intervening years. It is now the largest professional networking site in the world with over 100 million members, though over half of its members are in the United States. By June 2010, 4 million people in the UK had signed up to the service. For genealogy purposes the site can sometimes be useful to find living people if searches using conventional resources and Facebook have failed. It is free to set up a basic LinkedIn account. Advanced features are available for a fee but these will primarily be of interest to business users and employment agencies. Once you have registered with the site you can set up a basic profile page with details of your work experience. You can add your friends and colleagues to your list of contacts, join groups and follow companies. It is not a site you will need to visit on a frequent basis but is a useful resource to keep in mind.

Other social networking sites

There are, of course, many other online social networking websites, all of which operate in a similar way to Facebook and LinkedIn, but these tend to attract different users and will be of less relevance to family historians. MySpace, **www.myspace.com**, founded in 2003, was one of the earliest social networking websites and was used in particular by aspiring musicians and their fans. Bebo, **www.bebo.com**, was at one time especially popular with teenage girls. Users of both sites have gradually migrated to Facebook in the last few years. There are numerous other sites around the world. Some countries have their own favoured social networking websites, and there are a number of networks devoted to special interests and hobbies.

Google has had two failed attempts to enter the social networking scene with Google Wave and Google Buzz, both of which have now been retired. Google's third attempt, Google+, **http://plus.google.com**, was introduced in July 2011, and looks like it might prove to be more successful. The service was still in beta-testing at the time of writing and was being made available on an invitation–only basis, but has already attracted a loyal and enthusiastic user base. Each person was given up to 500 invites and the network acquired around 18 million users in its first two weeks. Google+ is rather like a cross between Facebook, Twitter and LinkedIn. Contacts are organised in circles. Although both Facebook and Twitter allow you to organise friends and contacts in lists, Google actively prompts you to categorise your contacts when you add them to your network. Google+ also features a useful new facility known as 'hangouts', which allow small groups of people to share a video chat. Genealogists were amongst the early adopters on Google+, but the majority of genealogists using the network in the early weeks were prominent bloggers and those who were already on Twitter. Amongst early Google+ users as a whole, there was also a marked gender imbalance with significantly higher proportions of men using the network. Most family historians seem to have little desire to move from Facebook to another service or to duplicate their social networking activities on two different websites. It therefore remains to be seen how Google+ will develop and how the other social networking websites respond and adapt to this new challenge, but it is certainly one to watch for the future.

Links

http://en.wikipedia.org/wiki/List_of_social_networking_websites A list of social networking sites from Wikipedia

www.familysearch.org/techtips/category/learn-about/social-media FamilySearch Tech Tips website on social media

10

Blogs

A blog is a personal website that is frequently updated. Blogs – a contraction of the word weblog – evolved from online journals and diaries and slowly began to increase in popularity from 1999 onwards, when the first blog-hosting tools became available to make the process of writing a blog as easy as updating a Word document. Each new blog post is dated and the posts are generally presented in reverse chronological order. An archive is usually provided where you can search for older postings either in date order or by topic. Most blogs provide a facility for readers to interact with the writer by posting comments. There are now literally millions of blogs with thousands more being started every day. Most of the genealogy bloggers are in America but a growing number of family historians in the UK are beginning to discover the joys of blogging. There is an increasing trend for genealogical societies and commercial organisations to use blogs as an easy way to keep their members or customers updated with the latest news. Ancestry.com, Findmypast and Genes Reunited are amongst the companies which now produce blogs. The Society of Genealogists launched a new blog at the beginning of 2009 and no doubt other family history societies will follow their example in time.

With so many blogs available it can be a challenge to find the ones that are of inter-est. Google provides a dedicated blog search at **http://blogsearch.google.co.uk**, which is useful if you are looking for references to a particular surname, but not so helpful if you're looking for blogs on a particular topic. Searches for keywords such as 'genealogy' and 'family history' will, for instance, return over 1 million hits. Fortunately a number of websites now provide directories of genealogy blogs. The most useful of these is the Genealogy Blog Finder, which is a directory of over 1,600 genealogy blogs organised by topic – such as personal research, single surname, associations and societies – and specialist topics – such as genetic genealogy and photography. Geneabloggers, the self-proclaimed 'genealogy community's resource for blogging' also maintain a directory of blogs organised by category at **www. geneabloggers.com/genealogy-blogs-type**. All of these directories rely on the

Figure 37 The Genealogy Blog Finder from Genealogue.

blogger to submit the URL for his or her blog, and there are possibly many other undiscovered gems that are not listed. Many blogs provide 'blog rolls' – lists of the bloggers' own favourite blogs. These blog rolls can also be a useful way to discover other blogs of interest. I have provided a list at the end of this chapter of some blogs, which will be of general interest to UK readers (see Figure 39). A separate listing of DNA-related blogs can be found in Appendix A.

RSS feeds

As blogs are updated frequently but irregularly it would be very time-consuming to keep visiting each blog on a daily basis to see if any new posts have been added. Fortunately, there are now a number of easier ways to keep up with your blog reading. The easiest solution is to use an online news reader (also known as an RSS reader or news aggregator) such as Google Reader (see Figure 38), or to use the RSS reader provided by some browsers. It is then a simple matter of subscribing to all your favourite blogs. Rather than checking each blog individually you simply log into the news reader on a regular basis to see which blogs have been updated, and you can click on the links in the reader to see the stories which are of interest. News readers can also be used on any website that provides an RSS feed, and provide a useful way of keeping up with pages that are frequently updated. RSS feeds can also be used

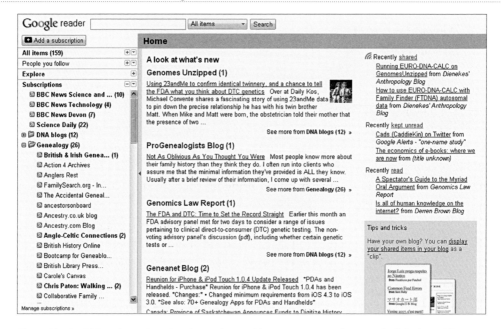

Figure 38   An RSS reader such as Google Reader provides an easy way to keep track of the latest blog postings. Simply subscribe to your favourite blogs and organise them into folders. You will then be able to see all the updates on one page.

to monitor updated blog postings for specific search terms, such as surnames which are of particular interest. Simply enter the search word into **http://blogsearch. google.co.uk** and then click on the RSS button at the bottom of the page. You will then be able to add the feed to your RSS reader. Alternatively, you can sign up for a Google Alert. Every time a new web page is published containing the search term you will receive an email with a brief extract from the webpage, or you can view the alerts in your RSS reader.

Some blogs provide an email subscription service by which new posts are automatically delivered to your inbox. Bulk emails can often get trapped as spam, and this is not always a reliable method to receive blog news. Even if you do subscribe by email it is still a good idea to maintain an RSS feed subscription to ensure you do not miss any important posts. Many bloggers now use Facebook and Twitter and will often post links to new blog posts for their Facebook friends and Twitter followers.

Writing your own blog

A blog is very easy to produce and is an effective way of creating an online presence, and it can be done completely free of charge. No special skills are required and anyone who can edit a Word document will have the necessary skills to edit a blog. A blog can easily be set up in half an hour, and then it is simply a question of writing your posts as and when you have the time. Once you have written the posts you click on the publish button and the page immediately goes live. If preferred, posts can be prepared in advance and scheduled to be published at a set time and date. Each blog post is created on a new web page, which is rapidly picked up by the various search engines. The more you write the more likely the search engines are to pick up your pages. If you make a mistake you can easily go back and correct it. Blogs usually provide an option for readers to leave comments and a blog can, therefore, often be a very interactive medium, bringing you into contact with researchers from around the world.

There are a number of companies that provide free blog hosting and storage. Easy-to-use software is provided to help you to create your blog, format the pages and upload pictures and videos. Templates are provided so that the design can be personalised. A variety of gadgets or applications can be added to give you extra functionality. There is usually an archive arranged in date order and a facility to categorise posts by user-generated labels, so that all posts on a particular subject can be viewed together.

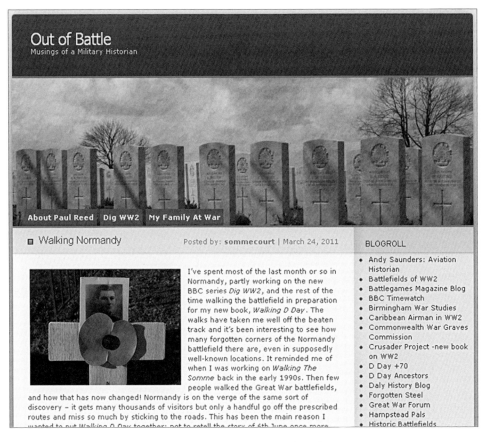

Figure 39 Out of Battle, the blog from the military historian Paul Reed.

Figure 40   Blogs can easily be created using one of the popular blogging services such as Google Blogger. The dashboard provides a range of easy-to-use tools, and writing a blog post is as easy as compiling a Word document.

Google's Blogger service is probably the most popular blogging service. It is very easy to use and ideal for beginners. WordPress and TypePad are popular with more experienced users who want a greater degree of customisation. Both WordPress and TypePad offer upgrades to a fee-paying premium service, which provides extra facilities such as a custom domain name and extra storage. There are a number of other providers listed at the end of this chapter.

A blog can be used to write up interesting stories and snippets that you discover in your family history research. Some bloggers focus on a single surname or a one-place study, while others will blog on topics of more general interest, such as general genealogy news, or provide specialist content on technical subjects such as photo restoration. Before you start it is always useful to have a look at other people's blogs to get some ideas about the design you prefer and the sort of content that you might like to produce.

I started writing my own blog back in January 2007. The blog is devoted to my one-name study of the very rare surname Cruwys and other variant spellings, which include Cruse and Crews. The blog is a very diverse collection of ramblings about my one-name study, with stories about some of the more colourful characters, transcriptions of letters and wills, photographs, postcards and other interesting documents. I sometimes digress and publish articles on DNA testing or visits to family history shows such as *Who Do You Think You Are? Live*. I tend to write as and when I have the time. Sometimes I will do several postings in one week, but if I am very busy I might not post anything for a month or so. I have found a blog to be a most effective way of communicating and reaching out to other researchers, and bringing in new contacts from all over the world. Often people will share their research with me and I can then publish their photos and stories on the blog as well.

To get your blog noticed you will need to ensure that it is listed in as many places as possible. The more pages that link to your blog the higher your blog will rise in the search engine rankings. Make sure you get your blog listed in all the blog directories noted below. Include the URL in your profile pages on the various social networking websites. If you post a message on a message board or mailing list you can include the URL in your signature. Many family history societies will have a page where members can promote their websites and blogs. Most blogging software will allow you to have a 'blog roll' of your favourite blogs. If you list some of your favourite blogs and your friends' blogs in your own blog roll you can then hope that they will return the favour and list yours.

Once you have a blog listed in all the available locations it is helpful to monitor the page views to give you an idea of the topics that your readers find of interest. It is also very encouraging to see the statistics so that you know that all your efforts are not in vain! Some of the blogging services provide basic statistics such as

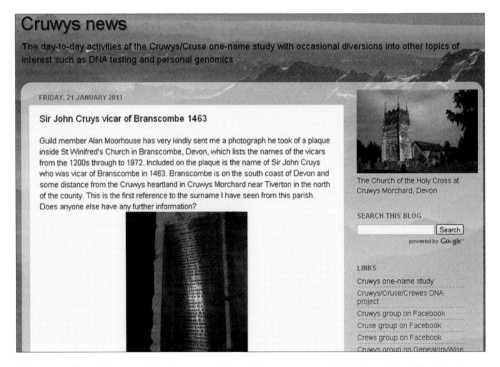

Figure 41   The author's own blog features articles on her one-name study with occasional diversions into the world of personal genomics.

the number of page views and the location of your visitors. It is, however, worth-while installing one of the free specialised utilities such as StatCounter or Google Analytics. These services will enable you to see not just the locations of your visitors but the referring link that led them to your blog. You can see the keywords that people use to reach your page, and which search engines and browsers they are using. It can also be quite exciting to see all the different countries that your visitors come from!

Blog directories

http://genealogy.alltop.com Alltop genealogy blog portal (mostly US)
www.cyndislist.com/blogs Cyndi's list blogs
http://blogfinder.genealogue.com Genealogy blog finder
www.geneabloggers.com/genealogy-blogs-type Geneabloggers
http://blogsearch.google.co.uk Google blog search
http://technorati.com/blogs/directory Technorati blog directory
http://hnn.us/blogs/entries/9665.html An extensive listing of history blogs from the History News Network

General genealogy blogs

http://ancestryinsider.blogspot.com Ancestry.com insider
http://anglo-celtic-connections.blogspot.com Anglo-Celtic connections
www.unlockthepast.com.au/australian-genealogy-history-blogs Australian genealogy blogs
http://blog.eogn.com Dick Eastman's blog
www.geneabloggers.com Geneabloggers
www.geneapress.com Genealogy press releases
http://growyourownfamilytree.wordpress.com Grow your own family tree
http://socialmediagen.com Carole Riley's social media and genealogy blog
http://scottishancestry.blogspot.com Scottish GENES (Genealogy News and Events)
http://wanderinggenealogist.wordpress.com Wandering Genealogist

Commercial and society blogs

http://blog.1911census.co.uk 1911 census blog
http://blogs.ancestry.com/uk Ancestry.co.uk
http://blogs.ancestry.com/ancestry Ancestry.com
www.familysearch.org/blog FamilySearch blog
http://blog.findmypast.co.uk Findmypast
http://genealogyblog.geneanet.org Geneanet
http://blog.genesreunited.co.uk Genes Reunited
http://blog.myheritage.com MyHeritage

http://labs.nationalarchives.gov.uk/wordpress The National Archives' labs blog

http://scotlandspeoplecentre.blogspot.com Scotland's People

www.societyofgenealogists.com Society of Genealogists

History

www.battleofbritainbeacon.org/pilots-blog Battle of Britain pilot's blog

www.bbchistorymagazine.com/blogs *BBC History Magazine* blogs

http://catsmeatshop.blogspot.com A miscellany of Victoriana from Lee Jackson

www.earlymodernwomen.blogspot.com Women in medieval and early modern history

www.georgianlondon.com Georgian London

www.thehistoryblog.com History blog

http://kithandkinresearch.posterous.com Luke Mouland's genealogy and history blog

http://medievalnews.blogspot.com Medieval news

www.medievalists.net Medievalists.net

www.pepysdiary.com Diary of Samuel Pepys

http://sommecourt.wordpress.com The musings of military historian Paul Reed

http://victoriandiary.blogspot.com Victorian diary

http://vichist.blogspot.com Victorian history

http://thevictorianist.blogspot.com The Victorianist

http://virtualvictorian.blogspot.com The Virtual Victorian

http://wwar1.blogspot.com First World War letters from an English soldier

http://womanlondonblitz.blogspot.com Second World War London Blitz diary 1939–45

http://worldwarone.wordpress.com Great War heroes' weblog

http://worldwar2daybyday.blogspot.com Second World War day by day

News readers

www.google.com/reader

www.google.com/alerts (Email alerts)

www.blogbridge.com

www.feedreader.com

www.netvibes.com

Blog hosting

www.blogger.com

www.livejournal.com

http://posterous.com

www.squarespace.com
www.tumblr.com
www.typepad.com
http://wordpress.org
www.xanga.com

Counters
www.google.com/analytics
http://statcounter.com

11

Wikis

A wiki is an easy-to-use collaborative community website that can be edited by anyone from a web browser on a home computer without the need to learn any specialist computer code or language. Wiki pages can be edited as easily as a Word document and updated instantaneously with a few quick clicks of the mouse. The first ever wiki, the Wikiwikiweb, a website about software development, was launched in March 1995 by Ward Cunningham, an American computer programmer. The website derived its name from the Wiki Wiki Shuttle, a bus service that links the airport terminals in Honolulu, Hawaii. *Wiki* is the Hawaiian word for quick, but it has now entered the English language as a general term for collaborative websites that use specialist wiki software. It was really only in the early years of the new millennium that wikis began to enter the public consciousness, largely due to the popularity of Wikipedia, the online encyclopaedia, which will be familiar to all internet users.

Specialist wiki software typically uses a WYSIWYG (what you see is what you get) interface to make the editing as easy as possible. There are many different types of wiki software available with different levels of functionality, but the important feature of most wikis is the ability to see the edit history of each page and to revert to previous versions as and when necessary. The entire history of an article is, therefore, preserved, no content is ever lost and mistakes can easily be rectified. Even if a page is deleted it can still be restored. Each wiki page will also have an associated talk page where issues relating to the article can be discussed. The other important feature of a wiki is that pages will typically have a large number of clickable 'wikilinks' to related pages of interest within the wiki.

Wikis are usually owned by a community rather than an individual. Personal websites come and go, and if the owner loses interest or the domain name registration expires the website, along with all its valuable content, will often disappear completely. Content submitted to a collaborative website is much more likely to be preserved in the long term as there will always be people within the community who are prepared to continue the work. However, as wikis are collaborative by nature no one person can claim ownership of an article, and anyone can change a page at any time. Although this might sound like a recipe for anarchy, there are a number of controls in place to ensure that standards are maintained. Wikis will usually have a team of trusted administrators who can perform special functions such as patrolling changes to recent pages, blocking vandals and spammers, protecting important or sensitive pages and restoring pages that have been accidentally deleted.

Wikis can simply be used as a source of information, but because they are so easy to edit I would encourage everyone to have a go at editing a wiki. We all have our own areas of expertise, and the more people who edit wikis and share their knowledge the more valuable the resources become. Some wikis allow pages to be edited anonymously by anyone who visits the website. Most wikis will require the user to create an account. There are also some wikis that are restricted to the members of a particular community or society. If you register to use a wiki you will need to choose a username, which will be associated with all your wiki edits. Usernames can either be a nickname or your real name. You are given a user page where you can provide information about yourself and your specialist interests on the wiki. Each user page also has an associated talk page where other wiki users can communicate with you. You can set up a 'watchlist' so that you can monitor pages that are of particular interest to you. Rather than checking each page individually, you will simply need to look at your watchlist every now and then to see if changes have been made by other editors to any of the pages you are watching. With some wikis it is possible to receive email notifications when edits have been made to pages on your watchlist.

If you have never edited a wiki before it is a good idea to experiment with a few minor edits before trying anything more ambitious. Most wikis will have an area known as a 'sandbox', an experimental area where new users can play around without changing the content of the main wiki. Once you have made an edit you can preview the page to check if your edits have come out as envisaged. You will need to write a brief summary of the edits you have done (for example, 'correcting spelling', 'adding a link'), then click on save, and the new page will be published instantaneously. If you make a mistake you can immediately go back and edit the page again. There are just a few basic formatting instructions that will need to be learned, such as the use of double square brackets to create wikilinks, but these are very easy to pick up. Some wikis provide a 'rich text editor', which has formatting tools similar to those used in Word, and even makes the more complicated formatting for features such as tables very easy to do. The important point to bear in mind about a wiki is that it is a work in progress. No page by definition will ever be finished. If you see something that needs correcting or a page that needs creating it is better to be bold and go ahead and make the edits. Over time other editors will come along and expand on your work. The more you edit the more you will learn.

Wikipedia

The wiki that every internet user will have encountered at some time or another is Wikipedia, which is now the largest encyclopaedia in the world and the most popular reference work on the internet with versions available in almost 300 different languages. The English language Wikipedia was first launched in 2001, and by 2003 it had grown to include 100,000 articles. It passed the 1 million mark in 2006 and had 3 million articles by August 2009.

The very open nature of Wikipedia is both its greatest strength and its greatest weakness. Pages can be edited by everyone and the edits of a schoolchild are just as acceptable as those of a university professor. Pages can sometimes be prone to vandalism and it can be difficult to reach a consensus on controversial topics. Inaccurate information can often go unchecked for some time and it has even been known for celebrities to find a premature announcement of their death! Despite its faults, Wikipedia is, nevertheless, an increasingly valuable resource with articles on a huge range of subjects. A Wikipedia page will often provide a good introduction to a topic with links to sources for further reading. For the family historian Wikipedia is a particularly useful reference for articles on places. There are pages on most of the villages, towns and cities in all major English-speaking countries, often with photographs. Some pages can be very detailed whereas newer pages will only have minimal content.

Wikipedia also has a range of genealogy articles, which are best accessed from the genealogy portal **http://en.wikipedia.org/wiki/Portal:Genealogy** (see Figure 42). There are articles on noble and notable families of all nationalities, as well as pages on genealogists, genealogy websites, relationships, family history software, haplogroups and many other subjects. If you want to check who has featured on *Who Do You Think You Are?* you will find full details of the participants in every series, including all the overseas editions. There is a huge category dedicated to surnames from around the world. The surname pages do not tend to contain much in the way of surname history but often include lists of notable people with the surname. There are articles on scutage, fee simple and escheat, and all the other archaic terminology associated with the feudal system, which you will often encounter when transcribing old documents. There are also detailed articles on most aspects of property and marriage law, such as the prohibited degrees of kinship, cousin marriage and the Married Women's Property Act. These articles do not come under the umbrella of the genealogy portal but pages on any such specialist terminology can easily be found by means of a general keyword search.

Care needs to be taken when using any Wikipedia article as the quality and accuracy can vary enormously. Some Wikipedia articles do undergo a peer review process by the community. The best articles, known as featured articles, are showcased on the Wikipedia home page and undergo a rigorous review process to achieve this status.

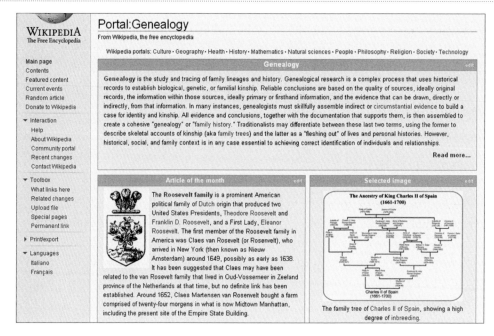

Figure 42   The Wikipedia Genealogy Portal.

Featured articles can be identified by the appearance of a small bronze star in the top right-hand corner. Good articles, identified by a small green cross, undergo a less rigorous review process but have to meet the strict 'good article criteria' agreed by the community. However, only a tiny percentage of Wikipedia articles qualify for good or featured article status. For other articles it is a question of exerting your personal judgement. The better articles will have a long list of references, which will enable you to go back to the original source and verify the content. It is also worth checking the article's talk page to see if other readers have raised any particular concerns.

As well as using Wikipedia for a reference, family historians should also consider contributing content to the encyclopaedia. If you have a good knowledge of a particular location, or an important historical figure who appears in your family history, you will no doubt have material that you could contribute. Wikipedia has a constantly evolving range of policies developed by the community to ensure that standards are maintained and that the content is encyclopaedic in nature. The principal requirement for a Wikipedia page is that the subject must be 'notable'. Notability is defined by coverage in multiple, reliable secondary sources. Original research is not permitted and the use of primary sources, such as unpublished manuscripts, parish registers and censuses, is discouraged. If you have an ancestor who has had an obituary published in a national newspaper or who is mentioned in a history book, then he will probably qualify for a Wikipedia entry. If you have an ancestor whose exploits, however heroic, are only recorded in unpublished documents at The National Archives, then he will not be eligible for a Wikipedia page. Wherever possible, and especially if creating a new page, you should provide sources. Places are by default considered notable, so if you find that your ancestral village does not have a Wikipedia page you might like to start one and perhaps even contribute a few photos. If you are researching a particular surname you might like to expand the existing page or create a new page if one does not already exist.

Genealogy wikis

Genealogy wikis began to appear from 2004 onwards but have only really taken off in the last couple of years. The majority of genealogy wikis use the same Mediawiki software that is used by Wikipedia. Anyone who is familiar with editing Wikipedia articles will, therefore, easily be able to edit any of these wikis. Nearly all the genealogy wikis require the editor to set up a user account. For some wikis run by specialist societies or research groups editing is restricted to members. Nearly all the genealogy wikis make their content publicly visible, but some wikis restrict access to members only.

Typically a large organisation or commercial company will install the wiki software on its own servers. The settings can then be customised as required and extensions can be added to provide extra features. However, specialist expertise is required to install and maintain wiki software, and such a task is probably beyond the capabilities of the average family historian. Fortunately, there are a number of companies that provide a free web hosting service for wikis on what is known as a 'wiki farm'. The wiki farm will install the wiki software on its own servers and then make space available for individuals and small societies to set up their own wikis. A wiki farm can often host hundreds if not thousands of individual wikis. Wiki farms are typically funded by advertising or by subscription. Fees are usually payable to have an advertising-free site or to add on extra storage. Popular wiki farms include Wikia, Wikispaces and PBWorks.

Genealogy wikis can be broadly divided into three main types:

1 Knowledge base wikis
Knowledge base wikis provide guidance on family history topics, or advice on records contained within collections held by large repositories. Many of these wikis have been set up by large institutions or organisations such as The National Archives or the Church of the Latter-Day Saints, and will often have paid staff members contributing content and acting as administrators. The main genealogy wikis tend to be of a more practical nature than Wikipedia. They cover topics that would not qualify for inclusion in Wikipedia, and often provide useful 'how to' articles, which are sometimes accompanied by screenshots or videos. Wikis provided by repositories such as The National Archives allow users to share their knowledge of the records and provide a space for researchers to publish transcriptions of wills and other documents.

GenWiki, **http://wiki-en.genealogy.net**
GenWiki was probably the first genealogy wiki to be established. It provides a genea-logical resource for researchers in German-speaking areas of the world, and is now available in English, German and Dutch. The German version was launched in 2003 and the English language version was set up in October 2004. Genwiki is run by the German genealogy organisation Genealogy.net and is maintained by their Society for Computer Genealogy.

The Encyclopedia of Genealogy, **www.eogen.com**
Dick Eastman launched the Encyclopedia of Genealogy in December 2004 as a sup-plement to his popular Eastman Online Genealogy Newsletter, **http://blog.eogn. com**. This was the first genealogy encyclopaedia to be established using wiki software. The basic shell of the encyclopaedia was created by Dick, and his newsletter readers were encouraged to add more content. Most of the entries are very short and there are no more than a few hundred articles. Although an innovative concept at the time, the encyclopaedia has largely been superseded by other resources and in particular by the success of Wikipedia, where much more detailed explanations of the many legal and technical terms used in genealogy can be found. The Antiquus Morbus website, **www.antiquusmorbus.com**, now provides much fuller coverage of archaic medi-cal terms. The Encyclopedia of Genealogy is, however, still a particularly useful resource for foreign language genealogical terms. I learnt, for instance, that *bestefar* is the Norwegian word for grandfather, and *oomzegger* is the Dutch word for nephew! The encyclopaedia also provides explanations for a number of obscure American abbreviations, for example, CDIB (Certified Degree of Indian Blood), which might occasionally crop up during the course of your research.

GeneaWiki, **www.geneawiki.com**
GeneaWiki is a genealogy encyclopaedia provided by the French genealogy web-site Geneanet. It is available in five languages – English, French, Spanish, Dutch and Swedish. The French language GeneaWiki was founded in June 2005 and is by far and away the largest with over 50,000 articles. The English language version is the second largest with 449 articles. GeneaWiki has particularly good content on genea-logical software and tools.

Jewish Genealogy Wiki, **www.jgene.org/wiki**
The Jewish Genealogy Wiki was established in 2006, but does not appear to have been updated for some time. The pages mostly consist of lists of external links.

Your Archives, **http://yourarchives.nationalarchives.gov.uk**
Your Archives is a wiki developed by The National Archives. It was launched in April 2007 and was the first wiki established by a large repository. By the end of 2010 the

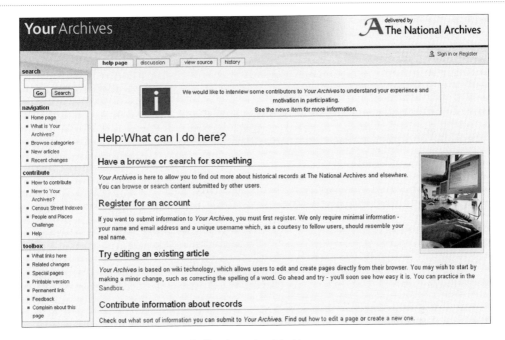

Figure 43   Your Archives, a wiki provided by The National Archives.

wiki had almost 200,000 pages in various stages of development. There are a number of useful research guides on a diverse range of subjects, such as transportation to Australia, dissolution of the monasteries and immigrants. There is a growing collection of will transcriptions provided by users, most of which are from the Prerogative Court of Canterbury wills in the Documents Online collection. One of the most useful features is the Historical Streets Project, which provides street indexes to the England and Wales censuses. Users are also encouraged to submit their own stories of places, streets, buildings, businesses and institutions.

FamilySearch Research Wiki, **http://wiki.familysearch.org**
FamilySearch – the genealogy service provided by the Church of Jesus Christ of Latter-Day Saints – launched its Research Wiki in July 2008. By the end of 2010 the wiki had over 45,000 articles, most of which were devoted to locations around the world and 'how to' articles on the practicalities of research. There are pages for most countries of the world and for most places in the UK. The content is good for some American states and some countries such as the Netherlands, but the UK content is still very sparse, though it will no doubt increase over time.

Ancestry.com Wiki, **www.ancestry.com/wiki**
Ancestry.com launched their wiki at the end of April 2010. Two key books, published by Ancestry.com in America, were used as the foundation of the wiki: *The Source: A Guidebook to American Genealogy* and the *Red Book: American State, County, and Town*

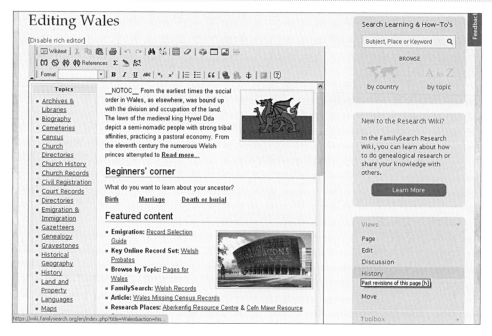

Figure 44 Editing the page on Wales in the FamilySearch wiki using the rich text editor.

Sources. Further pages are being added on a variety of topics such as censuses, archives and societies, but at the time of writing the content is virtually all related to America and American records. The World Archives Wiki, **www.ancestry.com/wiki/index. php?title=Ancestry_World_Archives_Project**, is a companion wiki, which provides instructions for transcribers involved with the World Archives Project.

ISOGG Wiki, **www.isogg.org/wiki**

This wiki, provided by the International Society of Genetic Genealogy, is a central resource for information and advice on DNA testing. I have to declare a particular interest in the ISOGG Wiki as I worked with Tom Hutchison, an ISOGG colleague in America, to set it up in July 2010, and we have since been joined by a small team of active editors. It has proved to be a very successful transatlantic collaboration.

Our Archives, **www.ourarchives.wikispaces.net**

Our Archives is a wiki set up by the U.S. National Archives and Records Administration (NARA) as a place for researchers, genealogists and NARA staff to share information and knowledge about the records of The National Archives and about their research. The Wiki was launched in July 2010.

In addition to the mainstream knowledge base genealogy wikis there are a number of specialist wikis provided by societies and user groups for the benefit of their members and users. The Guild of One-Name Studies was one of the first genealogical societies to set up its own wiki. It was established in 2006 and has now grown to be a valuable resource for Guild members on all aspects of one-name studies. Access to the Guild wiki is currently restricted to members.

The Families in British India Society (FIBIS) has a very successful public wiki, which can be found at **www.wiki.fibis.org**. The FIBIS wiki was started in 2007 and has grown to be an invaluable resource for anyone with ancestors who lived in British India. The Buckinghamshire Family History Society's public wiki was also set up in 2007 and can be accessed from their home page, at **www.bucksfhs.org.uk**. For anyone with Buckinghamshire interests the pages on Buckinghamshire postcards and photographers will be particularly useful.

There are also a number of dedicated wikis for users of family history software programs, such as the Family Historian Users' Group Knowledge Base, **www.fhug.org.uk/wiki/doku.php**; the Gramps wiki, **http://gramps-project.org/wiki**; the Next Generation wiki, **www.tng.lythgoes.net/wiki**; and the PhpGedView wiki, **http://wiki.phpgedview.net/en/index.php**.

2 Family tree wikis

Family tree wikis provide a collaborative facility to work on pages for shared ancestors. The ultimate dream would be to have one giant family history wiki with a page for every person who has ever lived, regardless of their notability. Rather than lots of individual researchers working alone on their own family trees, everyone would collaborate on a global family tree and all the known facts about any given person would all be easily located on one page. The idea of a global family tree wiki was discussed back in 2003 at Meta-wiki, the community site for Wikimedia Foundation projects, the organisation behind Wikipedia. The proposed project is currently named Wikipeople but discussions have been dormant since 2006. The project can be found at **http://meta.wikimedia.org/wiki/Wikipeople**. In the meantime, rather than one large wiki, several different wikis have been set up, all of which offer very similar services but with different functionality and emphases. Some wikis allow users to upload GEDCOM files. This results in large numbers of pages, often with minimal content, and lots of duplicate entries. Other wikis require pages to be created manually, either using a ready-made template or by writing a narrative Wikipedia-style article. The family tree wikis have not attracted anywhere near the number of users as the popular family tree-building websites such as Genes Reunited, Ancestry, Geni and MyHeritage. The dream of a single global family tree wiki is, therefore, a long way from reality.

Familypedia, **http://familypedia.wikia.com**

Familypedia was the first family tree wiki to be launched, with the first page appearing on the last day of December 2004. The site's original mission was to collect genealogies from the Muslim world, but it has since grown in scope and now has a broad spectrum of international articles. By the end of 2010 there were over 85,000 articles focusing mostly on people and surnames, with articles in a variety of different languages though mostly in English. There are a number of special projects dedicated to recording the genealogies of notable historical people, such as British monarchs, presidents of the United States, the descendants of Charlemagne and hereditary rulers of the Netherlands. However, most of the people pages have minimal content, and even the most well-written and complete articles are lacking in sources. The surname articles are mostly stubs, with little if any content other than links to other articles on the wiki on people with the surname in question. Users are required to use the site's own special templates to create new pages, which can look somewhat messy, especially if all the details have not been filled in. The site is hosted by Wikia, which is funded by advertising. The ads are very intrusive and make it difficult to navigate the articles.

Rodovid, **http://en.rodovid.org/wk**

Founded in September 2005, Rodovid is maintained by a team of administrators in the Ukraine. The name Rodovid comes from the Ukrainian word *rodovid*, which means lineage or genealogy. The wiki is available in a number of different languages. The Russian version has the most pages, followed by the English and French language versions. Data entry is done in a standardised fashion on ready-made templates. Most of the pages only have sketchy content with basic birth, marriage and death details, and charts showing the nearest relations from grandparents to grandchildren. Very few articles contain much in the way of sources.

WeRelate, **www.werelate.org/wiki**

WeRelate was launched in the spring of 2006 and now claims to be the world's largest genealogy wiki. By March 2011 WeRelate had wiki pages for over 2 million people. WeRelate is sponsored by the Foundation for On-Line Genealogy, a non-profit-making corporation in Utah, in partnership with the Allen County Public Library in Fort Wayne, Indiana. As one might expect from an American website, the majority of users are from the US and the pages are mostly devoted to American genealogies. WeRelate encourages users to upload GEDCOM files. Each person in the GEDCOM file is allocated a new page on the wiki. During the upload process if any of the people in your database have an existing WeRelate page you will be given the option to match that page and merge your data. The site has a number of dedicated volunteers who work hard to minimise the problem of duplication. The best articles are featured on the home page and these tend to be reasonably lengthy and well sourced. The majority of articles seem to be quite sketchy and only contain very basic life dates and census details where available.

Figure 45   The WeRelate wiki, a free service from the Allen County Public Library in Fort Wayne, Indiana.

Biographical Wiki, **www.biographicalwiki.com**

Established in February 2007, this wiki is hosted by a company in Utah by the name of Genealogical Enterprises. The wiki focuses on quality rather than quantity. By October 2010 it had only around 500 entries, but all of the pages have a lot of good content and a list of sources is provided for each article. The layout is simple and effective with a standard 'infobox' for the basic biographical information and a Wikipedia-style article as a biography. The biographies are nearly all American or Canadian.

Wikitree, **www.wikitree.com**

Wikitree was started in 2008 by Chris Whitten, the creator of WikiAnswers, and is run by a company called Interesting.com, Inc., based in New York. The site is free to use and is funded entirely by advertising. Most of the wiki pages are interspersed with Google Ads but they are much less intrusive than the ads on the Familypedia website. Wikitree operates in a different way from most wikis as the vast majority of pages are private with each page having its own 'profile manager'. If you wish to edit a page 'owned' by another researcher you need to send a message to the owner and ask to be added to their 'trusted list'. Such a system mitigates against the collaborative editing process as a major contributor will want to be able to take credit for their own contributions rather than having them obscured under someone else's name. The site provides a facility to upload data from a GEDCOM file, and most of the pages

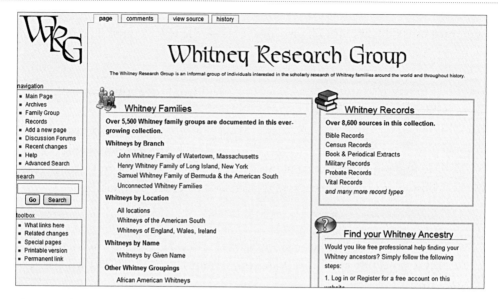

Figure 46   The Whitney Research Group wiki, an excellent example of the use of a wiki for a collaborative research project.

seem to have been started off in this way, which unfortunately does not make for very user-friendly reading. There is also currently no facility for GEDCOM export making it difficult to back-up your data externally or export it to other websites. As with many of the other family tree wikis, most of the contributors seem to be in the United States. The site has, however, grown steadily and by July 2011 Wikitree had over 32,600 registered 'Wikitreers' who had created around 2 million profiles.

3 Research group wikis

In addition to the large family tree wikis there are a small number of collaborative wikis set up by small groups of researchers. These wikis usually focus on the study of a single surname, or research into ancestors from a particular region.

Genealowiki, **www.genealowiki.com**
Genealowiki was set up by a team of Benedict researchers in North America in 2004, and was one of the earliest research group wikis. Their website is now home to a large collection of research into the Benedicts and a number of other associated surnames.

Whitney Research Group Wiki, **http://wiki.whitneygen.org/wrg**
The Whitney wiki provides an excellent demonstration of the possibilities of a collaborative group wiki. It was set up in the summer of 2006 and has built up a most impressive and well-organised collection of records. Family group records are provided for lineages from around the world. The site also hosts the group's archive collection, which consists of transcripts of family bibles, wills, newspaper articles and

numerous other documents. The group even uses the wiki to provide information about its DNA project and to publish the DNA results.

The Early North Carolina Phillips Families Wiki, **http://groupwiki.encphillips.com/wiki**
The Phillips wiki, run by a team of researchers in America, has also made effective use of the collaborative approach to investigate the many Phillips families from North Carolina in the early colonial period. The wiki went public in October 2010 and now hosts a growing collection of transcripts and family information.

Further reading and resources
www.ploscompbiol.org/article/info:doi/10.1371/journal.pcbi.1000941
   Ten simple rules for editing Wikipedia; written for scientists but has general application
www.cyndislist.com/wikis Wikis for genealogy on Cyndi's List
http://wikiindex.org The wiki directory of wikis
http://en.wikipedia.org/wiki/Comparison_of_wiki_farms Wikipedia page on wiki farms

12

Multimedia

The advent of the high-speed internet connection has brought a whole new dimension to family history research. Websites are no longer restricted to text and photos but are increasingly providing a wide range of rich multimedia content, such as videos and sound recordings, which can either be watched or listened to online, or downloaded on to a computer or portable media player such as an iPod. Along with the increasing availability of these resources, a number of new websites have been launched in recent years that make the process of finding, uploading and sharing photos and videos a straightforward process, which anyone can do from a home computer with an internet connection. Other new technologies covered in this chapter, such as webcasts and webinars, are still in their infancy but will become of increasing interest to family historians in the years to come.

Photo sharing

Many of the websites described in earlier chapters of this book, such as Facebook, Genes Reunited, Ancestry.com and Geni, provide the user with the ability to upload photos and videos to share with their friends and family. These websites will often have a range of settings so that access can be restricted to family members or fellow researchers or, if preferred, made publicly available on the internet. There are, however, a number of dedicated photo-sharing websites that provide an alternative option for sharing photos. It is much easier to share photos online rather than emailing photos to people individually or in group emails, which can often be very time-consuming and fraught with difficulties (such as bouncing emails and ISPs with limited upload and download limits). Once the photos are uploaded to the website of your choice it is simply a question of sharing the relevant link, or inviting people to join your photo group so that they can view your photos and download them as required. Most of the photo-sharing sites provide around 1 gigabyte of free storage, with a fee payable for additional storage space. Some have limits on the size of image that can be uploaded. Photo-sharing websites can also be good sources of photographs to illustrate your family history. You might well find photographs of your ancestral village or ancestral home readily available online. It will be necessary to check the copyright restrictions, and especially if you wish to publish the photographs. Some photographs are freely offered for reuse for non-commercial purposes under a licence such as the Creative Commons Licence. If the licensing details are not provided, you should always check with the owner.

Flickr, **www.flickr.com**

Flickr is the most popular and best-known photo-sharing website. Thousands of photographs are uploaded every minute and in September 2010 the site achieved the astonishing milestone of hosting 5 billion photographs. To get the best out of the website it is necessary first of all to create a free account. Flickr is owned by Yahoo, and if you already have a Yahoo account you can log in with your Yahoo ID. With a free account you can currently upload 100 megabytes of photos every month. Premium accounts are available for heavy users, institutions and commercial companies. Photos can be restricted either to friends or family or made public so that they can be viewed by anyone. Photos can be tagged by keyword so that they can easily be found by other users. Flickr accounts follow the standard social networking model. You get to choose a username and you are then given a profile page where you can provide as much or as little information as you feel is necessary. If you find photographs that you like you can add them to your favourites for easy retrieval. Comments and tags can be added to photographs uploaded by other users, though the ability to do so depends on their

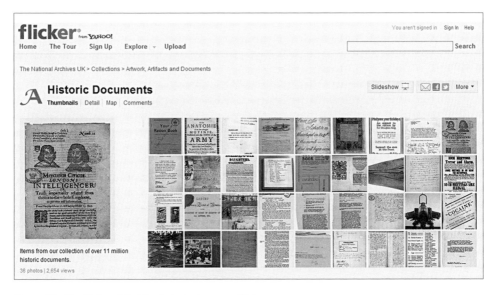

Figure 47 The National Archives' photostream on Flickr.

privacy settings. If you are interested in the work of a particular user or organisation you can add them as a contact so that you can follow their 'photostream'.

A number of public organisations, such as The National Archives, the Commonwealth War Graves Commission and the National Library of Scotland, have accounts with Flickr. Their photos can often be freely downloaded for non-commercial use provided that a suitable credit is provided. It is also possible to join a wide variety of specialist groups on Flickr covering a huge range of topics. Each group has its own discussion board where you can interact with other group members. There are groups photographing churches or villages in particular counties such as Devon and Durham. There are also many groups focusing on specific towns or villages.

Picasa Web Albums, **http://picasaweb.google.com**
A free photo-sharing website provided by Google, Picasa Web Albums operates in a similar way to Flickr. If you already have a Google account it can be integrated with your Picasa account. Users of Google's blogging service will find that any photos uploaded to their blog are automatically added to Picasa. These photos are unlisted on Picasa by default but can be made public if desired. In practice, once you have uploaded pictures on to a blog page these will be picked up anyway by image-searching engines such as Google Images. Picasa provides the facility to tag people in the photos and organise them into albums.

Other popular photo-sharing websites include Photobucket, **www.photobucket. com**, and Snapfish, **www.snapfish.com**. A comprehensive list of photo-sharing websites can be found on Wikipedia, at **http://en.wikipedia.org/wiki/List_of_ photo_sharing_websites**.

Photographic projects

The open and collaborative nature of the web has given rise to a number of volunteer photographic projects, with amateur and professional photographers alike contributing photographs for the public benefit. Some of these projects have a specific genealogical focus, whereas others are of a more general nature but are, nevertheless, useful resources for the family historian.

Geograph, **www.geograph.org.uk**
Geograph is probably the largest and most successful collaborative photographic project on the internet. The project was initiated in 2005 with the aim of collecting representative photographs and information for every square kilometre of Great Britain and Ireland. It has since grown to be a very valuable resource with photographs submitted by over 10,000 volunteer photographers. The 2 millionth photo

Figure 48   Geograph is an excellent resource for photographs to illustrate your family history research.

was uploaded in August 2010. The site now has excellent coverage of most of Great Britain. Ireland still has a long way to go, and is in the process of being split into a separate project at **www.geograph.ie**. Other Geograph projects have now been set up for Germany, **http://geo-en.hlipp.de**, and the Channel Islands, **http://channel-islands.geographs.org**.

Wikimedia Commons, **http://commons.wikimedia.org**
Wikimedia Commons is a sister site of Wikipedia and serves as a free media repository. It is a potentially useful resource if you are looking for photographs or videos for inclusion on a blog or website. Many of the images in Wikimedia Commons have been transferred from Geograph and Flickr under the Creative Commons Licence.

The Gravestone Photographic Resource, **www.gravestonephotos.com**
The aim of this ambitious project is to photograph gravestones from around the world. All the legible information is extracted, indexed and published online. Images are emailed on request free of charge to interested researchers. The project was founded in 1998 by family historian Charles Sale who initially indexed the gravestones in cemeteries in Norfolk and Suffolk near his home. The project has now expanded to cover the whole of the British Isles and many other countries, with particularly good coverage of Australia.

Teafor2, **http://teafor2.com**
This bizarrely named website is the American equivalent of the Gravestone Photographic Resource. It boasts a collection of over 200,000 photographs provided

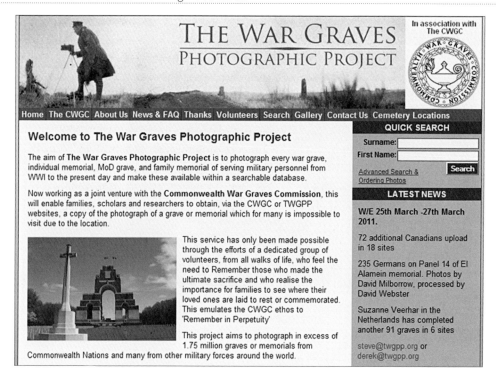

Figure 49   The War Graves Photographic Project is a collaborative project run in association with The Commonwealth War Graves Commission (CWGC).

by volunteers from numerous cemeteries across the country. The site was founded by family historian Allen Wheatley in 2002 and is hosted by RootsWeb.

The War Graves Photographic Project, **http://twgpp.org**
This project aims to 'photograph every war grave, individual memorial, MoD grave, and family memorial of serving military personnel from WWI to the present day and make these available within a searchable database'. The scope of the project was expanded in 2010, and submissions of images from pre-1914 from anywhere in the world are now also accepted. The project is run as a joint venture with the Commonwealth War Graves Commission, and relies entirely on volunteer help. The project is funded by levying a small charge for supplying photographs by email or post.

Videos

Roots Television, **www.rootstelevision.com**
Launched in 2006, Roots Television is now the home of hundreds of genealogy-related videos covering a wide range of subjects from photo restoration to DNA testing. Although a lot of the content is aimed at an American audience, there is still

much of interest to the British viewer, including a series of interviews from *Who Do You Think You Are? Live*, the big family history show held every year in London.

YouTube, **www.youtube.com**

The video-sharing website YouTube was set up in 2005 and is now, along with Google and Facebook, one of the most popular sites on the internet. Most of the videos are uploaded by individuals but an increasing number of genealogy companies are now setting up YouTube channels to promote their products and services. Videos uploaded by individuals must be no more than 15 minutes in duration. Videos can be viewed on YouTube free of charge without an account. If you set up a free account you will be able to bookmark your favourite videos and subscribe to your favourite channels. With a channel subscription you can opt to receive an email alert every time a new video is uploaded. If you create an account you also have the option to link it with other social networking sites such as Facebook and Twitter so that you can share your favourite videos with your friends and followers.

Genealogy channels on YouTube

www.youtube.com/user/AncestryCom Ancestry.com
www.youtube.com/user/britishlibrary British Library
www.youtube.com/user/fibiswebmaster Families in British India
www.youtube.com/user/familysearch FamilySearch
www.youtube.com/user/familytreemagazine Family Tree Magazine (US)

Figure 50   The FamilySearch channel on YouTube.

www.youtube.com/user/GenealogyGems Genealogy Gems
www.youtube.com/user/NationalArchives08 National Archives Channel
www.youtube.com/user/SoGGenealogist Society of Genealogists
www.youtube.com/user/usnationalarchives US National Archives Channel

YouTube Time Machine, **http://yttm.tv**
This is an enterprising website that allows the viewer to select a year and travel back in time to see a hand-picked selection of YouTube clips from that year. The first clip in the collection dates from 1860 and is the earliest known sound recording. Other delights are a pixellated 24-second clip of Queen Victoria's funeral in 1901, and some real footage of the *Titanic* in Belfast before her fateful maiden voyage. Users are encouraged to add their own videos to the collection.

British Pathé, **www.britishpathe.com**
Pathé is a wonderful archive collection of over 90,000 videos with newsreels, sports footage, social history documentaries, musical clips, comedy sketches and much more from 1896 to 1976. The clips can be viewed free of charge online. If you create an account you can create a page of your favourite video clips by saving them to your 'workspace' for future viewing.

Podcasts

A podcast, a short form of 'personal on-demand broadcast', is a pre-recorded digital audio file, which is made available on the internet. The podcast can either be listened to online or downloaded on to a home computer or a portable media player, such as an iPod, to be played at your own convenience. The term podcast strictly speaking refers to both audio and video files, but the term is more often used to refer to audio files. Podcasts with video content are generally referred to as video podcasts. To play a podcast on your computer you will need to install the appropriate media player, such as Real Player, Windows Media Player or iTunes, which are all freely available as downloads.

The first genealogy podcasts began to appear in 2005 in America. One of the best known and most enduring genealogy podcast series is 'The Genealogy Guys', presented by George G. Morgan and Drew Smith. A new podcast is uploaded around once or twice a month, and the show now has a large international audience. Each programme has a mixture of genealogy news and reviews combined with answers to questions submitted by listeners. The content is not just focused on the US. There is often coverage of new genealogy software, social networking websites and general computing tools that have an application in family history research.

In the UK The National Archives have led the way by providing an extensive and regularly updated podcast collection on their website, covering a diverse range of subjects such as apprenticeship records, transportation to Australia, manorial documents and DNA testing. There are even podcasts about the UFO and MI5 records held at The National Archives! A separate podcast series from The National Archives is dedicated to their 'Voices of the Armistice' collection.

BBC radio family history programmes such as 'Tracing your Roots' and 'Digging up your Roots' are made available as podcasts after transmission, but will need to be downloaded fairly promptly as they are only archived for a few weeks after the broadcast. The *BBC History Magazine* produces a monthly podcast covering a wide range of historical topics and periods from the Anglo-Saxons to the Second World War.

The American *Family Tree Magazine* has been running a free monthly podcast since June 2008 as a complement to their journal, though most of the content is of more interest to American researchers. No doubt the UK family history press will follow their example in due course.

There are two main ways to keep up with a regular podcast series. Firstly, you can subscribe to the podcast's RSS feed in your RSS reader (see Chapter 10). In this way, if you check your RSS reader on a regular basis you will be notified automatically

Figure 51   The iTunes store has a wide selection of genealogy podcasts, which can be downloaded onto a computer or played on an iPod.

of any new broadcasts. Alternatively, you can subscribe to a podcast series using specialist podcast software (known as a 'podcast client' or 'podcatcher') such as iTunes. iTunes is a free download and will work on both PCs and Macs. You can subscribe to a series manually or automatically, and then either listen to the programme on your computer or transfer it to your iPod. The major broadcasters, such as The National Archives and The Genealogy Guys, have all made their programmes available on iTunes. The iTunes Store, which is accessible through iTunes, also has a huge directory of over 100,000 free podcasts covering a wide variety of subjects, although only a small number will be of direct relevance to the family historian. The only caveat is that iTunes is a proprietary Apple format and any file downloaded on iTunes will probably not play on any portable media player other than an iPod or iPad.

In addition to the regular podcast series a variety of other podcasts can also be found. There are a number of podcast directories listed below, which can be searched for programmes of interest.

Genealogy and history podcasts

www.bbchistorymagazine.com/podcast-page *BBC History Magazine* podcasts

http://blog.eogn.com/eastmans_online_genealogy/podcasts Dick Eastman's podcasts

www.familytreemagazine.com/Info/Podcasts *Family Tree magazine* (US) podcasts

http://genealogyguys.com The Genealogy Guys

http://historicalpodcasts.blogspot.com Historical podcasts blog

www.nationalarchives.gov.uk/podcasts The National Archives podcast collection

www.nationalarchives.gov.uk/armistice 'Voices of the Armistice' podcasts

www.naa.gov.au/info/rss/podcasts.aspx The National Archives of Australia podcast service

Podcast directories

www.apple.com/itunes
www.bbc.co.uk/podcasts
www.cyndislist.com/podcasts
www.genealogytoday.com/audio
www.learnoutloud.com
www.podcastalley.com
www.podcastblaster.com/directory/
www.podcastdirectory.com

Webcasts

A webcast is a broadcast that is transmitted, or 'streamed', live over the internet. The first webcasts were radio shows but the word is now more often used to describe a video broadcast, also known as a videocast. A webcast can also be recorded so that it can be viewed on demand at any time after the event. A webcast is a one-way transmission and there is no opportunity for interaction with the presenters. Often, however, viewers will watch a webcast and provide their own commentary on Twitter or Facebook. As the costs of producing and hosting webcasts come down, we can increasingly expect to see webcasts used by genealogy companies and family history societies. A conference might only have the capacity for a few hundred people, but if a webcast is provided interested researchers from all over the world will be able to listen to the speeches as they are presented. You might, therefore, one day be able to watch the annual conference of your local family history society live on your computer from the comfort of your own home. The Association of Professional Genealogists in America has formed a trial partnership with FamilySearch to make webcasts of their conference presentations available online. The DNA testing company 23andMe has also pioneered the use of webcasts, and they provided video recordings on their website of the presentations made at their Policy Forum meeting in June 2010. Webcasts were also transmitted live during the first Rootstech conference in Salt Lake City, Utah, in February 2011. Selected webcasts from this conference have now been archived on the FamilySearch website.

Links
www.apgen.org/publications/pmc_webcast.html Webcasts from the US Association for Professional Genealogists
http://rootstech.familysearch.org/video.php Selected webcasts from the Rootstech 2011 conference in Salt Lake City, Utah
www.23andme.com/policyforum 23andMe Policy Forum
www.genome.gov/10001292 National Human Genome Research Institute's webcasts

Webinars

The somewhat clumsy name webinar is a contraction of 'web seminar': a presentation, lecture, workshop or seminar that is transmitted over the internet. A key feature of a webinar is its interactive elements, with the audience having the opportunity to provide feedback and ask questions. In the family history world the use of webinars has been pioneered by Ancestry.com. The American family history software program Legacy also hosts a number of general genealogy webinars on its website. In January

2011 the American genetic genealogist Elise Friedman began to broadcast regular webinars on the subject of DNA testing with a mixture of free and paid webinars. In February 2011 the American blogger and radio broadcaster Pat Richley, who is known by the name DearMYRTLE, set up a new blog called Geneawebinars, which provides a central resource to notify genealogists of forthcoming webinars and provides some useful instructions on how to use the new technology. Unfortunately for family historians in the UK the schedules are arranged with an American audience in mind and, unless you are prepared to stay up late, there will be little chance to participate. The webinars are, however, archived online for viewing at your own convenience. With faster internet connections webinars will no doubt soon become more popular in the UK.

Links

http://blog.geneawebinars.com Geneawebinars blog
http://learn.ancestry.com/LearnMore/Webinars.aspx. Ancestry webinars
www.legacyfamilytree.com/Webinars.asp Legacy webinars
http://relativeroots.net/webinars Relative Roots webinars

13

Collaborative tools

The focus of the second half of this book has been on the methods used by genealogists to make contact with other researchers and the networking sites that help to keep people in touch. We will now take a brief look at a few additional tools, which can be very useful once you have established contact with your newly found friends and relatives from around the world. The list is by no means comprehensive and I have chosen to focus on the tools that I have found the most useful from my own personal experience.

Collaborative editing

There are a number of programs that allow files such as Word documents, Excel spreadsheets and PowerPoint presentations to be stored online in the 'cloud', in a private or public workspace, and shared with one or more people for viewing or collaborative editing. Google Docs, **http://docs.google.com**, is probably the best known and most popular free tool for collaborative editing. A free Google account is required to use the service. Files can be uploaded to Google Docs from your computer or you can create new documents online using the proprietary Google Docs office software. The revision history of each document is stored so that you can revert to a previous version of the document in the case of any disasters. The Google Docs office software does not have the full functionality of the equivalent Microsoft products, but it is more than adequate for most purposes.

There are four different settings for the sharing of documents. Documents can be kept private for your own personal viewing, shared with named people by email invitation, made accessible on the web to anyone with the link, or made public on the internet so that the document will appear in search engine results. The service can, therefore, by very handy if you are, for example, having trouble reading a will or a census page and want to share the image with a mailing list which cannot accept

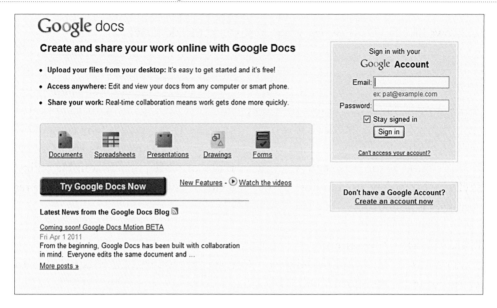

Figure 52   Google Docs can be used for collaborative editing or for online storage.

attachments. If you have a large document that you want to send to a lot of people it can often be easier to upload it to Google Docs and then send people the link so that they can download it themselves. Google Docs can also be a convenient way to have ready access to a document while travelling.

Occasionally, I find that other family history researchers send me files that I am unable to open on my PC because they are in an unusual or out-of-date file format such as OpenOffice or an ancient version of Word. Google Docs seems to have the capacity to deal with any file format. If you upload the file to Google Docs and convert it into the equivalent Google Docs format, the file should open without any trouble and can then be downloaded back on to your computer and saved in the corresponding format in your own software. Google Docs can also be used to convert PDF files into text files using optical character recognition (OCR) software.

Google Docs also doubles up as an online storage facility. One gigabyte of storage is currently provided free of charge, and additional storage can be purchased for a fee. Any type of file format can be uploaded and saved online, including Word documents, Excel documents, PowerPoint presentations, image files and PDF files. For the family historian it is particularly useful to have the facility to upload a back-up GEDCOM file and store it online on Google Docs. The subject of online back-up is beyond the scope of this book, and there are, of course, many other popular sites that provide online storage including Mozy, Dropbox and Box.net.

Windows Live SkyDrive, **www.windowslive.co.uk/skydrive**
SkyDrive is Microsoft's answer to Google Docs. Documents can be created online in Microsoft Word, Excel, PowerPoint and One-Note using the web-based versions of the programs. Files can also be uploaded from your computer for online editing or storage. SkyDrive is able to handle Microsoft documents with complicated formatting that Google Docs will not recognise. It is, however, not fully compatible with non-Microsoft browsers and works best in Internet Explorer. As with Google Docs, documents can be shared with collaborators or made publicly available online. SkyDrive can also be used to store photos and videos online. A generous 25 gigabytes of storage is provided free of charge.

Docs.com, **http://docs.com**
Docs.com is a similar online Microsoft Office tool designed for integration with Facebook and aimed at students.

Zoho, **www.zoho.com**
Zoho is another alternative that provides a suite of collaborative online applications aimed at the business market. The services include Zoho Docs, which is very similar to Google Docs, and offers one gigabyte of online storage space free of charge.

ScribD, **www.scribd.com**
ScribD, pronounced 'skribbed', describes itself as a 'social publishing site' and can be used to share PDF, Word and PowerPoint documents. Tags can be added to documents for ease of searching. Users can create profile pages, follow other users and 'readcast' the works of other users to show that they have read them.

SlideShare, **www.slideshare.net**
SlideShare is a useful website for sharing presentations, and can also be used to share documents and videos. A basic account is free and provides the user with unlimited uploads for documents and presentations and a profile page. A subscription is required for advertising-free content and to upload more than three videos. Additional features for subscribers such as analytical tools will mostly be of interest to business users.

Links
www.youtube.com/user/docs The Google Docs channel on YouTube
http://googledocs.blogspot.com Google Docs blog
http://blogs.zoho.com/category/docs Zoho Docs blog
http://en.wikipedia.org/wiki/List_of_online_backup_services Wikipedia
   article on online back-up services

Social bookmarking

As your family history research progresses, you will find that you acquire a large collection of favourite websites. Internet browsers provide a facility for you to save these links as 'bookmarks' or 'favourites' so that they can be easily retrieved, and so that you do not have to enter a long and complicated URL every time you want to return to a particular site. As you collect more links you will probably organise them into folders, perhaps with separate folders for particular topics such as wills, newspapers, counties and countries. As your link collection grows you will probably accumulate a large collection of folders, and perhaps even a hierarchy of subfolders. Once your bookmark collection reaches a reasonable size it can sometimes be quite difficult to navigate your folder collection, thus defeating the whole object of the exercise. Browsers are becoming increasingly sophisticated, and omnibars, the enhanced address bar available on some browsers such as Firefox and Google Chrome, will now search for keywords in your bookmark collection – but will only suggest matches if the word is contained within the website's URL. If all your bookmarks are stored locally on your own computer, every time you want to share your bookmarks with other researchers you will have to copy all the links individually and paste them into an email or other document. If you regularly use more than one computer you will need to export your bookmarks file to your laptop and your work or home computer. Few browsers provide a successful system for synchronising bookmarks between multiple computers so you will generally need to keep one master file and export it on a regular basis.

An alternative solution is to use what is known as a 'social bookmarking' website, which allows you to store all your bookmarks online and share them easily with your friends and fellow researchers. Most sites will allow you to have a mix of personal and private bookmarks. Instead of organising your bookmarks in folders you will be encouraged to add 'tags', or labels, to each bookmark to categorise them. Multiple tags can usually be added to each URL. It is then a simple matter of searching the tags to find the relevant bookmarks rather than having to negotiate a maze of folders. Most of the social bookmarking sites will allow you to import your existing favourites file from your browser. There is usually an extension that can be added to your browser to make it easy to save and tag new websites as you find them. The social aspect comes into play because you can use the tagging system to find other people who share your interests. You can then add yourself to their network or follow their bookmark collection to discover new websites of interest. Most bookmarking sites will also provide an RSS feed (see Chapter 10) so that you can subscribe to the feed of your favourite users or monitor a particular search term in your RSS reader without having to visit the website. Social bookmarking can be particularly useful when working on collaborative wiki-style projects.

Figure 53   A Delicious bookmark collection.

One of the most popular social bookmarking websites is Delicious, **www. delicious.com**, the website that pioneered the use of tagging and reputedly coined the term social bookmarking. Delicious was founded in 2003 as del.icio.us. It was acquired by Yahoo in 2005, but was sold in April 2011 to Chad Hurley and Steve Chen, the founders of YouTube. Delicious has a very simple, clean and easy-to-use interface. Bookmarks can be imported from most of the major browsers. Links are imported as private by default. The names you have used for folders are converted to tags. Once your bookmarks are uploaded to Delicious you can then use the 'bulk edit' tool to change the settings of your folders and make selected folders publicly available. Tags can easily be renamed globally and each URL can have multiple tags. Links can also be sorted chronologically or alphabetically. There is a number displayed against each URL, which is an indication of the number of people who have saved that link and made it public. As you come across other users who share your interests you can add them to your network so that you can search their public bookmark collection and keep track of their updates, or you can become a 'fan' of other users. Alternatively, you can subscribe to particular tags of interest. Popular tags such as 'genealogy' and 'DNA' will result in a large number of hits, and a subscription will be more manageable if you subscribe to fewer common search terms.

Other free social bookmarking sites include Diigo, **www.diigo.com**, and Faves, **http://faves.com**. Historio.us. **http://historio.us**, provides a trial account for up to 300 bookmarks free of charge, but a small monthly or annual subscription is required to store unlimited bookmarks. Pinboard, **http://pinboard.in**, describes itself as the 'social bookmarking site for introverts'. It charges a small one-off registration fee. There are other sites such as StumbleUpon, **www.stumbleupon.com**, which work on a system of user recommendations to suggest sites you might like to visit. LinkaGoGo, **www.linkagogo.com**, is a free service, which describes itself as an 'online favourites manager'. It does not use tags but instead bookmarks can be searched by keywords, viewed in a directory-style structure or sorted in a variety of ways – such as by folder name, URL or date last visited. The website also has a particularly useful bookmarks importer, which will convert bookmarks from a variety of different browsers into a standard format for use on LinkaGoGo or elsewhere. This feature can be particularly helpful if you have a large collection of bookmarks trapped in a browser such as AOL, which does not provide a facility to export to other browsers. The basic LinkaGoGo service is provided free of charge. A small subscription is required for additional facilities such as bookmark synchronisation and a regular back-up file sent by email. If you do decide to store your bookmarks online, make sure that you make regular offline back-ups. One of the social bookmarking websites by the name of Gnolia.com (formerly Ma.gnolia.com) famously lost its members' bookmarks in 2009 and the site has since been closed down.

Links

http://en.wikipedia.org/wiki/Social_bookmarking Wikipedia article on social bookmarking with a link to a list of social bookmarking sites

Voice and video chat

Family history research will bring you into contact with lots of new members of your family, and you will make friends with researchers all over the world who share your interests. Most of the time you will probably stay in touch by email or Facebook, but every now and then you might like to speak to your relatives and friends on the telephone. If your family and friends are in the UK then the cost of a telephone call will not be a problem. Often, however, your research will bring you into contact with relatives overseas and especially in Australia, Canada, New Zealand and America. Now, thanks to the wonders of modern technology, it is possible to make free voice calls and even video calls without even using a telephone. Instead of using a traditional landline, calls are made on a computer, over the internet, using special Voice over the Internet Protocol (VoIP) software. To enable you to make a call you will need to download some free VoIP software and invest in a webcam or an audio headset. New laptops will often have an inbuilt webcam and speakers, and a basic miniature webcam can now be bought for as little as £10.

There are a number of companies that make VoIP software but the most popular service is provided by Skype, **www.skype.com**. Calls to other Skype users can be made free of charge. Once you have an account set up you can upload your email address book to see which of your friends and relatives are already on Skype. You can

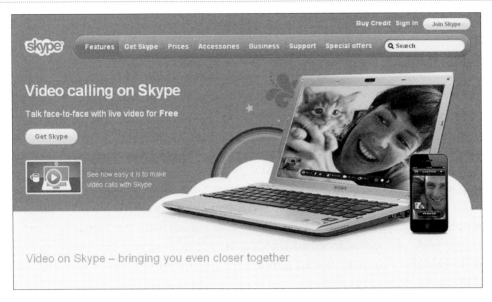

Figure 54 Skype is a convenient, free method of hosting video chats with family and friends over the internet.

also search for people by username or email address. Skype can now optionally be integrated with Facebook so that you can see your Facebook newsfeeds in Skype. You can also input your Facebook username and see which of your Facebook friends have accounts. Once you are set up, all you have to do is sit down at your computer, fire up the Skype software, select the person you want to ring from your contact list and press the call button to make the call. It is usually a good idea to pre-arrange a convenient time in advance, especially if you are planning to make a video call, so that you do not catch the caller at a difficult time while they are still in their pyjamas or eating their dinner! One of the big advantages of video calls is that the whole family can gather round the webcam and join in the conversation. It is, therefore, an ideal way to keep up with a son or daughter at university or on a gap year, or for grandparents to chat with their grandchildren on the other side of the world. Skype can also be used to conduct free conference calls between multiple users, to send instant messages and to make cheap calls to traditional landline telephones and mobile phones.

Similar services are provided by Yahoo Messenger, **http://messenger.yahoo.com**; Windows Live Messenger, **http://explore.live.com/windows-live-messenger**; and Google Chat, **www.google.com/chat/video**. The Google service is integrated with Google Mail and iGoogle. Apple Mac enthusiasts can use FaceTime for Macintosh, **www.apple.com/mac/facetime**. With all these services both parties must have the same software installed on their computers.

Appendix A

DNA websites

General

www.isogg.org International Society of Genetic Genealogy (ISOGG)

www.isogg.org/wiki ISOGG Wiki

www.jogg.info *Journal of Genetic Genealogy*

www.dna-testing-adviser.com Richard Hill's independent guide to DNA testing

www.worldfamilies.net Educational resources for project administrators and project listings by haplogroup, surname, size and geographical area

www.scientific.org/tutorials/articles/riley/riley.html DNA testing for non-scientists

www.kerchner.com/dna-info.htm Charles Kerchner's genetic genealogy resources page

Deep ancestry and haplogroups

www.bradshawfoundation.com/journey An interactive map showing the migration of man out of Africa and around the world

www.buildinghistory.org/distantpast/peoplingeurope.shtml The peopling of Europe

www.eupedia.com/genetics The genetics pages on Eupedia include migration maps and information on European haplogroups, their distribution and frequencies

www.genebase.com/learning Genebase haplogroup tutorials

https://genographic.nationalgeographic.com/genographic/atlas.html Atlas of the human journey

http://en.wikipedia.org/wiki/Haplogroup Wikipedia haplogroup page with links to pages on all the Y-DNA and mtDNA haplogroups

Y-DNA tools

www.hprg.com/hapest5/index.html Whit Athey's haplogroup predictor

http://members.bex.net/jtcullen515/haplotest.htm Jim Cullen's haplogroup predictor

www.mymcgee.com/tools/yutility.html Dean McGee's Y-DNA comparison utility for calculating genetic distance and TMRCA (time to the most recent common ancestor)

www.smgf.org/ychromosome/marker_standards.jspx Y-DNA marker standards and conversion values

mtDNA

www.ianlogan.co.uk Ian Logan's mtDNA pages and information on GenBank

www.phylotree.org The mtDNA phylogenetic tree

www.cambridgedna.com/genealogy-dna-ancient-migrations-slideshow.php An mtDNA view of the peopling of the world

http://vps1.jameslick.com/dna/mthap James Lick's tool for mtDNA haplogroup analysis

Genetics primers

www.dnaftb.org DNA from the beginning

http://stevemorse.org/genetealogy/dna.htm From DNA to genetic genealogy

http://learn.genetics.utah.edu Genetic Science Learning Centre from the University of Utah

www.thetech.org/genetics/index.php A guide to understanding genetics from Stanford University

http://en.wikipedia.org/wiki/Introduction_to_genetics Wikipedia introduction to genetics

DNA databases

www.ncbi.nlm.nih.gov/genbank GenBank (for full sequence mtDNA results)
www.mitosearch.org A public mtDNA database sponsored by Family Tree DNA
www.smgf.org The Sorenson Molecular Genealogy Foundation
www.ysearch.org A public Y-DNA database sponsored by Family Tree DNA
www.yhrd.org The Y-chromosome Haplotype Reference Database

Scientific research projects

www.ahobproject.org Ancient Human Occupation of Great Britain
http://genographic.nationalgeographic.com The Genographic Project
www.peopleofthebritishisles.org The People of the British Isles research project
www2.le.ac.uk/projects/roots-of-the-british Roots of the British 1000 BC – AD 1000
www.smgf.org The Sorenson Molecular Genealogy Foundation

Mailing lists and forums

http://dna-forums.org DNA forums
http://lists.rootsweb.ancestry.com/index/other/DNA/GENEALOGY-DNA.html Genealogy DNA list for advanced users
http://groups.yahoo.com/group/DNA-NEWBIE ISOGG DNA newbie mailing list
http://groups.yahoo.com/group/ISOGG ISOGG project administrators' mailing list
http://lists.rootsweb.ancestry.com/index/other/DNA/AUTOSOMAL-DNA.html Autosomal DNA mailing list
http://lists.rootsweb.ancestry.com/index/other/DNA/Y-DNA-PROJECTS.html Y-DNA projects mailing list

DNA blogs

Anthropology and history blogs
http://anglosaxonnorseandceltic.blogspot.com Cambridge University's Anglo-Saxon, Norman and Celtic blog
http://dienekes.blogspot.com Dienekes Pontikos' anthropology blog provides news and commentary on anthropology and deep ancestry

http://eurogenes.blogspot.com European genetics and anthropology blog

http://evoandproud.blogspot.com Peter Frost's anthropology blog, with special reference to sexual selection and the evolution of skin, hair and eye pigmentation

http://johnhawks.net/weblog John Hawks' anthropology blog provides news and commentary on paleoanthropology, genetics and evolution

http://norseandviking.blogspot.com Norse and Viking ramblings

Commercial DNA blogs

www.decodeyou.com Decode blog

http://blog.genetree.com GeneTree blog

http://blogs.nationalgeographic.com/blogs/genographic The Genographic Project blog

http://spittoon.23andme.com The Spittoon – the 23andMe blog

DNA testing blogs

http://genealem-geneticgenealogy.blogspot.com Emily Aulicino's genetic genealogy blog

www.thegeneticgenealogist.com A blog from Blaine Bettinger, editor of the *Journal of Genetic Genealogy*

www.yourgeneticgenealogist.com CeCe Moore's blog specialising in genetic genealogy and personal genomics

Personal genomics blogs

www.wired.com/wiredscience/geneticfuture A personal blog from Daniel MacArthur, a scientific researcher at the Sanger Institute in Cambridge, who writes about the latest developments in human genetics and personal genomics

www.genomicslawreport.com A blog produced by a team of lawyers in America who write on the legal aspects of genomics and personalised medicine

www.genomesunzipped.org A group blog from a team of researchers in various fields of genetics who have made their own genetic data freely available. The blog provides independent and informed analysis of developments in the field of genetics and the genetic testing industry

Appendix B

Testing companies

The International Society of Genetic Genealogy provides three useful charts to compare the tests and services provided by the main testing companies:
www.isogg.org/ydnachart.htm Y-DNA testing comparison chart
www.isogg.org/mtdnachart.htm mtDNA testing comparison chart
www.isogg.org/features.htm Project management facilities

23andMe, **www.23andme.com**
Founded in 2006. 23andMe is a pioneering personal genomics company based in Mountain View, California. Their personal genomics test is primarily a health test, but the Relative Finder component of the test is of interest to genealogists.

Ancestry.com DNA, **http://dna.ancestry.com**
Founded in 2007. Ancestry.com DNA is the genetics testing service provided by Ancestry.com. Testing is done in the laboratories of Sorenson Genomics in Salt Lake City, Utah. The company offers three basic products: a medium-resolution HVR mtDNA test; a 33-marker Y-STR test; and a 46-marker Y-STR test.* No SNP testing is provided. Ancestry.com inherited the database of the now-defunct company Relative Genetics.

DNA Heritage, **www.dnaheritage.com**
2003–2011. DNA Heritage was a British DNA testing company based in Weymouth, Dorset. It was acquired by Family Tree DNA in April 2011. DNA Heritage offered two Y-STR tests at 23 and 43 markers and a high-resolution HVR mtDNA test. A 58-marker Y-STR test was introduced at the end of 2010. The testing was done in the laboratories of Sorenson Genomics in Salt Lake City, Utah. Following the acquisition, former customers were given the option of transferring their Y-DNA results to the Family Tree DNA database. As DNA Heritage tested a different range of markers from FTDNA only 25-marker results can be added to the FTDNA database.

Customers were given the option to upgrade to 37 markers for a nominal fee to make their results compatible with the larger FTDNA database. Kit numbers from DNA Heritage customers are prefixed by the letter H in the FTDNA database.

Ethnoancestry, **www.ethnoancestry.com**

Founded in 2005. Ethnoancestry, registered in Scotland, specialises in deep ancestry testing. The haploview test combines a 20-marker Y-STR test with a range of SNPs. SNP tests are available for the major haplogroups for subclade determination, and custom SNPs can also be ordered individually. A low-resolution mtDNA test is also offered and mtDNA SNP testing is available separately for subclade analysis.

Family Tree DNA, **www.familytreedna.com**

Founded in 2000. Family Tree DNA (FTDNA) is the current market leader offering the widest range of tests and benefiting from the largest database. The company is based in Houston, Texas. Some tests are done at their Personal Genomics Center in Houston with the balance carried out in their labs at the University of Arizona. A range of Y-STR tests is offered from 12 through to 111 markers. Deep clade tests are available for subclade analysis for the major haplogroups, and additional SNPs can be ordered individually if required. Low and high-resolution mtDNA tests are available. SNP tests for accurate mtDNA haplogroup confirmation are included in the price. A full-sequence mtDNA test is also available. The new autosomal Family Finder test was launched in February 2010. FTDNA hosts a wide range of surname projects, geographical projects and haplogroup projects.

FTDNA has a number of affiliate companies around the world, which include African DNA in the US, iGENEA in Switzerland, DNA Worldwide in the UK, and DNA Ancestry and Family Origin in the Middle East. Kits ordered through these companies are included in the FTDNA database, but it is much more expensive to order tests from these companies rather than ordering direct from FTDNA.

GeneBase, **www.genebase.com**

Founded in 2005. GeneBase is the ancestry division of Genetrack Biolabs. The company is based in Vancouver, Canada, and also has offices in Seattle in the US. The company offers a range of Y-STR tests from 20 to 91 markers. Y-SNP haplogroup backbone tests are offered for subclade analysis. Low and high-resolution mtDNA tests are available. An mtDNA haplogroup backbone SNP test can be ordered as an extra. There is also an option to upgrade to a full-sequence mtDNA test. There are some excellent haplogroup tutorials on the GeneBase website.

GeneTree, **www.genetree.com**

Founded in 2007. GeneTree, based in Salt Lake City, Utah, is the commercial arm of the non-profit-making Sorenson Molecular Genealogy Foundation. The company offers two basic products: a high-resolution mtDNA test and a 46-marker Y-STR test.* The tests are done in the Sorenson Genomics laboratory in Utah. In April 2011 GeneTree introduced a range of specialty DNA tests, which are custom-designed to suit individual requirements. The new tests include an option to order additional Y-STR markers and Y-SNP testing for accurate haplogroup classification. A relationship test using up to 53 autosomal STR markers is available for confirming or disproving close relationships. A specialist X-STR chromosome test is available to confirm relationships on the X-chromosome line.

The Genographic Project, **http://genographic.nationalgeographic.com**
The Genographic Project is a major five-year global research project that was launched in April 2005 to explore the genetic history of the human species, and to trace the journey of mankind out of Africa and around the world. The project is a partnership between National Geographic and IBM with support from the Waitt Family Foundation and is led by the population geneticist Dr Spencer Wells. The project aims to collect and analyse DNA samples from over 100,000 indigenous people from around the world. The project also invites participation from the general public who can join by purchasing a Genographic Project Public Participation Kit. Participants can take either a 12-marker Y-DNA test or an HVR1 mtDNA test. The testing is done in the Family Tree DNA laboratories at the University of Arizona. Genographic Project participants have the option of adding their results to the Family Tree DNA database, where they can order upgrades and also join the relevant surname, geographical and haplogroup projects.

Oxford Ancestors, **www.oxfordancestors.com**
Founded in 2000. Oxford Ancestors was founded by Professor Bryan Sykes of Oxford University. The company offers a basic low-resolution mtDNA test and a 15-marker Y-DNA test at almost double the price of the equivalent tests offered by other companies.

---

* The 33-marker and 46-marker Y-DNA tests offered by Ancestry.com DNA and GeneTree include 3 markers that normally have null values and are, therefore, of no relevance for genealogical purposes. Other companies will test for these markers and provide results on the rare occasion when a value is reported. The Ancestry.com and GeneTree 46-marker test is identical to the 43-marker test formerly provided by DNA Heritage.

Appendix C

DNA projects

Surname projects

The majority of surname projects can be found at **www.familytreedna.com**. The database can be searched by surname and the alphabetical lists can also be browsed at **www.familytreedna.com/projects.aspx**. Some surname projects can also be found at **http://dna.ancestry.com**, though many of these surnames are also represented in larger projects at Family Tree DNA.

An incomplete list of surname projects can also be found on the Cyndi's List website at **www.cyndislist.com/surnames/dna**.

Surname projects mentioned in this book

www.familytreedna.com/public/carden Carden DNA Project
www.isogg.org/wiki/Creer_Y-DNA_Project Creer DNA Project
www.familytreedna.com/public/CruwysDNA Cruwys/Cruse DNA project
**http://freepages.genealogy.rootsweb.ancestry.com/~hjohnson/New%20
   Index/index/j-j-j_index.htm** The Johnson/Johnston/Johnstone DNA Project
http://meates.accessgenealogy.com Meates DNA Project
www.phillipsdnaproject.com Phillips DNA Project
www.plant-fhg.org.uk/dna.html Plant DNA Project
www.one-name.org/profiles/pomeroy.html Pomeroy DNA Project
www.worldfamilies.net/surnames/pitts Pitts DNA Project
www.savin.org/dna Savin DNA Project
www.familytreedna.com/public/Swinfield Swinfield DNA Project
http://williams.genealogy.fm Williams DNA Project

Special projects

www.familytreedna.com/public/adopted The Adopted Y-DNA and mtDNA
   project
www.familytreedna.com/public/donor_conceived The Donor Conceived
   DNA project – a project for adults conceived by sperm donation who are seeking
   their biological roots
www.familytreedna.com/public/Romnchel The Romany DNA Project

Geographical projects

England
www.familytreedna.com/public/Birmingham_Midlands Birmingham and
   West Midland mtDNA project
www.familytreedna.com/public/cornwall-mtDNA Cornwall mtDNA
   Project
www.familytreedna.com/public/Devon Devon Y-DNA and mtDNA project
www.weston-genealogy.net/eagdna/frame_set.html East Anglia Y-DNA and
   mtDNA project
www.familytreedna.com/public/Hampshire-County-England Hampshire
   Y-DNA project
✳ **www.familytreedna.com/public/northumberland-england** Northumberland
   Y-DNA and mtDNA project

Ireland
www.familytreedna.com/public/IrelandHeritage Ireland Heritage Y-DNA
   Project
www.familytreedna.com/public/Ireland%20-%20MtDNA Ireland Heritage
   mtDNA Project
www.ulsterheritage.com Ulster Heritage Y-DNA Project
www.familytreedna.com/public/ulsterheritagemtdna Ulster Heritage
   mtDNA Project
www.clansofireland.ie The Clans of Ireland website maintains a database of DNA
   projects for Irish clans

Isle of Man
www.manxdna.co.uk Manx Y-DNA Project

Scotland

www.scottishdna.net Scottish DNA Project

http://scottishdna.blogspot.com The companion blog to the Scottish DNA project. The blog maintains a useful list of individual Scottish clan projects

www.ourfamilyorigins.com/scotland/dna.htm The Scotland Y-DNA project and mtDNA project

http://freepages.genealogy.rootsweb.ancestry.com/~gallgaedhil/elliott_border_reivers_dna.htm Border Reivers Y-DNA project

www.familytreedna.com/public/isleofislay Isles of the Hebrides Y-DNA and mtDNA project

www.davidkfaux.org/shetlandislands Y-DNA Shetland Islands Y-DNA and mtDNA project

Wales

www.familytreedna.com/public/WalesDNA Wales Y-DNA and mtDNA Project

British Isles DNA Project

If there is no surname project for your surname, and none of the geographical projects listed above meets your requirements, another alternative is to test with the British Isles DNA Project, which can be found at **www.familytreedna.com/public/BritishIsles**. This is the largest geographical DNA project in the world with over 4,500 project members by the end of 2010. It accepts results for both Y-DNA and mtDNA tests. The project is very broad in its scope. It is 'open to persons whose family history or surname indicates a paternal or maternal lineage originating in the British Isles, or who have a family tradition pointing back to the British Isles'.

European geographical projects

An alphabetical listing of geographical DNA projects can be found on the Family Tree DNA website at **www.familytreedna.com/projects.aspx**. For anyone of Jewish origin a comprehensive listing of Jewish DNA projects is provided on the JewishGen website at **www.jewishgen.org/DNA/genbygen.html**.

The following is a selective list of the larger European geographical projects:

www.familytreedna.com/public/Czech Czech Y-DNA and mtDNA project
www.familytreedna.com/public/Denmark Denmark Y-DNA and mtDNA project

www.familytreedna.com/public/Danish_Demes Danish Demes Y-DNA and mtDNA project

www.familytreedna.com/public/Finland Finland Y-DNA and mtDNA project

www.familytreedna.com/public/Flanders Flanders and Flemish Y-DNA and mtDNA project

www.familytreedna.com/public/frenchheritage French heritage Y-DNA and mtDNA project

www.german-dna.net Germany Y-DNA and mtDNA project

www.familytreedna.com/public/Greece Greek Y-DNA and mtDNA project

www.familytreedna.com/public/Italy Italy Y-DNA and mtDNA project

www.familytreedna.com/public/Netherlands Netherlands Y-DNA and mtDNA project

www.familytreedna.com/public/Norway Norway Y-DNA and mtDNA project

www.familytreedna.com/public/polish Polish Y-DNA and mtDNA project

www.ourfamilyorigins.com/portugal/dna.htm Portugal Y-DNA and mtDNA project

www.familytreedna.com/public/russiadna Russian Y-DNA and mtDNA project

www.familytreedna.com/public/ScandinaviamtDNA Scandinavian mtDNA project

www.familytreedna.com/public/scandinavianydna Scandinanvia Y-DNA project

www.familytreedna.com/public/Casa-de-Espana_HouseofSpain-DNA Spanish DNA project

www.familytreedna.com/public/switzerland Switzerland DNA project

Appendix D

Surname resources

Surnames

www.americanlastnames.us American last names
www.britishsurnames.co.uk The British surnames website
www.one-name.org The Guild of One-Name Studies
www.surnamestudies.org.uk Surname studies website – a continuation of the former Modern British Surnames website created by the late Philip Dance
http://www.taliesin-arlein.net/names/search.php The surnames of England and Wales: how common (or rare) is your surname?

Surname mapping and distribution

www.archersoftware.co.uk Archer Software has created two useful tools for mapping British surnames. The nineteenth-century Surname Atlas plots surname distributions in England, Wales and Scotland from the 1881 census. GenMap UK is a useful tool for compiling maps based on historical or genealogical data relating to the British Isles
http://gbnames.publicprofiler.org Great Britain family names profiler
http://worldnames.publicprofiler.org World names public profiler
www.members.shaw.ca/geogenealogy Howard Mathieson's surname-mapping website
www.mapyourname.com Map your name – a global name-mapping website
www.wykes.org/usdist US surname distribution analysis
http://hamrick.com/names US surname distribution tool
www.gens-us.net US surname maps

Glossary

Ahnentafel numbers
A numbering system used in genealogy, which assigns numbers to a person's ancestors in a particular order. The root person is number 1, the father is number 2, the mother is number 3, the paternal grandfather is number 4 and so on. Ahnentafel numbers can be a convenient method for charting the inheritance of the X-chromosome, if the appropriate numbers are known.

Allele
The value of a particular genetic marker. In genetic genealogy the term is mostly used to describe the number of short tandem repeats (STRs) for specific markers on the Y-chromosome. These are the numbers that are reported when you receive your Y-DNA results from the testing company.

Autosomal DNA
The DNA in autosomes. Autosomal DNA is inherited from both parents and undergoes a process of recombination or genetic shuffling. Autosomal DNA is examined in the Family Finder test from Family Tree DNA and the Relative Finder test from 23andMe.

Autosomes
Chromosomes that are not sex chromosomes. Humans have twenty-two pairs of autosomes and one pair of sex chromosomes (XX or XY).

Bases
The four building blocks or units of DNA. Bases are designated by the four letters in the DNA alphabet – A (adenine), T (thymine), G (guanine) and C (cytosine). In genetics, bases are also referred to as nucleotides.

Base pair
A pair of bases or nucleotides. The four bases – A, T, G and C – are arranged in pairs to form the rungs of the two strands of the DNA ladder. A always pairs with T, and G always pairs with C.

Cambridge Reference Sequence (CRS)
The first published sequence of the 16,569 base pairs that comprise the human mitochondrial genome. The sequence was published in 1981 by a team of scientists from Cambridge University. A revised version was issued in 1999. Mitochondrial DNA test results are compared against the revised Cambridge Reference Sequence (rCRS).

CentiMorgan (cM)
A measurement used to determine how likely a segment of DNA is to recombine from one generation to the next. A single centiMorgan is equivalent to a 1 per cent chance that a segment of DNA will recombine within one generation. One centiMorgan is generally equivalent to about 1 million bases, but this varies depending on the chromosome.

Chromosome
A structure that contains genetic material. Humans have twenty-three pairs of chromosomes, consisting of twenty-two pairs of autosomes and one pair of sex chromosomes (XX or XY).

Deoxyribonucleic acid (DNA)
A double-stranded, ladder-shaped molecule in the shape of a double helix which contains the blueprint of life.

FTDNATiP™
An acronym for Family Tree DNA Time Predictor, a proprietary program that calculates the time to the most recent common ancestor using marker-specific mutation rates.

GEDCOM
An acronym for Genealogical Data Communication, a method of exchanging genealogical data between different family history software programs. The GEDCOM format was developed by the Church of Jesus Christ of Latter-Day Saints as an aid to genealogical research.

Gene
A stretch of DNA on a chromosome, which determines a particular hereditary characteristic.

Generation

The number of years between the birth of the parents and the birth of their children. Different studies use different numbers of years per generation, ranging from twenty to thirty-five years.

Genome

The total complement of genetic material contained in an organism or a cell. The human genome consists of around 3 billion base pairs.

Haplogroup

A group of people who descend from the same branch of the human family tree. A new branch is formed when a single-nucleotide polymorphism (SNP) occurs in an individual, which is then passed on to all of his or her descendants. There are twenty haplogroups labelled from A through to T in the Y-chromosome tree, and twenty-six haplogroups labelled A through to Z in the mitochondrial DNA tree.

Haplotype

A string of numbers representing the values for a set of Y-STR markers that make up the result of a Y-chromosome DNA test. A collection of differences from the revised Cambridge Reference Sequence that constitute the results of a mitochondrial DNA test.

Hypervariable region (HVR)

The section of mitochondrial DNA that is most prone to mutation. It is also known as the control region. The HVR is sequenced in part or in its entirety in a standard mitochondrial DNA test.

ISOGG

The International Society of Genetic Genealogy, **www.isogg.org**, a non-profit-making volunteer-run organisation founded in 2005. Its aim is 'to advocate for and educate about the use of genetics as a tool for genealogical research, and promote a supportive network for genetic genealogists'.

Marker

A location on a stretch of DNA that is subject to change. The term is often used colloquially in genetic genealogy to refer to the Y-STR markers used in Y-chromosome DNA testing.

Mitochondria

The plural of mitochondrion. Small structures in the cytoplasm of a cell (the area outside the nucleus) which generate energy.

Mitochondrial DNA (mtDNA)
DNA found in mitochondria. Mitochondrial DNA is passed on from a mother to her sons and daughters, and can be used to trace the direct maternal line.

Mitochondrial Eve
The most recent common ancestor on the direct maternal line of all humans alive today. She is estimated to have lived between 180,000 and 200,000 years ago.

Mutation
A random heritable change in a DNA sequence. A mutation can involve a change in one of the letters in the DNA alphabet or a different number of repeats in a sequence of DNA. Mutations can be used to distinguish between different ancestral lines.

Mutation rate
The rate at which random changes in DNA occur. Mutation rates are used to make estimates of the time to the most recent common ancestor (TMRCA) between two people or a population group. The result is given in terms of the number of generations or number of years.

Non-paternity event (NPE)
A catch-all term used to describe a situation in which the link between the Y-chromosome and the surname is broken. NPEs can be caused by illegitimacy, adoption, marital infidelity, name changes, etc.

Nucleotide
A single unit or building block of DNA. *See* bases.

RSS reader
An online news reader or news aggregator such as Google Reader, which can be used to keep track of changes in websites and blogs that are regularly updated.

Short tandem repeat (STR)
A short pattern in a DNA sequence, which is repeated a number of times in succession. Sometimes, as a result of a random mutation, the number of repeats changes, either upwards or downwards. The locations where these changes occur on the Y-chromosome are known as Y-STR markers.

Single-nucleotide polymorphism (SNP)
Pronounced 'snip', a location in a sequence of DNA where a change sometimes occurs in one of the four letters of the DNA alphabet; for example an A is replaced by a G. SNPs are used to define haplogroups.

Subclade or subhaplogroup

A branch of a haplogroup.

Time to the Most Recent Common Ancestor (TMRCA)

A statistical calculation to determine the most likely time that two people, or a group of people, shared a common ancestor based on their DNA results. It is a complicated calculation, which requires knowledge of marker-mutation rates, generation intervals and effective population sizes.

Unique-Event Polymorphism (UEP)

A mutation occurring at such a low frequency that it is generally thought to be an event that happened only once in the history of mankind. Most single-nucleotide polymorphisms (SNPs) are UEPs.

Walk Through the Y (WTY)

An ongoing consumer-funded research program at Family Tree DNA, which aims to discover new subclade-defining single-nucleotide polymorphisms in the Y-chromosome.

X-chromosome

One of the two sex chromosomes, X and Y. Women inherit two X-chromosomes, one from each parent. Men inherit an X-chromosome from their mother and a Y-chromosome from their father.

Y-chromosomal Adam

The most recent common ancestor on the direct paternal line of all men alive today. He is estimated to have lived around 80,000 to 130,000 years ago.

Y-chromosome

One of the two sex chromosomes, X and Y. The Y-chromosome is handed down from father to son, and is used to trace the direct paternal line, especially in the context of a surname project.

Y-DNA

A shorthand term for the DNA found on the Y-chromosome.

Y-STR marker

A location on the Y-chromosome where changes in the number of short tandem repeats (STRs) are prone to occur. The number of differences determines the degree of relatedness between individuals or populations. Y-STR markers are used in genetic genealogy in Y-chromosome DNA tests. The number of repeats is counted on each marker included in the test.

Bibliography

DNA testing

Fitzpatrick, Colleen and Yeiser, Andrew, *DNA and Genealogy*. Rice Book Press, 2005.

Pomery, Chris, *DNA and Family History: How Genetic Testing Can Advance Your Genealogical Research*. National Archives, 2004.

———, *Family History in the Genes: Trace Your DNA and Grow Your Family Tree*. National Archives, 2007.

Savin, Alan, *DNA for Family Historians*. Privately printed, 2000–03. Available from: **www.savin.org/dna/dna-book.html**

Smolenyak, Megan and Turner, Ann, *Trace Your Roots with DNA: Using Genetic Tests to Explore Your Family Tree*. Rodale Books, USA, 2005.

Whitehead, Jill, *Genetic Genealogy – Expanding the Jewish Family Tree*. The Jewish Genealogical Society of Great Britain. (Available to members only in the Members' Corner at **www.jgsgb.org.uk**)

Deep ancestry

Harding, Stephen, Jobling, Mark and King, Turi, *Viking DNA: The Wirral and West Lancashire Project*. Countywise Ltd and Nottingham University Press, 2010.

McKie, Robin, *Face of Britain: How Our Genes Reveal the History of Britain*. Simon & Schuster, 2007.

Moffat, Alistair and Wilson, James F., *The Scots: A Genetic Journey*. Birlinn Ltd, 2011.

Oppenheimer, Stephen, *The Real Eve: Modern Man's Journey out of Africa*. Carroll & Graf, 2004.

———, *Out of Eden: The Peopling of the World*. Robinson Publishing, 2004.

———, *The Origins of the British: A Genetic Detective Story*. Robinson Publishing, 2007.

Roberts, Alice, *The Incredible Human Journey*. Bloomsbury, 2009.

Sykes, Bryan, *Adam's Curse. A Future without Men*. Corgi, 2004.

————, *The Blood of the Isles*. Bantam Press, 2006.

————, *The Seven Daughters of Eve: The Science that Reveals Our Genetic Ancestry*. Corgi, 2004.

————, *DNA USA: A Genetic Biography of America*. W.W. Norton, 2011.

Wells, Spencer, *The Journey of Man: A Genetic Odyssey*. Penguin, 2002.

————, *Deep Ancestry: Inside the Genographic Project*. National Geographic Society, 2006.

————, *Deep Ancestry Second Edition: How DNA Reveals the Roots of Your Family Tree*. National Geographic Society, 2011.

————, *Pandora's Seed: The Unforeseen Cost of Civilization*. Allen Lane, 2010.

Surnames

Black, George Fraser, *The Surnames of Scotland: Their Origin, Meaning and History*. Birlinn, 2007.

Davis, Dr Graeme, *Research Your Surname and Your Family Tree*. How To Books, 2010.

Dorward, David, *Scottish Surnames*. Mercat Press, 2002.

Hay, David, *Family Names and Family History*. Carnegie Publishing, 2000.

McKinley, Richard, *A History of British Surnames*. Longman, 1990.

MacLysaght, Edward, *The Surnames of Ireland*. Irish Academic Press, 1985.

Redmonds, George, *Surnames and Genealogy: A New Approach*. Federation of Family History Societies, 2002.

Redmonds George, Hey, David and King, Turi, *Surnames, DNA, and Family History*. Oxford University Press, 2011.

Reiney, P.H. and Wilson, R.M., *A Dictionary of English Surnames*. 3rd edition. Oxford University Press, 2005.

Rogers, Colin D., *The Surname Detective: Investigating Surname Distribution in England, 1086–Present Day*. Manchester University Press, 1995.

Sturges, Christopher M. and Haggett, Brian C., *Inheritance of English Surnames*. Hawgood Computing Ltd, London, 1987.

Rowlands, John and Rowlands, Sheila, *The Surnames of Wales: For Family Historians and Others*. Genealogical Publishing, 1996.

Titford, John, *Penguin Dictionary of British Surnames*. Penguin, 2009.

Index

Page numbers in bold indicate tables or figures

Other titles published by The History Press

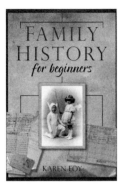

Family History for Beginners

KAREN FOY

£13.49

Dabbling in family history is a pastime anyone of any age can enjoy, but the massive proliferation of websites, magazines and books in recent years can baffle the would-be genealogist to a standstill. This is an ideal introduction to the tools and processes of researching your past. It will teach you how to get the most information from living relatives, how to negotiate the vast quantities of census data with ease, and the best way to store, catalogue and present the information you discover.

978-0-7524-5838-0

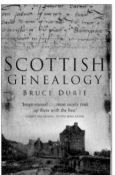

Scottish Genealogy

BRUCE DURIE

£13.49

Scottish Genealogy is the comprehensive guide to tracing your family history in Scotland. The work is based on established genealogical practice and is designed to exploit the rich resources that Scotland has to offer. After all, this country has possibly the most complete and best-kept set of records and other documents in the world. Addressing the questions of DNA, palaeography and the vexed issues of Clans, Families and tartans, Bruce Durie presents a fascinating insight into discovering Scottish ancestors. Informative and entertaining, this updated edition is the definitive reader-friendly guide to genealogy and family history in Scotland.

978-0-7509-4569-1

A Viking in the Family: and Other Family Tree Tales

KEITH GREGSON

£9.99

Genealogist Keith Gregson takes the reader on a whistle-stop tour of quirky family stories and strange ancestors rooted out by amateur and professional family historians. Each lively entry tells the story behind each discovery and then offers a brief insight into how the researcher found and then followed up their leads, revealing a range of chance encounters and the detective qualities required of a family historian. *A Viking in the Family* is full of unexpected discoveries in the branches of family trees.

978-0-7524-5772-7

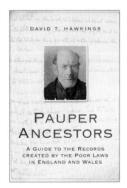

Pauper Ancestors: A Guide to the Records Created by the Poor Laws in England & Wales

DAVID T. HAWKINGS

£27.00

From the sixteenth century onwards, many laws were enacted to provide support for the poor and needy; some parishes established poor houses and later workhouses, which gained a reputation for cruelty in the eyes of the public. Detailed records were kept of everything: rate-payers, collectors of rates, the staff and inmates of workhouses, and those given assisted passage to Australia. David T. Hawkings, one of Britain's leading genealogists, explains how these records can be used to discover details of your ancestry, providing a must-have resource for genealogists and family historians who want to make use of this comprehensive repository of information.

978-0-7524-5665-2

Visit our website and discover thousands of other History Press books.

www.thehistorypress.co.uk